The Seafarers THE U-BOATS

TIME
LIFE ®
BOOKS

The Cover: Carving a foamy path
through North Atlantic waters in 1917,
the German submarine *U-53* makes
a surface run in an oil painting by marine
artist Claus Bergen. During both world
wars, deadly U-boats constantly prowled
the sea-lanes leading to Great Britain,
striking at merchant vessels and warships
alike with torpedoes and gunfire.

The Title Page: A brass patrol badge,
showing a U-boat encircled in a laurel
wreath and surmounted by an eagle
symbolizing the German Reich,
was awarded to submarine officers and
crewmen who completed three or
more enemy missions in World War II. A
similar medal—bearing the Kaiser's
crown instead of the swastika—had been
given to U-boat men of World War I.

THE U-BOATS

by Douglas Botting
AND THE EDITORS OF TIME-LIFE BOOKS

TIME-LIFE BOOKS, ALEXANDRIA, VIRGINIA

Time-Life Books Inc.
is a wholly owned subsidiary of
TIME INCORPORATED

FOUNDER: Henry R. Luce 1898-1967

Editor-in-Chief: Henry Anatole Grunwald
Chairman of the Board: Andrew Heiskell
President: James R. Shepley
Editorial Director: Ralph Graves
Vice Chairman: Arthur Temple

TIME-LIFE BOOKS INC.

MANAGING EDITOR: Jerry Korn
Executive Editor: David Maness
Assistant Managing Editors: Dale M. Brown (planning),
George Constable, George G. Daniels (acting),
Martin Mann, John Paul Porter
Art Director: Tom Suzuki
Chief of Research: David L. Harrison
Director of Photography: Robert G. Mason
Senior Text Editor: Diana Hirsh
Assistant Art Director: Arnold C. Holeywell
Assistant Chief of Research: Carolyn L. Sackett
Assistant Director of Photography: Dolores A. Littles

CHAIRMAN: Joan D. Manley
President: John D. McSweeney
Executive Vice Presidents: Carl G. Jaeger,
John Steven Maxwell, David J. Walsh
Vice Presidents: George Artandi (comptroller);
Stephen L. Bair (legal counsel); Peter G. Barnes;
Nicholas Benton (public relations); John L. Canova;
Beatrice T. Dobie (personnel); Carol Flaumenhaft
(consumer affairs); Nicholas J. C. Ingleton (Asia);
James L. Mercer (Europe/South Pacific); Herbert Sorkin
(production); Paul R. Stewart (marketing)

The Seafarers

Editorial Staff for The U-boats:
Editor: Jim Hicks
Picture Editor: John Conrad Weiser
Designer: Herbert H. Quarmby
Text Editors: Anne Horan, Gus Hedberg
Staff Writers: Michael Blumenthal, Kathleen M. Burke,
Stuart Gannes, Sterling Seagrave, Mark M. Steele
Chief Researcher: Charlotte A. Quinn
Researchers: W. Mark Hamilton, Mindy A. Daniels,
Philip Brandt George, Barbara Levitt, Kimberly K. Lewis,
Elizabeth L. Parker, Trudy W. Pearson
Art Assistant: Michelle René Clay
Editorial Assistant: Ellen P. Keir

Special Contributors
Champ Clark (text); Martha Reichard George,
Barbara Hicks, Betty Ajemian (research)

Editorial Production
Production Editor: Douglas B. Graham
Operations Manager: Gennaro C. Esposito,
Gordon E. Buck (assistant)
Assistant Production Editor: Feliciano Madrid
Quality Control: Robert L. Young (director), James J. Cox
(assistant), Daniel J. McSweeney, Michael G. Wight
(associates)
Art Coordinator: Anne B. Landry
Copy Staff: Susan B. Galloway (chief), Sheirazada Hann,
Diane Ullius Jarrett, Celia Beattie
Picture Department: Nancy Cromwell Scott

Correspondents: Elisabeth Kraemer (Bonn);
Margot Hapgood, Dorothy Bacon, Lesley Coleman
(London); Susan Jonas, Lucy T. Voulgaris (New York);
Maria Vincenza Aloisi, Josephine du Brusle (Paris);
Ann Natanson (Rome).
Valuable assistance was also provided by: Janny Hovinga
(Amsterdam); Helga Kohl, Martha Mader (Bonn); Enid
Farmer (Boston); Brigid Grauman, Chris Redman
(Brussels); Judy Aspinall, Brian Davis (London); Carolyn
T. Chubet, Miriam Hsia (New York); Marie Thérèse
Hirschkoff (Paris); Mimi Murphy (Rome); Janet Zich
(San Francisco); Nancy Friedman (Washington, D.C.)

The Author:
Douglas Botting knows well the British waters once prowled by the U-boats: He circumnavigated Great Britain as part of a coastline conservation project for The Times of London and the BBC. The author of The Pirates in The Seafarers series and a number of other historical works, he has also traveled to remote corners of the earth on exploratory and scientific expeditions.

The Consultants:
John Horace Parry served with the Royal Navy during World War II, rising to the rank of commander. He is now Professor of Oceanic History at Harvard University.

Karl-Wilhelm Grützemacher was first engineer on the U-427 during World War II patrols in the North and Arctic Seas. An electrical engineer, he is owner and president of a Munich electronics firm.

Thomas O. Paine served in World War II aboard a United States Navy submarine. A student of submarine technology ever since, he has amassed a private library of 3,000 volumes. An engineer by profession, he served as administrator of NASA during the first manned lunar expedition in 1969, then embarked on a distinguished business career in the field of aviation.

Antony Preston is naval editor of Defense magazine and a known expert and writer on warship design and naval history.

Leonard Stoehr spent 19 years on submarine duty in the United States Navy. Now a civilian, he supervises naval tactical studies for a research and development company in Washington, D.C.

William Avery Baker, an engineer, naval architect and writer on maritime history, is curator of the Hart Nautical Museum at the Massachusetts Institute of Technology.

For information about any Time-Life book, please write:
Reader Information, Time-Life Books,
541 North Fairbanks Court, Chicago, Illinois 60611.

TIME-LIFE is a trademark of Time Incorporated U.S.A.

Library of Congress Cataloguing in Publication Data
Botting, Douglas.
   The U-boats.
   (The Seafarers)
   Bibliography: p.
   Includes index.
   1. Submarine warfare—History. 2. European War,
1914-1918—Naval operations—Submarine. 3. World
War, 1939-1945—Naval operations—Submarine.
I. Time-Life Books. II. Title. III. Series.
V210.B67   359.8'3   79-17043
ISBN 0-8094-2675-7
ISBN 0-8094-2724-9 lib. bdg.

Contents

Prowling the seas in slivers of steel

Propagandists and romantics called them gray wolves. Their victims cursed them as barbaric pirate vessels. The men who served on board were more likely to refer to them as steel coffins. By any name, the *Unterseeboote*, or U-boat submarines, were Germany's foremost naval weapon in two world wars—so devastating that in both conflicts they came within an ace of choking off entirely the vital sea-lanes to Great Britain.

In the two wars nearly 8,000 merchant ships and warships were sunk by U-boats, with a loss of hundreds of thousands of lives. That the U-boats did not prevail was due in both wars to overwhelming Allied force, and to their own terrible vulnerability. By the end of the second war, 962 U-boats had been destroyed; half of all the U-boat crewmen, some 33,300, went down with their craft. The individual actions in this brutal struggle were almost all small-scale: a handful of determined men in tiny steel splinters, seeking out the enemy in the vastness of the sea. Theirs was a solitary and desperate war, waged in extreme hardship, far from the fields of glory.

But the officers and crews of the U-boats became national heroes, like the medieval knights of German legend, because of the very individuality of their kind of warfare. Claus Bergen, an artist who recorded German Navy exploits during World War I, helped to immortalize the U-boat men in paintings that cast them as heroic figures dominating vast seascapes from their gray steel chargers. Bergen accompanied the *U-53* on a bold, long-distance mission into the North Atlantic in June and July of 1917. Sailing with Lieutenant Hans Rose to the crucial Allied shipping lanes off Ireland's coast, Bergen carefully observed and sketched for later painting all the exhilaration, boredom, sadness and satisfaction of a two-month patrol.

The artist encountered subchasers, withstood depth-charging and watched as enemy ships were torpedoed, scuttled or gunned to the bottom. The prospect of battle was always close at hand, and death was a constant companion in the long night of war beneath the sea.

Bergen painted because he knew there would be few other memorials to those who died in U-boats. The ocean, he wrote, "reveals nothing of the fates of men and ships. No crosses or flowers mark the last resting places of many heroes who lie in their riddled and shattered steel coffins."

As dawn colors the North Atlantic, the U-53's commander, Hans Rose, hails a comrade homeward bound from patrol. "How small the gray object looked in that expanse of ocean," said Bergen. "Both crews swarmed to the conning towers, eager to witness this happy meeting." While a crewman on the U-53 signals with semaphore flags, Rose speaks to the other U-boat through a megaphone, seeking reports of the enemy.

CLAUS BERGEN

8

Firing across the bow of the British full-rigger *Atlantic*, the U-53's gunners force her to heave to off the Hebrides. After her crew had abandoned the *Atlantic*, the U-boat sank her with the deck gun. "Only the necessity of sinking every ship within the blockade zone," said Bergen, "could master the sadness natural to every true seaman at the sight of the destruction of so splendid a vessel."

Having dispatched an Allied freighter with explosive charges after her crew took to their boats, the German demolitions team rows back to the U-53. "The pressure of air and water," wrote Bergen, "flung a little black cloud of soot from the funnel, the so-called 'black soul'—the farewell of a steamer on its way to the bottom."

Howling with glee and yelling epithets, the crew of the U-53 derides the passing periscope of a British sub, the J-6, that tried unsuccessfully to sink their vessel near the Shetland Islands. Having missed with torpedoes at close range, the J-6 gave up the attack and cruised off underwater. The infrequent incident of sub attacking sub occurred six weeks before Bergen signed on the U-53, but he reconstructed the triumphant scene at the urging of the U-boat's crew.

Chapter 1

Time of trial for an awesome new weapon

In November 1945 the courtyard of the Nuremberg Palace of Justice was littered with empty machine-gun cartridges strewn among the fallen autumn leaves. Two German SS divisions had made their last stand in this city, hanging on for almost a week until American artillery and fighter-bombers had blasted them out. Now, six months after Germany had surrendered, the place still looked as if it were under siege. The shattered city was encircled by American infantry and antiaircraft guns, and fighter aircraft stood on alert not far away. Five Sherman tanks guarded the Palace of Justice, and in its courtyard and corridors soldiers armed with machine guns crouched at the ready behind sandbag emplacements. In the prison block next door to the courthouse, where 21 Nazi leaders were awaiting trial before the International Military Tribunal, steel-helmeted soldiers kept close guard night and day.

Among those incarcerated in this oppressive place was one of Germany's most distinguished naval officers—former Grand Admiral Karl Dönitz. A U-boat captain in World War I, Commander in Chief of the U-boat Navy in World War II, then head of the German Navy and finally Hitler's successor as chief of the German state, Dönitz occupied a cell measuring 13 feet by six and a half feet, with a chill stone floor and dirty brick walls. The only furniture was a rickety plywood table, a chair, an iron bed with a musty mattress and five United States Army blankets, and a toilet without a seat. By day, a wan twilight filtered in through a tiny window set high in the cell wall, and at night a powerful electric light filled the place with a brilliant, tormenting glare that made it exceedingly difficult to sleep. Night was the worst time. There was never a moment's peace from the endless chatter of the young American soldiers outside the door, the echoing clangs and bangs along the stone-flagged prison corridor, the rattling of the chain at the spy hole in the steel door, and the heavy, measured tramp of Hermann Göring's boots as he paced up and down in his nearby cell, three steps one way, three steps back, over and over again.

Karl Dönitz was not a troublesome prisoner. He took prison life quite well, kept his cell clean and his notebooks and pens in good order. His IQ was well above average—138, according to a United States Army psychiatric test—and he displayed a high level of creative ability that won the notice of his fellow prisoners. He spent much of his time reading volumes of English poetry and prose. But Dönitz was a bitter and disillusioned man. For he did not believe that he should be a prisoner at all, let alone that he should stand trial for his life. In his own estimation he was guilty of no crime.

Major Airey Neave, the British officer whose job it was to serve Dönitz with his indictment in his cell, recalled that when Dönitz saw the charges against him—conspiracy, crimes against peace, and war crimes—his dull eyes flashed suddenly, turning from gray to a sharp, cold blue. A look of intense disdain swept over his face.

"With what conspiracy am I charged?" he snapped. "I waged an honorable war against your country."

Later, at his trial, he was to declare, "I kept the Navy decent and clean down to every nook and corner." But what Karl Dönitz seemed never to

With the bleak-eyed intensity of veteran hunters, two lookouts stand watch on a U-boat, ignoring a fellow crewman emerging from belowdecks. At least four men—two are out of sight here—were on lookout duty any time a U-boat was on the surface, scanning all 360 degrees of the horizon for signs of enemy shipping.

understand was the underlying nature of the accusations. It was for his very success as the U-boat leader that he was brought before the International Tribunal. It was as history's most brilliant exponent of underwater warfare that he stood charged. And, in a sense, his place in the dock at Nuremberg was shared by the thousands of men who had served in the German U-boat Navy during the War, and during the War before that as well. Under indictment too was the weapon they used: the German U-boat, something unique in modern warfare, and the most feared and hated vessel in naval annals.

Twice in the space of 25 years, at the most critical stages of both world wars, U-boats alone had the power to decide the outcome for Germany. Twice they came within a whisper of victory in their attempt to isolate Britain and force her to terms. Twice they were prevented from doing so by the intervention of the United States. So close were the U-boats to winning the war in 1917 and 1942 that the very course of history could be said to have depended both times on a few score German submarines and the courageous men inside them.

In the sense that the U-boat was directed primarily against civilian shipping, it represented the vanguard of that modern phenomenon called total war—a state of absolute, all-out warfare waged by virtually any means that might bring down the enemy. Inevitably the U-boat men's slaughter of merchant ships and private citizens raised the question of the legality of their actions under international law. But purely legal debate was overwhelmed by a tide of hatred and loathing among the victim nations. The excessive military zeal and downright callousness of certain U-boat commanders, the accidental tragedies and the transparently deliberate atrocities—all the dark facets of U-boat warfare roused howls of execration. The U-boat men, justly or unjustly, were vilified as barbarian pirates in World War I and as fanatical Nazis in World War II. But were they pirates, or were they merely professional sailors doing their duty?

The very characteristics of the U-boat were partly to blame for the question. The U-boat was invisible; it did not play according to the rules; it had advantages that were considered unsporting; it waged war at sea like the commando on land—striking and then disappearing. So much was it feared and so deeply was it reviled that in World War II the British Empire and the United States together deployed nearly half the industrial might of the world against it in a campaign that was given the highest priority. But though the U-boat losses were substantial in both wars— about 45 per cent in World War I, 60 per cent in World War II—the U-boat Navy was not defeated in either. Disciplined, loyal and defiant to the bitter end, the U-boat men fought on against fearsome odds until the collapse of Germany deprived them of their bases and their cause.

In their moments of triumph and their downfall, the U-boat men proved themselves seafaring warriors of the highest order. Few men in modern times have been in more intimate contact with the sea in all its moods: exposure to the elements and nearness to the water made the men on a surfaced U-boat's bridge almost a part of their environment. In a true Atlantic storm the water would break over the bridge as solid as wet cement. The force and weight of the seas were so great that on

Fitful progress into an alien realm

Alexander the Great begins a solo dive in this medieval picture. Another account said two draftsmen went along.

Man doubtless began to dream of conquering the deep as soon as he put to sea, and tantalizing hints of progress toward that goal appear in several ancient chronicles. In the Fifth Century B.C., the historian Herodotus told of a Greek diver named Scyllias, who "plunged into the sea at Aphetes, and did not come to the surface until Artemesium"—a distance of nine miles. "I can only suppose," Herodotus added, "that he made the journey in some sort of vessel."

Scarcely a century later, courtiers of Alexander the Great reportedly devised a submersible glass barrel (*above*) to enable their Emperor to observe undersea mysteries. Ensconced in the vessel, Alexander could be raised and lowered by means of ropes, breathing the limited supply of air sealed inside.

By Renaissance times men were beginning to formulate the principles that eventually would make extended underwater travel possible. In the 16th Cen-

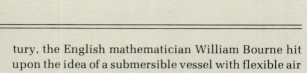

tury, the English mathematician William Bourne hit upon the idea of a submersible vessel with flexible air chambers that could alter the craft's displacement so that it "may goe under water unto the bottome, and so to come up againe at your pleasure"; the scheme, although never put into practice, foreshadowed the ballast tanks used in submarines nearly 300 years later.

Two Americans, David Bushnell and Robert Fulton, pioneered military subs based on Bourne's concept—and included a means of lateral underwater propulsion. Bushnell's submersible, an egg-shaped wooden vessel called the *Turtle*, rose and sank by means of a manual water valve and pump combination that controlled displacement. Navigating in New York Harbor with the aid of a hand-cranked propeller, the *Turtle* attempted to sink a British warship in 1776 with a keg of gunpowder attached to a timing device, but was thwarted by strong currents. In a French port 25 years later, Fulton's 21-foot-long *Nautilus*, featuring a horizontal rudder for better control, blew up an old schooner as a demonstration for Napoleon's benefit; unfortunately the Emperor declined to invest in the newfangled weapon.

The next 70 years of the 19th Century saw limited progress, and prolonged submarine navigation still seemed the stuff of fantasy when Jules Verne introduced his fictional sub *Nautilus* in the 1870 epic, *Twenty Thousand Leagues under the Sea*. Although one critic sneered at the tale for containing "not a single bit of valid speculation," less than four decades would pass before the first U-boats turned some of Verne's improbable imaginings into reality.

occasion men were swept overboard. In such weather the view from the bridge was petrifying—a vast wilderness of mountainous waves whipped white by the roaring wind. The duration of bridge watches had to be cut by half in these storms, for no man could stand more than two hours of battering by the seas and laceration by spray. Conditions were little better belowdecks. The violent corkscrewing, rolling, pitching and yawing motions of the boat, the brutal jolt as the bow hit a wave, and the steam-hammer clang of the sea smashing down on the hull made it difficult to relax for a minute.

Only when the U-boat dived was there any respite. Once the vessel was below the surface, all was peace and quiet. "A solemn stillness reigns," recalled Claus Bergen, a German marine artist who had traveled with a U-boat on a wartime patrol in 1917. "The adjustment of the periscope and the movement of the submarine steering gear are the only sounds in the vessel that are audible in the conning tower. The commander uses both hands to swing the greased and glittering periscope, now dripping with water. In his eye, the only eye in the vessel that is still in communication with the upper world, is the bright and shining reflection of the light of day."

Whether the U-boat was on the surface or was submerged, the interior lights burned 24 hours round the clock, effectively blurring the distinction between day and night. On long patrols especially, crews lived in an atmosphere of increasing squalor. The heat was oppressive, the air stale and foul and reeking of bilge water, wet oilskins, rubber boots, sweat, and diesel fumes so thick that a man's hair became a pitchy mire. The U-boat grew steadily damper from the intense condensation and the frequent leakage of water through the hatch of the conning tower. Bunks smelled moldy and charts began to rot. A gray-green film of mildew coated shoes and shirts. Sausages sprouted luxurious overcoats of mold overnight. In this environment a man could easily grow irritable and morose and, under stress, even paranoiac or violent—*Blechkoller* it was called, tin-can neurosis.

Yet through all this the U-boat men persevered. Hardship and deprivation were their constant companions; they contended with storm, ice and tropical heat, and lived continuously with the threat of death by asphyxiation, drowning or explosion. Only youth, camaraderie, discipline and a dogged heroism kept them going through an ordeal that many men would have found unendurable.

In the beginning, no one knew for certain how effective a weapon the submarine would be—or whether it would be effective at all. For this reason, the German U-boat Navy, which twice came so near to shaping history, had an exceptionally mean and niggardly start. In 1901, while other nations were developing underwater craft, Admiral Alfred von Tirpitz, creator of the modern German Navy, declared flatly that "Germany has no need of submarines." Later he explained: "I refused to throw money away on submarines so long as they could only cruise in home waters." The first U-boat—for *Unterseeboot*—to enter Naval service was not completed until December 1906, several years after the rival navies of Britain, France, Russia and the United States had acquired

fledgling submarine fleets. The *U-1* was a slow diver and poorly armed, with only a single torpedo tube in the bow. But she handled well on the surface—where most submarines, in spite of their name, spent most of their time—and in 1908 she successfully completed a 600-mile cruise from Heligoland around the Danish peninsula to Kiel. This achievement helped to convince the conservative German high command that the submarine was worthy of more consideration—although it remained essentially an experimental weapon.

Germany quickly outstripped other nations in submarine technology. In 1909, her shipyards turned out two new subs boasting a 12-knot surface speed and armament consisting of four torpedo tubes and a gun. By 1910, German U-boats could cross the North Sea, carry out a patrol and return to base without refueling. By 1913, U-boats of the *U-19* class, equipped with more efficient diesel engines, optically superior periscopes and powerful wireless transmitters, were capable of cruising 5,000 miles at eight knots—capable, in other words, of operations in the waters around the entire coast of Great Britain.

The implications of this capability were not entirely lost on the British. In July 1914, a month before the outbreak of World War I, Admiral Sir Percy Scott wrote a prescient letter to the London *Times*:

Fifteen sleek submarines stand ready for a taste of combat at the Kiel naval base in May 1914—three months before the War. The four in the foreground boasted new fuel-efficient diesel engines that enabled them to run 5,000 miles—from their home base to Great Britain and back.

"All war is, of course, barbarous, but in war the purpose of the enemy is to crush his foe; to arrive at this he will attack where his foe is most vulnerable. Our most vulnerable point is our food and oil supply. The submarine has introduced a new method of attacking these supplies. Will feelings of humanity restrain our enemy from using it?"

Scott's logic could not be faulted, but even the First Lord of the Admiralty, Winston Churchill, who had few illusions about feelings of humanity in war, rejected the possibility of a submarine campaign on merchant shipping. "I do not believe this would ever be done by a civilized power," he declared. And the rest of the Admiralty agreed. As they saw it, a submarine was bound by the same set of rules as a surface warship. These rules, the so-called Prize Regulations, dated back to the 16th Century but were still accepted as international law by almost all maritime powers. According to the regulations, a warship could stop an unarmed merchant ship for a search by firing a shot across its bow. If the ship turned out to be a neutral, it should be let go. If it belonged to a belligerent, both ship and cargo could be taken as prizes and the passengers and crew kept as hostages. If no prize crew could be provided, the ship could be sunk. Under all circumstances the passengers and crew of the ship had to be treated with every possible care.

Plainly, submarines were ill suited to observance of the Prize Regulations; a submarine could not search a merchant ship without exposing itself on the surface, and it could not spare men for a prize crew or accommodate prisoners on board for a long time. Therefore, true to Churchill's assumptions, a campaign against merchant vessels did not figure in Germany's plans for her small force of U-boats—only 20 prepared for combat compared with Britain's total of 74 submarines—when, on August 1, 1914, war began.

Though at this point Germany had declared war only on Russia, in the east, it was to the west that the U-boats turned their bows when they formed their first patrol line on the edge of the Heligoland Bight in the early hours of August 1. Among the U-boats that were moored on the surface along this static defensive position was the *U-9*, commanded by the man who was destined to become Germany's—and the world's—first submarine ace, Lieutenant Otto Weddigen. As the day passed and the crimson glow of sunset spread over the horizon in the direction of the British Isles, Weddigen turned to his first officer on the bridge, Johannes Spiess, and said:

"Spiess, you see how red the sky is. The whole world seems bathed in blood. Mark my words—England will declare war on us."

On August 4, England did so, and two days later 10 U-boats left Heligoland on the first submarine war patrol in history. Unlike the British, who saw the submarine only as a defensive weapon to be used in support of a surface fleet, the Germans suspected that the vessel had great offensive potential, and they intended to lose no time in putting it to the test. Weddigen and the other U-boat captains in that first patrol had no less a mission than attacking the British Grand Fleet.

In line abreast the U-boats slid out into the North Sea, then dispersed northward and westward till they formed a moving arc 40 miles across. Two days later they had traveled 400 miles and were nearing the Orkney

Islands. There the adventure rapidly went sour. One U-boat ran into a minefield and disappeared without trace. Another, the *U-15*, took on three British dreadnoughts with torpedoes but missed each time; later, afflicted with mechanical trouble, the *U-15* was caught on the surface by the light cruiser *Birmingham* and rammed and sunk.

This pioneering patrol had been far from successful. The group had lost 20 per cent of its vessels and had failed to sink a single victim. "Our submarine fleet was as good as any in the world," one U-boat officer remarked wryly, "but not very good."

Nonetheless, in the weeks that followed, more U-boats were sent out, singly and in pairs, to hunt warships in England's eastern waters. Sightings of periscopes by British sailors became a daily occurrence, and this state of affairs so alarmed the Commander in Chief of the Grand Fleet, Admiral Sir John Jellicoe, that he ordered Britain's big dreadnought battleships to abandon the anchorage at Scapa Flow in favor of a remote sea loch on the northwest side of Scotland. Other British ships continued their patrols, however, and on September 5, barely a month after the beginning of the War, the light cruiser *Pathfinder* was hit by a single torpedo fired by another future ace, Lieutenant Otto Hersing, and sank after her magazine blew up.

Far worse was to follow for the Royal Navy. Shortly after dawn on September 22, some 20 miles off the Dutch coast, Johannes Spiess, still the first officer on Weddigen's *U-9*, spotted a small masthead coming over the horizon. "It looked like the mast of a warship," he wrote later. "Could this be our first sight of the enemy in the War?" He had the

In a cloud of smoke, the torpedoed British cruiser Pathfinder plunges bow first into the North Sea in September 1914, taking 259 of her crew with her. The 2,940-ton vessel, which took only four minutes to go under, was the first warship to be sunk by a U-boat.

diesels stopped and called Weddigen from his breakfast below. Although the ship Spiess had spotted was miles away, Weddigen ordered the *U-9* to submerge immediately; when the sea closed over them, he took his position at the periscope. As the submarine drew closer, the periscope was raised above the surface just a few seconds at a time so that its white, feather-shaped wake would elude detection.

Suddenly Weddigen clapped Spiess on the shoulder. "Spiess," he said, "there are three English battle cruisers. They are of the same class as the *Birmingham*"—the ship that had rammed and sunk the *U-15* the month before. "Revenge!" replied Spiess.

The three ships were, in fact, not at all like the *Birmingham* but were old armored cruisers, the *Aboukir*, *Cressy* and *Hogue*. Any victims at all, however, would be sweet revenge for U-boat men who, thus far in the War, had lost more vessels than they had sunk.

Weddigen chose as his first target the *Aboukir*, the middle of the three cruisers. The torpedo tubes were made ready for action. "First tube," he ordered. "Bow shot."

Spiess unscrewed the safety cover over the electric firing mechanism and held his thumb ready on the appropriate button.

"Periscope out," Weddigen said. "First tube stand by."

The men of the *U-9* had never fired a torpedo in combat, never seen a ship blow up. They did not know what to expect. They were only about 500 yards from the *Aboukir*, and some of them half-feared that at that close range the explosion of the torpedo would send them to the bottom along with their victim.

"First tube fire," Weddigen ordered. Then: "Periscope in."

Spiess pressed the firing button, simultaneously ran the periscope down with his other hand and called out: "First tube fired." He automatically checked the depth indicator to be sure the U-boat did not break through the surface because of the momentary lightening of her bow between the time the torpedo burst from the tube and the time the sea water rushed in to fill it. Then he clung to the periscope with both hands, fearing the worst.

Thirty-one long seconds passed before the torpedo hit the target and the sound traveled back. Spiess heard a dull blow and then a louder explosion. Everyone cheered.

The periscope went back up. The *Aboukir* was sinking stern first. Her companion ship, the *Hogue*, closed to pick up survivors and was herself hit by two torpedoes from the *U-9*. "Those of us in the conning tower," Spiess recalled, "tried, by cursing the English, who had incited the Japanese and all Europe against us, to dispel the gruesome impression made on us by the drowning men struggling in the midst of floating wreckage and clinging to the upturned lifeboats."

Now the last of the three cruisers, the *Cressy*, steamed up to rescue the survivors from the other two. She, in turn, was hit twice by the *U-9*. "The periscope revealed a fearful picture," Spiess remembered. "The giant with four funnels turned slowly over to port. Men climbed like ants over her side and then, as she turned turtle completely, they ran about on her broad flat keel until, in a few minutes, she disappeared beneath the waves." Spiess watched this scene through the periscope "with a sense

With the unwavering gaze that led a fellow officer to characterize him as a "man of iron," U-boat ace Lieutenant Otto Weddigen displays on his chest the Iron Crosses he won for sinking three British cruisers in a single day, September 22, 1914. Weddigen's exploits were later to earn him Germany's highest award for valor, the Pour le Mérite (bottom).

of tragic horror. For long minutes we were lost as if in some kind of a trance." As well they might be, for they had not only sunk three cruisers totaling 36,000 tons but had killed 1,460 human beings in little more than the space of an hour.

Germany went wild with joy at the news. Every member of the submarine's crew was awarded the Iron Cross Second Class. Weddigen also received the coveted Iron Cross First Class, and to the *U-9* went the right to have the Iron Cross painted on her conning tower. In Britain the deadly ease with which a U-boat had destroyed three armored cruisers astounded the Admiralty. Senior Navy officers derided the sinkings as somehow underhand and unsporting, but they also knew that henceforth the U-boat Navy was a force to be reckoned with. This new weapon had inflicted more damage on the British Navy in one attack than had Germany's entire High Seas Fleet.

Soon U-boats were to demonstrate their potency in another, even more ominous way. On October 20, 14 miles off the Norwegian coast, the *U-17* sank a British cargo ship, the *Glitra*—the first merchant vessel ever lost to a submarine. The *U-17* acted strictly within the Prize Regulations, allowing the crew to take to the lifeboats before opening the vessel's sea cocks and scuttling her. But the incident presented the German high command with its first glimpse of a new concept of U-boat warfare, one that—if diligently pursued—would inevitably lead to departures from naval convention.

Up to this point, the only violations of international maritime law had been committed by the British—or so the Germans claimed. Britain's alleged misdeed was her imposition of an extremely stringent naval blockade on the enemy. British vessels were stopping and searching all ships, including neutral ones, for contraband cargoes bound for Germany; the British definition of "contraband" was so broad that it even included food. Royal Navy warships also barred the exit routes to the Atlantic for German shipping.

Such a blockade was at that time virtually the only means a sea power such as Britain had of attacking a major land power like Germany. Germany's logical riposte was to impose a counterblockade on Britain. But the few German surface raiders that ventured near British waters were soon driven off by the Royal Navy. For the Germans the U-boat was the only practical solution. Even at this early date, some of the admirals in the high command were beginning to speak of the U-boat as Germany's chief offensive weapon. The characteristics of a submarine made it perfect for patrolling the sea routes unseen and lying in ambush at the vulnerable points of convergence for ships heading toward British ports. Correctly handled, the U-boat had the capability to sever Britain's maritime life lines.

The sea was at once the main source of Britain's power and her main weakness. A large percentage of her food had to be imported by sea, along with all the oil and most of the raw materials necessary for her industry and war effort. If these imports were drastically reduced by cutting the island's sea communications, then the British would be forced to sue for peace or face starvation and defeat. It was true that Germany had few U-boats available for this mammoth task—only 29 by

The deadly dart of the sea

With a snout packed full of explosive, the German self-propelled torpedo that came of age during World War I could blast a gaping hole in even the heaviest of hulls. And it could deliver its subsurface wallop through turbulent seas from a distance of three miles—although U-boat men usually launched their seagoing missiles from a much shorter range for deadly accuracy.

The torpedo's reciprocating engine, automatically activated on firing, was driven by compressed air stored in a large tank just abaft the warhead. A burner heated the air, increasing its pressure and adding about 30 per cent more power to the system.

A shaft transmitted the power to a gearbox at the stern of the torpedo. The gears turned two propellers—one rotating clockwise and the other counterclockwise, ensuring that the torpedo did not pick up a spin that could cause it to stray.

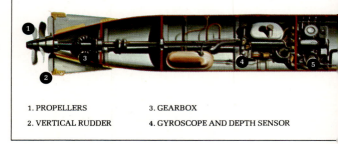

1. PROPELLERS   3. GEARBOX
2. VERTICAL RUDDER   4. GYROSCOPE AND DEPTH SENSOR

The tandem propellers sent the torpedo streaking through the water at a speed of about 40 knots.

Two sets of tail fins guided the missile. Rudders on a vertical pair of fins, controlled by a gyroscope sensitive to the slightest change in direction, kept the torpedo on course. Proper depth was maintained by rudders on a horizontal pair of tail fins, which were in turn regulated by a pressure-sensing diaphragm in the hull casing.

Upon striking the target, the warhead was exploded by a simple trigger device protruding from its nose and leading inside to a highly volatile detonating charge, such as fulminate of mercury. The trigger mechanism included an ingenious safeguard against the terrifying possibility of an inadvertent detonation: It was capped by a safety lock in the form of a tiny propeller that spun itself off a threaded shaft and fell away after the torpedo had run about 30 yards on its course.

5. ENGINE
6. COMPRESSED-AIR TANK
7. WARHEAD
8. TRIGGER WITH SAFETY LOCK

the end of 1914—and that Britain's mercantile fleet was enormous, amounting to almost half the merchant ships in existence in the world. But fully one third of her imports were brought in by ships of neutral countries, and here lay Britain's Achilles' heel. If Germany declared an unrestricted U-boat campaign that turned the waters around the British Isles into a war zone where all ships could be sunk without warning, neutral ships would be frightened away from trade with Britain, and that nation would inexorably wither and die.

The German government was divided on this issue. Some Germans feared that the reaction of neutral countries—the United States above all—might adversely affect Germany's interests. They pointed out that there was a crucial difference between Britain's blockade and the proposed German one: in the British blockade, only the cargo was lost; in the German one, both the ship itself and the human beings on board would be lost as well.

By early 1915, German hopes for a quick victory on land had faded, and the Kaiser decided that a decisive victory must be sought at sea: on February 4 he declared the waters around the British Isles a war zone. Any enemy ships entering this zone would be sunk without warning, and no guarantee could be given for the safety of their passengers and crews. Moreover, neutral ships also ran the risk of being sunk in this zone, though some effort would be made to spare ships flying the colors of neutral countries, unless there was other evidence to suggest that these colors were false.

So the first unrestricted U-boat campaign began its brutal course. Over the next two months some 20 U-boats set out from German bases for the waters around Britain. Within a week of the start of the offensive, four of them reached their patrol areas, attacked 11 ships and sank seven of them. From that point forward the toll on Allied and neutral shipping began to soar. The total tonnage lost in January 1915, before the unrestricted campaign began, had been 47,900 tons. In March the total leaped to 80,700 tons, in May to 120,000 tons, and by August it had reached a formidable 185,800 tons, representing a huge loss of foodstuffs and war materials—and more to the point, a steady reduction in the number of hulls that were available to the Allies for carrying further war materials, food and troops.

If the U-boats were proving themselves to be more effective weapons than anyone in Germany had supposed before the War, they were also deepening Germany's reputation for ruthlessness. In April 1915 the British ship *Harpalyce*, en route to America to pick up food for the relief of the starving people of Belgium, was torpedoed without warning even though she was flying a white flag and bearing the words COMMISSION FOR BELGIAN RELIEF painted in large white letters along her side. The British public was horrified, viewing the incident as the logical continuation at sea of the brutality meted out by the German Army against Belgian civilians on land. Britain's government fanned these sentiments by launching a propaganda campaign in which the U-boat men were vilified as pirates and barbarians.

International opinion was no less outraged, especially in the United States. Already an American had died as a result of the unrestricted

campaign: Leon C. Thrasher drowned when the British liner *Falaba* was torpedoed by the *U-28* in St. George's Channel on March 28. American newspapers called this attack "a crime against humanity" and described Germany as "a frenzied beast at bay."

Hitherto America had taken an ambivalent attitude toward the war in Europe. Determined to have nothing to do with any foreign conflict, the United States, as a peaceful neutral, reserved the right to trade with either side and send its ships anywhere in pursuit of lawful business—war or no war. American businessmen initially had been displeased with the way the British blockade was interfering with their trade with Germany. As the War progressed, however, their trade with the British and French in war materials and goods of all kinds grew more lucrative than any possible commerce with Germany, and their indignation at the U-boats' interference waxed accordingly. As the U-boats continued to take American lives, opinion turned from indignation to full-blown wrath, but the United States nonetheless remained determined to keep out of the War at all costs.

Four German submariners form a tense control-room tableau in this 1915 depiction of a U-boat's descent. One U-boat man, remembering the anxious moments of wondering whether an enemy had spotted his sub, wrote: "We stare into the emptiness and wait. Everything depends on the judgment and ability of the commander."

It would take a major catastrophe at sea before American opinion finally shifted far enough for the country to seriously entertain the possibility of joining in the struggle. That catastrophe occurred in May 1915, when a lone German submarine had a fateful encounter with a luxury liner called the *Lusitania*.

The 30,000-ton Cunard liner *Lusitania* was one of the largest, fastest, most popular transatlantic passenger ships of her time. In addition to her speed (26 knots flat out), she provided luxury unsurpassed by any of the world's finest hotels. Moreover, so her owners claimed, the *Lusitania* was unsinkable: her double bottom and watertight compartments guaranteed that.

The outbreak of the War did not unduly disrupt the *Lusitania*'s sailings. She had been looked over by the Admiralty for possible use as an armed cruiser but was found to burn too much coal for war duties. However, the *Lusitania* was required to reserve cargo space for the express purpose of conveying American war materials across the sea. And this she dependably did.

On April 17, 1915, she left Liverpool at the start of her 101st round trip, docking in New York on April 24. She prepared to start on the return voyage to England a week later.

The United States government's reaction to the German declaration of a war zone around the British Isles, and the fury with which the American press had greeted the subsequent torpedoing of the *Falaba*, had alarmed some German-Americans, who were fearful that they would become pariahs within their adopted country. A group of leaders from the New York German community conferred with a representative of the German embassy and decided that the way to avoid the loss of American lives and the attendant recrimination would be to discourage Americans from challenging the U-boat blockade. On the morning of May 1, the day the *Lusitania* was due to sail, this group published an advertisement on the shipping page of various New York newspapers warning travelers that British ships, even those that were carrying passengers, were "liable to destruction" in the war zone. On the advice of the embassy representative, the advertisers signed the notice "Imperial German Embassy." The warning was printed right next to a notice of the *Lusitania*'s sailing time.

The juxtaposition of the two notices caused some furor among press, public and passengers alike. A swarm of reporters and cinema newsreel teams gathered round the main gangway as the *Lusitania*'s passengers embarked. The newsmen cheerfully announced that they were there to record "the last voyage of the *Lusitania*."

Anxiety spread like contagion among all on board the *Lusitania*—all, that is, except her master, 58-year-old Captain William "Bowler Bill" Turner, a broad, bluff, taciturn martinet with immense experience of the sea and total contempt for all passengers, whom he described as "a lot of bloody monkeys." To reassure them now, Captain Turner chose more diplomatic language: "There is always a danger, but the best guarantees of your safety are the *Lusitania* herself and the fact that wherever there is danger your safety is in the hands of the Royal Navy."

Picturing a noose of submarines tightening around the British Isles, a poster calls upon German citizens to "buy bonds for the U-boat war against England." The poster was part of a propaganda effort coinciding with the Kaiser's proclamation in February 1915 that merchant ships bound for Britain would be destroyed without warning.

A little after midday, two hours later than scheduled, the *Lusitania* sailed. On board were 1,257 passengers, 197 of them American. Several were public figures, most notably the 37-year-old multimillionaire and amateur sportsman, Alfred G. Vanderbilt, traveling to London to attend a meeting of the International Horse Show Association. In addition to the bona fide passengers, three Germans were discovered hiding in a steward's pantry shortly after sailing and were put under arrest to be questioned when the ship got to England. Whether they were German agents or merely stowaways has never been decided; their presence was simply one of the many mysteries surrounding the voyage.

Another mystery, never cleared up, involved the liner's cargo. According to the manifest, the *Lusitania* was laden with a miscellany of sheet brass, copper ingots, cheese, beef, bacon, Connecticut oysters, confectionery, leather hides, furs, machinery, auto parts, dental equipment—and 4,200 cases of small-caliber rifle ammunition (amounting to about 10½ tons of explosives), 1,248 cases of shrapnel shells and 18 cases of fuses. Subsequent investigations have produced indications—though no proof—that the *Lusitania* was carrying even more munitions than this, that the ammunition in reality totaled six million rounds, and that 323 bales listed as raw furs were in fact a volatile type of gun cotton that exploded when brought into contact with water. Moreover, rumor at the time had it that some six million dollars in gold bullion lay locked in strongholds on the lower decks. One way or another, more than a little intrigue attended the ship that left for England on that calm and sunny first day of May 1915.

While the *Lusitania* was heading eastward for her usual landfall, Fastnet Rock, off the southern tip of Ireland, the *U-20* under Lieutenant Walther Schwieger was traveling down the west coast of Ireland toward the same point, looking for large troop transports—legitimate targets of war. The U-boat's presence was known to the Admiralty. Her radio signals to Germany had been intercepted and decrypted by the Naval Intelligence Division in London and passed on to both the First Lord of the Admiralty, Winston Churchill, and the First Sea Lord, Admiral Sir John Fisher. At 9 a.m. on May 5 the *U-20* was plotted by the Admiralty as hovering a few miles to the northwest of Fastnet. The *Lusitania* was still almost two days' steaming to the west.

The next two days brought intermittent fog to the Fastnet area, but in the occasional clear patches Schwieger sank three vessels. By the evening of May 6, Admiral Sir Charles Coke at the Royal Navy's nearby Queenstown base thought the situation so grave that he sent a signal to all British ships: "Submarines active off south coast of Ireland." On board the *Lusitania*, Captain Turner was given the message at 7:50 p.m. as he was about to go down to dinner and a gala end-of-voyage concert. At 8:30 an Admiralty message reiterating the warning was handed to Turner. The captain promptly had the lifeboats swung out on their davits, posted double lookouts, closed as many watertight doors as possible, imposed a black-out and reduced speed so that he would clear Fastnet by night. "On entering the war zone tomorrow," he told his jittery passengers, "we shall be securely in the care of the Royal Navy."

At that moment the *U-20* was lying on the surface, out of sight of land,

A warning signed by the German embassy in the New York newspapers on May 1, 1915, adjacent to an ad for the British luxury liner Lusitania, gave notice that Americans on the vessel would enter the war zone "at their own risk."

Attended by a bevy of tooting tugs, the Lusitania steams out of New York Harbor on her final voyage. In answer to one passenger's worries about the U-boats lurking ahead, the captain confidently stated that the Lusitania was "safer than the trolley cars in New York City."

recharging her batteries. The U-boat was low on fuel and had only three torpedoes left, two of which Schwieger intended to reserve for the long homeward trip he would begin on the next day. By 11 o'clock the next morning, Friday, May 7, the fog had dispersed, and Schwieger decided to submerge until noon. At about the time he dived, the Admiralty issued yet another warning to all British ships: "Submarines active in southern part of Irish Channel. Last heard of 20 miles south of Coningbeg Light. Make certain *Lusitania* gets this."

The *Lusitania* did get it, and Captain Turner made a fateful 20-degree alteration of course north toward land—partly because he wanted to get a proper navigational fix at the end of the ocean crossing, partly because a course closer to land seemed safer. Meanwhile the *U-20* had begun her long voyage home. She was now traveling at full speed on the surface—and on a course that would intercept the great liner's.

Sitting jacketless on his bridge in the brilliant sunshine, Walther Schwieger, young and blond, ate his lunch of potato soup and sausage as he listened to the popular ballad "Rose of Stamboul" wafting up from the boat's gramophone through the conning-tower hatch. Shortly after 1 p.m., he noticed a smudge of smoke on his starboard bow; peering intently through his binoculars, he watched it grow into what looked at first like the masts and funnels of two destroyers. But the distant image quickly resolved itself into the four funnels and two masts of a steamer making toward land.

"Diving stations!" Schwieger yelled down the voice pipe. "Flood!"

The *U-20* submerged and set a course that would take her ahead of the
unsuspecting *Lusitania.*

The liner steered toward the 256-foot headland called the Old Head of
Kinsale until 1:40 p.m. Then Captain Turner, only 25 miles from
Queenstown and safety, ordered a sharp turn to starboard and began to
take a four-point bearing to determine his exact position. This alteration
brought the *Lusitania* exactly into the *U-20's* path. For the next 25 minutes the U-boat labored at her maximum underwater speed of nine knots
to gain an attack position off the *Lusitania's* bow. Shortly before
2:10 p.m. the Cunarder moved into Schwieger's periscope firing sight
for a perfect torpedo shot. The liner's orchestra was still beating out the
"Blue Danube Waltz" for the second-sitting lunch guests when Walther
Schwieger quietly said, "Fire."

To his navigation officer standing beside him in the conning tower,

Schwieger dictated a log entry: "Clean bow shot at 700 meters' range (G torpedo three meters' depth adjustment), angle of intersection 90 degrees, estimated speed 22 knots."

The lookout on the starboard side of the *Lusitania's* forecastle saw the white streak in the water and cried out to the bridge: "Torpedoes coming on the starboard side!"

At almost the same moment another lookout stationed high in the crow's-nest telephoned the bridge, where the second officer repeated the report to Captain Turner:

"There is a torpedo coming, sir."

Captain Turner looked up and he, too, saw the white wake speeding in toward his ship. It was so close that he had time to take only one step toward the helmsman before it struck.

Lieutenant Schwieger watched the result of his attack through the periscope, dictating log notes all the while:

"Shot hit starboard side right behind bridge. An unusually heavy detonation follows with a very strong explosion cloud (high in the air just in front of the first smokestack). The explosion of the torpedo must have been followed by a second one (boiler or coal or powder?). The superstructure above the point of impact and the bridge are torn asunder, fire breaks out, and smoke envelops the high bridge. The ship stops immediately and heels over to starboard very quickly, immersing simultaneously at the bow."

Within seconds of the explosion, which had thrown a column of coal, wood and steel splinters 150 feet above the liner's radio aerial, her wireless operator was tapping out his SOS: COME AT ONCE, BIG LIST, 10 MILES SOUTH OLD HEAD KINSALE.

The hole torn just aft of the bridge by the torpedo had flooded the nearly empty starboard coal bunkers and caused the ship to list 15 degrees almost instantly. The second, internal explosion, which occurred immediately afterward, did not destroy the bridge or set the ship on fire, as Schwieger had suggested in the log, but it did cause massive damage in the bow. As a result the *Lusitania's* foredecks were underwater within a few minutes of the blast.

There has been much speculation as to the cause of this second explosion. The boilers may have ruptured, or coal gas from the forward bunkers may have ignited. But some have cited the secret cargo of contraband munitions that they suspect the liner carried (the official cargo of explosives was insufficient to cause such mortal damage). Whatever the reason, the consequences of the second blast were more serious than the original torpedo explosion.

Though steam pressure was falling and the engine room flooding fast, the *Lusitania's* momentum kept her forging ahead out of control, listing over to starboard as she went and going steadily down by the bow. Captain Turner gave the order to abandon ship, but the *Lusitania's* speed made it difficult to launch the lifeboats, and several were overturned when they hit the water, spewing out their occupants, who were either crushed against the side of the ship or left struggling in the sea far astern. Because of the heavy list, lifeboats on the port side had no clear drop down to the sea, while those on the starboard side had swung so far out

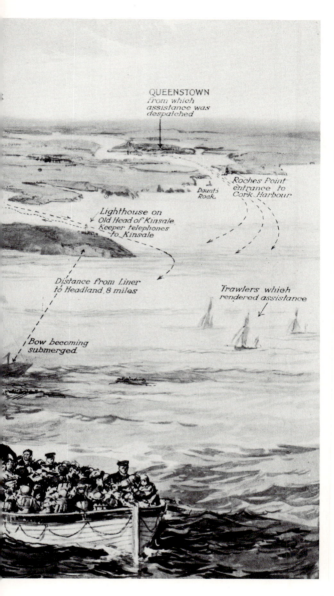

The stricken Lusitania—seen here in a contemporary magazine drawing—begins to slide beneath the surface moments after a torpedo from the U-20 struck her starboard side near the bow. Of the efforts to launch lifeboats and reach the nearby Irish coast, one survivor said simply: "There was infinite confusion."

that passengers were afraid to climb out to them. Several port-side boats bumped down the side of the ship and had their bottoms torn out by the large rivet heads protruding from the liner's plates. The *Lusitania* had lifesaving equipment for 2,605 people—far more than were actually on board. But the launching of the lifeboats was so difficult that only six of the 48 stayed afloat, and only a small proportion of the passengers were able to find a place in them.

In vain, Captain Turner tried to head his great ship for the shore, hoping to beach her. He also tried unsuccessfully to reduce her headway so that the liner could be abandoned with greater safety. There was no response from engines or rudder. Appalled by the endless cascade of bodies plunging headlong out of smashed or inverted lifeboats, Turner gave an order temporarily halting their launching. This infuriated one panicky New Yorker who, with a group of passengers and crew, had been trying to lower a port-side boat. "To hell with the captain!" he yelled, drawing a revolver. "The first man that disobeys my orders to launch the boat I shoot to kill." A sailor knocked out the retaining pin, and the boat slid down the sloping deck, scything its way through a crowd of passengers and crushing more than 30 of them to death before it toppled over and spilled its occupants into the sea.

The *Lusitania* was clearly doomed. The bow was invisible below the water and the sea was pouring into the ship through the forward hatches and starboard portholes—at a rate later calculated to be three and three quarters tons per minute per porthole.

The slope of the deck was now so steep that people were sliding across it, fetching up against the railings. The sea was thick with flotsam and bodies, both the living and the dead. Above the lifeboats and the swimmers, the *Lusitania's* four huge funnels loomed menacingly, threatening to topple down on them at any moment. People were leaving the ship by any means they could: by climbing down ropes or the ship's wire log line, or by diving overboard—a sheer dive of 100 feet for those who jumped from the rising stern. Others stayed: people who could not swim or who were resigned to death, women who would not abandon their helpless infants, and men like the London reporter of the International News Service who continued to take photographs until the ship went down, exclaiming, "These will be the greatest pictures ever!" (They were lost in the sinking.)

Alfred G. Vanderbilt, who could not swim a stroke, was one of those who stayed. He was seen on B deck vainly attempting to rescue a hysterical woman. He was heard telling his valet, "Find all the kiddies you can, boy!" He was seen again later in the ship's great entrance hall quietly tying life jackets to a collection of bassinets containing babies from the nursery. He was last observed lighting a cigarette and strolling forward after giving his life jacket away to a young nurse. Vanderbilt's body was never found.

At 2:25 Schwieger decided to call it a day. "It seems as if the vessel will be afloat only a short time," he noted in his log. "Submerge to 24 meters and go out to sea. I could not have fired a second torpedo into this throng of humanity attempting to save themselves."

As the great ship slid slowly forward and downward, the sea swirled

Coffins fill a mass grave of Lusitania victims in Queenstown, Ireland. Business in the city was suspended for the day, and mourners came from every part of the country to attend the services for the 130 unidentified casualties of the sinking.

over her bridge and around Captain Turner's legs. Pulling his cap tight over his head, he began to climb up a ladder from the bridge to the signal halyards, but the ship sank faster than he could climb. He was overtaken by the encroaching sea and floated off clutching a chair. It would help keep him afloat until his rescue.

Pointed steeply downward, her four slowly revolving propellers and great 65-ton rudder sticking high into the air, the *Lusitania* suddenly stopped dead in her dive and quivered throughout her length. Her bow had hit the rocky bed of the sea. At this extraordinary angle, the great ship stood and pivoted for a long moment, her boat decks still crowded with people hanging onto railings and struggling to launch the remaining boats. Then her stern slowly settled with ''a thunderous roar''—as one survivor put it—''as of the collapse of a great building during a fire.'' At least two passengers were sucked into the dreadful black vortexes of the funnels as they dipped beneath the surface—and were shot out again when a boiler blew up. The boiler explosion was followed by a ''long, lingering moan,'' recalled a survivor. ''Those who were lost seemed to be calling from the very depths.'' The surface where the ship had gone down boiled as if from an underwater volcano, then quieted, leaving a calm and sunlit sea covered by wreckage and people scattered in a circle half a mile across. The *Lusitania*, pride of the Cunard line, had taken just 18 minutes to sink.

By the time the last survivor had been fished out of the Atlantic by a fleet of rescue boats from Queenstown late that evening, 1,198 people had lost their lives, including 785 passengers; 94 of them were children (and 35 of those, infants), 128 of them Americans. Fast and supposedly unsinkable, the *Lusitania* had been the best the British had to offer in the way of attack-proof passenger ships. She now lay on the bottom, and the U-boat—the curious-looking vessel that just a year earlier had been regarded by the Germans as no more than a promising experiment—had in a stroke established itself in the eyes of an aghast world as a devastatingly effective war machine.

In Germany, the press generally acclaimed the sinking, although some German accounts held that Schwieger had mistaken the *Lusitania* for a troop transport. (Schwieger was killed before the end of the War, and it was never determined for certain whether he knew he was attacking a passenger liner before he fired the torpedo.) In the United States, the news was received with horror. President Wilson wept in the White House garden when he was told. Former President Theodore Roosevelt denounced the sinking as ''piracy on a vaster scale of murder than any oldtime pirate ever practiced.'' He added: ''It seems inconceivable that we can refrain from taking action. We owe it to humanity, to our own national self-respect!''

The day after the sinking, the United States Ambassador in Britain, Walter Hines Page, telegraphed President Wilson a summary of British opinion: ''The unofficial feeling is that the United States must declare war or forfeit European respect. If the United States do come in, the moral and physical effect will be to bring peace quickly and to give the United States a great influence in ending the war and in so reorganising the world as to prevent its recurrence.''

But Americans were not ready to declare war. The President merely issued a note of protest to Germany, reaffirming his determination to safeguard by any means the rights of Americans to travel anywhere on the high seas in any ship they chose, even if that ship belonged to a belligerent nation. In Britain, both the United States and her President were lampooned as cowards. Audiences booed and hissed when the word ''America'' was mentioned in the theaters, and British soldiers fighting on the Continent began calling a dud shell a ''Wilson.''

Nevertheless, the *Lusitania* case was a smoldering fuse. It contributed mightily to anti-German feeling in America; eventually it would help to change the minds of the people and the President.

The furor that arose over the sinking of the *Lusitania* took a long time to die down. Indeed, if Schwieger had survived the War—he was killed in 1917 when his new command, the *U-88*, struck a mine—he would undoubtedly have been put on trial at the insistence of the Allies as Germany's No. 1 war criminal.

The U-35: first in a mighty fleet of equals

By any measure, the most famous U-boat to fight in World War I was the *U-35*, captained by Germany's quintessential ace, Lothar von Arnauld de la Perière *(page 36)*. But aside from her record, there was little that was unusual about the *U-35*; she was, in fact, typical of the remarkable breed of ship built by the hundreds for the Kaiser's undersea Navy.

Launched at Kiel in 1913, the *U-35* was 212 feet in length, with a beam of 20.5 feet and a keel-to-deck depth of 11.7 feet. She displaced about 800 tons, mounted two torpedo tubes at her bow and two at her stern, and carried a total of six torpedoes. Two diesel engines, each producing 1,700 horsepower, spun her dual propellers and recharged the storage batteries that drove her when she was submerged.

The *U-35*—like her sister submarines—was a stunning technological achievement. She could undertake missions only dreamed of in former wars, dropping beneath the sea's surface to attack ships 10 or 20 times larger. Moreover, unlike the submarines of other nations, the *U-35* and the other U-boats were marvelously trim vessels on the surface.

The principles of hydrodynamics dictated that, to withstand the enormous water pressure deep beneath the sea's surface, the hull of a submarine had to be shaped like a tube tapered at both ends. Britain and its allies built tube-shaped vessels that performed well enough submerged, but wallowed horribly on the surface. The Germans, however, sheathed a tubular internal pressure hull with a second hull shaped like that of a sleek destroyer *(overleaf)*. The shape of the outer hull enabled German subs to cut through the waves at about 18 knots and keep a steady keel in seas that would force a cigar-shaped submarine to seek refuge below.

When a U-boat submerged, water flooded the space between the hulls so the outer casing was not subjected to crushing pressures. Her surface-ship configuration made her more difficult to manage underwater than the tube-shaped subs. But this disadvantage was negligible because a submarine on patrol usually spent nearly all of its time on the surface, going under only to hide or attack.

Until the very last days of the War, German sub builders kept striving for improvements. They lengthened the vessels, gave their bows a more sweeping profile and added heavier guns. But these were only minor modifications, and all the while the shipyards kept turning out boats for duty like so many knackwursts on a string. So felicitous was the basic design that years later, when Germany again went to war, the U-boats she turned loose on Britain were not substantially different from the *U-35*.

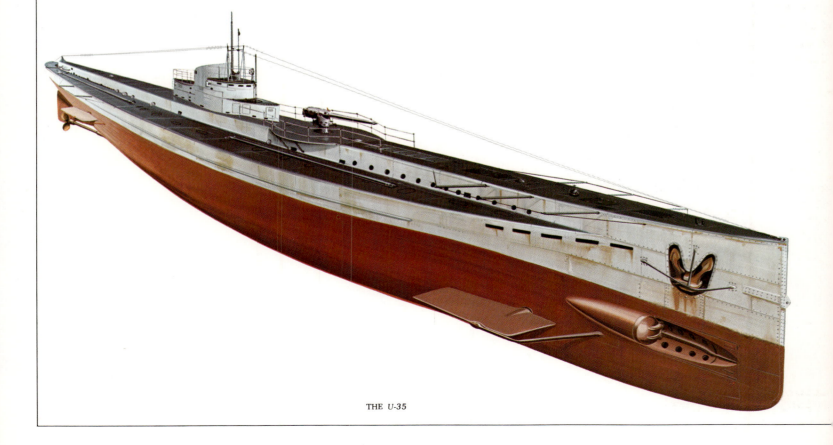

THE *U-35*

The German Navy regarded the U-boat more as a weapon that happened to be manned than as a vessel that happened to be armed. Every ton of displacement was devoted primarily to the submarine's fighting capability—the weapons and equipment that contributed to her firepower, speed and radius of action. The crew of 35 men aboard had to make do with the narrow spaces and oddly shaped gaps left between the machinery.

The conning tower, which sat atop the hull amidships, and the control room immediately beneath it together formed the nerve center of the U-boat. Two periscopes, one for aiming the torpedoes and one for guiding the ship, were used from inside the conning tower, where the U-boat captain was stationed during battle. To prevent the lenses from fogging when the boat submerged, the whole periscope tube was filled with dry air and sealed. A heavy glass plate was mounted midway down the tube to hold out the sea in case the upper end of the periscope was shot off in combat.

A hatchway joined the tower to the control room, where the chief engineer and his asssistants operated the engines, tanks and hydroplanes. These three systems acted in concert when it came time for the *U-35* to submerge. Enough water was let into the ballast tanks mounted on the outside of her pressure hull *(cross section at right)* to bring the U-boat to diving trim—just at the point of sinking. Then, by means of her engines and hydroplanes, the vessel was propelled forward and downward. She normally maintained neutral buoyancy throughout her dive and returned to the surface in the same way, like a graceful sea creature in underwater flight; but in an emergency the water could be forced from the ballast tanks by compressed air, causing her to rise rapidly.

Just aft of the control room, through a circular door mounted in a hefty watertight bulkhead, lay the engine room, lair of the great diesels that drove the U-boat when she was on the surface. Here, in a murky, fume-laden atmosphere where every surface dripped with grease, the trained ears of the crewmen listened intently for any irregularity in the rhythm of the engines. "It was a little hell of rattling, whirring tumult," recalled an engineer.

Aft of this compartment lay the hushed room that housed the electric motors used to power the vessel when she was submerged (using diesels underwater would have burned up all the air inside the boat's hull in a matter of seconds). The batteries for the electric motors were located below the compartment's floor; fully charged, they could keep the boat running for nearly two hours at a speed of six to eight knots. The electric motors were linked to the diesels by a reversible coupling. When the batteries needed recharging, the vessel surfaced and the diesels spun the electric motors in reverse, causing them to act as generators.

At the U-boat's stern and bow were the two sets of torpedo tubes that dealt her dreaded sting, and scattered throughout the boat were the vest-pocket spaces where the crew members lived and toiled, more like miners in a pit than sailors on the ocean wave.

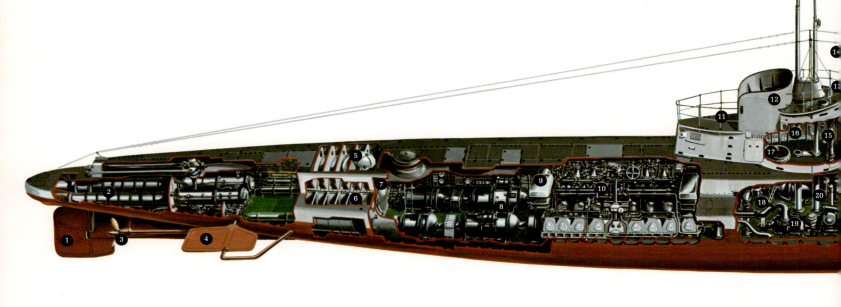

1. RUDDER
2. STERN TORPEDO TUBES
3. PROPELLER
4. HYDROPLANE
5. HATCH FOR LOADING TORPEDOES
6. FUEL TANK
7. WATERTIGHT DOOR
8. ELECTRIC MOTORS
9. VENTILATOR
10. DIESEL ENGINES
11. CONNING-TOWER DECK
12. WEATHER SCREEN
13. DECK STEERING WHEEL
14. VOICE PIPE
15. CONNING TOWER
16. PERISCOPE EYEPIECE
17. CONNING-TOWER HATCH
18. CONTROL ROOM

19. COMPRESSOR
20. PERISCOPE WELL
21. DEPTH CONTROL
22. GALLEY
23. CAPTAIN'S CABIN
24. BATTERIES
25. OFFICER BUNKS
26. OUTER HULL
27. 10.5 CM. DECK GUN
28. PRESSURE HULL
29. FLOOD PORT
30. PUMPS
31. COMPRESSED-AIR TANKS
32. SPARE TORPEDO
33. CAPSTAN
34. FORWARD TORPEDO TUBES
35. TORPEDO PORT
36. ANCHOR

A cross section of the U-35 reveals the shape of the outer hull, the circular inner pressure hull and the ballast tanks set between the two like saddlebags.

Appalled by the violence of the American reaction, Germany ordered the U-boat force on June 6 to stop attacks on large passenger ships, and on September 18, the Kaiser called a halt to the unrestricted U-boat war on merchant shipping in British waters. For the greater part of the year that followed, Britain enjoyed a respite from U-boat predations—apart from the continued laying of minefields outside British harbors and in the shipping lanes, an activity that went on without interruption until the end of the War.

Anxious not to waste its submarine potential, the German Admiralty diverted its U-boats from the Atlantic and North Sea to the Mediterranean. There the submarines could support Germany's allies, the Turks, in their struggle against British and Empire forces trying to obtain a foothold in the Dardanelles at Gallipoli.

With flotillas based in the Adriatic, the U-boats launched a new campaign against transports taking troop reinforcements to the Gallipoli front and against British and neutral merchant ships bringing cargoes from India and the Far East. The pickings were good, the opposition light and the U-boats' exploits spectacular. At Gallipoli, Lieutenant Otto Hersing on the *U-21* torpedoed the battleship *Triumph*, which had been bombarding the Turkish lines, and then escaped counterattack from nearby vessels by diving under the sinking battleship and making good his retreat on the other side. Two days later he torpedoed another British battleship, the *Majestic,* in full view of the hard-pressed Turkish soldiery on the shore. Hersing's two scores persuaded the British to withdraw all capital ships from their bombarding squadrons.

Another U-boat commander, Lothar von Arnauld de la Perière, turned the Mediterranean theater into his personal hunting estate. On board the *U-35 (pages 33-35),* Arnauld performed the greatest feat of arms ever achieved by a submariner when, between July 26 and August 20, 1916, he sank 54 ships totaling 91,150 tons, expending 900 shells and only four torpedoes in the process. When he put into port in the Adriatic with 54 pennants—one for each of the ships he had sunk—the waiting crowd applauded wildly. But Arnauld stoutly insisted that he had done nothing at all remarkable. "My record cruise was quite tame and humdrum," he later recalled. "We stopped ships. The crews took to the boats. We examined the ship's papers, gave sailing instructions to the nearest land and then sank the captured prize." By the time he left the *U-35* to assume another command, this modest ace of aces had scored a staggering total of 195 sinkings—two warships, one armed merchant cruiser, five troopships, 125 steamers and 62 sailing ships. By the end of the War, he had accounted for more than 200 vessels totaling nearly half a million tons. And throughout his career Arnauld adhered to the strictest code of naval chivalry.

The Mediterranean was not the only distant theater in which U-boats became active. In July 1916, as a demonstration of Germany's desire to trade with the United States, a peculiar vessel known as a mercantile U-boat and named the *Deutschland* arrived in Baltimore. The *Deutschland,* carrying a cargo of chemicals, dyes and precious stones, had broken through the British blockade and crossed the Atlantic via the Orkneys in a little under four weeks. Built like a normal U-boat

Carrying a cargo worth one million dollars from pro-German businessmen in Baltimore, the submarine freighter Deutschland arrives in Bremen harbor to an exuberant welcome in August 1916, having managed to slip beneath the British blockade. All seven U-boats designed as freighters were eventually converted to service as standard U-boats.

but without guns or torpedo tubes and with a broader beam to accommodate her cargo, the *Deutschland* was a privately sponsored blockade runner that was being operated as a business concern by a German shipping company—though it was clear she could easily be converted for use as a war vessel.

In August the *Deutschland* left for home with a million dollars' worth of precious nickel, tin and crude rubber in her hold. But the good will engendered by her visit soon evaporated. The next U-boat to cross the Atlantic was a conventional war boat, the *U-53*. In an impudent and belligerent demonstration of the submarine's long-range capabilities, she coolly sank five merchant ships—three British, one Norwegian and one Dutch—just outside the limits of American territorial waters while United States destroyers stood by, powerless to intervene.

Although the American reaction to U-boat activity remained one of anger without action, the British sought desperately for an effective means to strike back. By mid-1916, more than a million tons of shipping had been sent to the bottom, with a loss of only 32 U-boats. Minefields were of little use because British mines had faulty firing apparatuses and often failed to explode. Obviously something better would have to be found. But what? The best hope—an unlikely answer to an unprecedented plight—was an ancient idea that the British had revived more than a year earlier: the decoy ship.

Chapter 2

A desperate campaign of ruse and disguise

Aboard the *U-27*, one of three German submarines sent to wage unrestricted warfare in the western approaches to the English Channel, members of the crew were topside sunning themselves as they steered a westward course about 80 miles off the Scilly Isles on August 19, 1915. It was only 3 o'clock in the afternoon, but among them the three U-boats had already done a full day's work. They had sunk six British cargo ships, badly mauled another and, in a flagrant violation of international law, sunk the 15,801-ton White Star liner *Arabic,* with a loss of 44 lives.

The day was perfect for such lethal labors. A fresh breeze blew out of the southeast, stirring the surface of the sea just enough to obscure a periscope among the dipping wavelets, and the horizon was a hard-edged line of contrasting blues against which a distant ship would be distinctly visible.

Suddenly the lookout on the U-boat's conning-tower bridge cried out and pointed. Over the horizon to the west hung a faint patch of smoke, and binoculars revealed two masts as fine as needle points moving against the sky. Lieutenant Bernhardt Wegener instantly ordered his men inside the *U-27,* and in a moment the submarine had descended to just beneath the surface of the water and was stealthily making her way toward this new mark.

The ship—a legitimate target—was the Leyland liner *Nicosian,* a 6,369-ton converted transport returning home to England from New Orleans with a cargo of 800 American mules purchased by the British Army. Also aboard were 80 American muleteers.

Sizing her up from a nearer vantage point, Wegener decided not to expend a torpedo on the *Nicosian.* She was obviously unarmed, and he could easily destroy her with his deck gun—a much cheaper if somewhat more time-consuming procedure. Accordingly, he brought his vessel to the surface about half a mile off the *Nicosian's* port quarter. No sooner had the water washed from the deck of the submarine than the gun crew of his bow-mounted 22-pounder had taken their positions and were ready to begin firing. At Wegener's command, the crew let loose a series of ranging shells.

Panic broke out aboard the *Nicosian* as the first shells came whistling down, narrowly missing the broad white flank of the liner's hull. Her skipper, Captain Chester Manning, took the only protective measures available to a vessel such as his. Throwing his engines to full speed ahead, he steered a wild zigzagging course through the sea, making his ship at least a more difficult target for the pursuing U-boat. He had his wireless operator flash distress signals. Ship and cargo, he was sure, were doomed, but at least there was a chance that a passing vessel would hear his call for help and pick up what survivors there might be after the German submarine had finished with the *Nicosian.*

A few minutes later the situation worsened considerably when the U-boat gunners found their range. The *Nicosian* took several shots below the water line in her No. 1 hold and rapidly began filling with water. One of her boilers was knocked out, and she was holed in several places aft. Another wireless message was sent out: CAPTURED BY ENEMY SUBMARINE. CREW READY TO LEAVE. LAT. 50.22 N., LONG. 8.12 W.

Disguised by stacks of hay, a Royal Navy Q-ship, posing as an innocuous merchant vessel, blasts away at an unwary U-boat. Such Q-ship disguises, although long rumored, were not publicly acknowledged by the Admiralty until August 1918. Italian artist Achille Beltrame painted this watercolor from a news report of the Admiralty revelations.

The muleteers and some of the crew had, in fact, already been lowering the boats in an effort to get clear of the foundering ship and the storm of shellfire that was tearing up her deck. At 3:20 the *Nicosian* came to a full stop. Then the main transmitter blinked off and the stricken ship's battery-powered emergency set was activated to send a last desperate call: HELP! HELP! FOR GOD'S SAKE, HELP.

All this while the U-boat crewmen had been so preoccupied with their dogged bombardment of the fleeing liner that they failed to notice that to the west a third ship had entered the arena of action. This vessel was a ragged-looking tramp steamer flying an American flag from her stern and wearing two large signboards painted with the Stars and Stripes at either side of her hull to emphasize her claim to the rights of a neutral power. Her crew stood about the deck in clusters, pointing and waving at the men fleeing from the *Nicosian*.

When Wegener spotted this ship, she was about as far off the *Nicosian's* starboard quarter as was the *U-27* from the liner's port quarter. She appeared to be headed for the lifeboats that were bobbing ahead of the *Nicosian*. Surprised by the temerity of the American tramp, Wegener immediately moved to intercept her before she could reach the *Nicosian's* fleeing crew. With binoculars he could read the name *Baralong* stenciled on the rusty bow of the intruding vessel, and on her bridge he saw the ship's captain—an unprepossessing figure with long straggly hair falling from under his hat.

It was too late for him to strike at the newcomer while they were both astern of the *Nicosian*; the *Baralong* was just passing out of sight on the other side of the liner's hull. So Wegener sped ahead down the port side of the smoldering liner, intending to turn his gun on the *Baralong* when she came into view again beyond the *Nicosian's* bow. The ships would then be only a few hundred yards apart, and at that range—almost point-blank for naval warfare—the meddlesome American would be completely at his mercy.

But on the far side of the *Nicosian*, unseen by Wegener, a marvelous transformation was taking place. The moment they had passed out of sight of the U-boat, the seamen who had been idly watching at the *Baralong's* rail suddenly stiffened and sprang to action, moving about the ship with a concerted precision that suggested months of practice and a rote mastery of carefully plotted roles. On the bridge the captain flung off his cap—throwing with it his long, unkempt wig—and began barking orders into a voice pipe at his side. The handrails at the stern of the ship were yanked from their sockets and thrown overboard. A wooden sheep pen on the poop suddenly collapsed like a house of cards, and eight men stepped to their positions at the long, 12-pound deck gun that had been hidden therein. Just forward of this, what had appeared to be a large brown life-belt locker was instantly dismantled to unveil another 12-pounder, and a second crew took up positions around it.

The *Baralong* was now nearing the *Nicosian's* bow and, in the seconds that were left before she would greet the U-boat, the color boards were dropped from her sides and the American flag at the stern was run down. In its place the white ensign—the flag of a fighting ship in the Royal Navy—was sent up the pole.

Meanwhile, aboard the *U-27* on the other side of the *Nicosian*, Wegener's gun crew stood ready to fire on command. But as the two vessels slid past the bow of the *Nicosian*, emerging broadside to broadside, Wegener and his men recoiled in shock. What moments before had appeared to be a harmless tub flying neutral colors was now a dangerous enemy ship in an excellent position to do the *U-27* grievous damage. Before Wegener could utter either an order to fire or a command to dive for safety, both guns on the *Baralong* opened up. The first shot flew wide and sent up a plume of water just to the submarine's stern, but the second shell caught the sub at the base of her conning tower, gashing her hull plates. She was now unable to dive.

The remainder of the scene was played out quickly. Wegener was able to get off only one shot; it fell short. While riflemen aboard the *Baralong* picked off the Germans on the U-boat's deck, at least 34 more shells were fired from the 12-pounders, many of them striking their target. Finally the *U-27* heeled over and, with an enormous noisy escape of air from the interior, disappeared beneath the surface, never to rise again.

Captain Wegener had fallen victim to one of the most extraordinary weapons Britain was to employ against the German U-boat menace in World War I: the Royal Navy's Q-ships. The *Baralong*, with her hidden ordnance and crew of mummers, was not a one-of-a-kind experimental vessel manned by eccentrics. She was part of a growing fleet of deadly decoys, each carefully disguised and fitted out to destroy German submarines by means of an elaborate *ruse de guerre*. Posing as an ocean-going tramp, coastal freighter, fishing trawler or any other vessel that appeared innocent and helpless, a Q-ship sought to lure a predaceous, unsuspecting U-boat in close; it would then drop the guise and try to blast the submarine out of the water.

For nearly two years, between 1915 and 1917, the Q-ships were among the more effective answers England had to Germany's U-boat campaigns. In all, they actually destroyed only 14 U-boats, about 10 per cent of the 145 German submarines lost in enemy action during the War. But they damaged 60 more, some so severely that they were lucky to escape and spent weeks being repaired before returning to operational status. These engagements were among the most exciting and dramatic naval battles of the War—although the world was largely unaware of them at the time that they were taking place. The British government kept the Qs shrouded in a veil of secrecy and, in fact, refused even to admit that such ships existed until the War was almost over. This secrecy did not remain completely intact, however, and one reason for its being broken was what happened next on that August afternoon off the Scilly Isles.

As the *Baralong*'s captain, Lieutenant Commander Godfrey Herbert of the Royal Navy, welcomed aboard the incredulous muleteers and crew from the *Nicosian*, someone noticed that a number of the German sailors who had been standing on the U-boat's deck when it went down were now climbing up the side of the *Nicosian* on rope falls that had been left hanging when the ship was deserted. Neither Herbert nor his men were in any mood to be lenient. They had heard what had happened to the passengers aboard the *Arabic* earlier that day, and they carried with them the bitter memory of the torpedoing of the *Lusitania* three months before. Herbert had the Germans—among them Lieutenant Wegener—shot at as they climbed, and those who reached the deck were hunted down and executed on the spot.

Later, after the *Nicosian* had made it safely to port, British security tried desperately to keep any mention of the top-secret *Baralong*, or the bloody epilogue of her fight with the *U-27*, under wraps. But the American muleteers were irrepressibly loquacious. Once home, they related the story in vivid detail to the American press, and it instantly became international news. In Germany, where the propaganda machine reported that the British sailors had thrown the U-boat men live into the *Nicosian's* boilers, the incident provoked a howl of outrage. But more important to the future of the Q-service, it also alerted every U-boat commander in the North Sea and the Atlantic to keep a weather eye out for British warships in disguise.

Although the Q-ships were never really an effective answer to the U-boat menace, and many historians have come to regard them as little more than a kind of quixotic sideshow in the history of naval warfare, they nonetheless were for a time the best answer available. Airplanes and airships were still too short on range, speed and weaponry, too vulnerable to bad weather and mechanical breakdown, to provide effective air defenses far out of sight of land. Groups of fast Navy destroyers and patrol boats scurried hither and thither in their search for submarines, but a U-boat could submerge within minutes of sighting such warships, and all that the patrols usually found was a shelled wreck that marked the spot where a U-boat had been.

Antisubmarine defenses such as minefields across vital channels, steel nets and massive booms across harbor mouths, and defensive armament for merchant ships were easier to arrange. But so long as U-boats could make themselves invisible by submerging, they remained almost invulnerable to any offensive action the British might take. Away from coastal waters, out at sea where the water was too deep for mines to be anchored in place, a U-boat was virtually free to come and go, taking a horrible toll of the merchant shipping that was the lifeblood of the British nation and the British Army in France.

All sorts of solutions to the U-boat problem poured into the Admiralty uninvited, some ingenious, others bizarre. They ranged from the claims of one man that he could divine oil underwater by using a phosphor-bronze tuning fork, to a suggestion by a patriotic citizen that if the right opportunity arose little hammers could be used to smash the lenses of periscopes. Incredibly enough, the Admiralty took this latter suggestion to heart. Some picketboats patrolling the English coast were armed not only with hammers but with little canvas sacks as well. Should an enemy periscope pop out of the water nearby, the sack was to be immediately slipped over its lens and secured with a drawstring. This would prompt the baffled U-boat man to raise his auxiliary periscope to discover what had blinded him, and when this happened an Englishman waiting at the ready with his hammer would smash both scopes, putting the enemy out of commission for the time being.

Such measures, of course, served only to provide humorous footnotes to the grim history of the War. On the other hand, the Q-ship, although its very nature bordered on the preposterous, was actually a quite logical—and, considered in a certain light, obvious—solution to a grave threat.

The Q-ship was not the brain child of any one man but grew out of various ideas put up to the Admiralty by naval officers at the end of 1914. These decoys were known initially as special-service ships; only later in the War were they given their enigmatic Q designations, for reasons never explained. The first of them was the S.S. *Vittoria*, a merchant vessel commandeered by the Royal Navy, fitted out with a few quick-firing guns and commissioned in November of 1914. Her captain was instructed to take her out into the heavily trafficked British shipping lanes and fly neutral colors—a legitimate act under international law, provided that she ran up the white ensign before opening fire. The comings and goings of the *Vittoria* at British ports were so hush-hush that even servicemen on other Royal Navy vessels referred to her as the "mystery ship." After a three-month tour without sighting a single submarine, the *Vittoria* was brought home and paid off in January 1915, and the Sea Lords then addressed themselves to the task of planning a better decoy strategy.

Would-be wonder weapons against the submarine menace

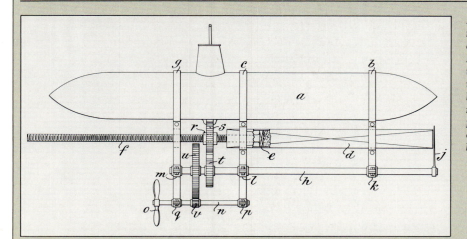

A patented Rube Goldberg-like drawing reveals the workings of Thomas Mill's decoy submarine, meant to fool birds into locating U-boats. As the device was towed through the water, the propeller (o) turned a shaft (h) together with the blade on its end (j). By means of a threaded rod (f), the same power advanced a pusher (e) that forced offal from the end of a tube (d), where it was sliced into bite-sized bits by the whirling blade (j).

Seeking ways to find and fight U-boats in World War I, the British Admiralty's Board of Inventions and Research entertained any and all suggestions from the public. One citizen advised trapping U-boats on the ocean floor with massive magnets. Another urged effervescing them to the surface with Eno's Fruit Salts, a fizzy laxative.

One of the zaniest proposals came from a man named Thomas Mills. In 1917 Mills proposed that sea gulls be trained to congregate over submerged U-boats, thus revealing the concealed menaces. Mills invented a submarine-shaped training decoy fitted with a mechanism *(above)* that emitted morsels of meat as the model was towed. In theory, once gulls were conditioned to finding tasty tidbits near the decoy's dummy periscope, they would hungrily head for any periscope their sharp eyes detected.

Although Mills spent a year towing his decoy off the coast of Devon, he failed to win over the board. Nevertheless, he always insisted that if his device had been adopted the Germans would have given up their nasty business "within four or five weeks."

During the spring of 1915, another series of disappointing forays were made by armed fishing trawlers. But in July of that year, the Q-ship idea finally bore fruit. U-boat activity had been particularly savage in the waters off the northern coast of Scotland. There, a steady stream of small colliers traveled back and forth between the mainland and the mist-enshrouded Orkney Islands, where Great Britain's Grand Fleet made its base at Scapa Flow. During the early part of that summer, a handful of these little coal ships were converted to decoys. One of these was the *Prince Charles*, a 373-ton collier under the command of Royal Navy Lieutenant Mark Wardlaw. Her peacetime captain and crew of five deck hands, two engineers and two firemen had volunteered to stay with her and assist the 10 servicemen who were aboard to operate her hidden guns in the perilous tour of duty that was proposed.

On the evening of July 24, after cruising for three days in waters where submarines had recently been spotted, the *Prince Charles* came upon the Danish steamer *Louise*, stopped in midocean about 10 miles northwest of Rona Island. Lying alongside the neutral Dane was a U-boat.

Lieutenant Wardlaw kept the *Prince Charles* on course as if he had not seen the submarine, and a few minutes later the U-boat—she was the *U-36*—started up her engines and struck out at full speed for the passing collier, leaving the Danish ship that she had been menacing. At a range of about three miles, the *U-36* fired her first shell, which fell about 1,000 yards beyond the *Prince Charles*. Wardlaw stopped his engines and turned his bow head on into the Atlantic swell. Behind screens that had been set up on deck, his gun crews waited for the word to drop their covers and open fire.

But first a bit of carefully prepared theatrics was in order. Generally, when under submarine attack, the crew of a defenseless merchantman would lower boats and paddle off some distance from the ship in the hope that the German marauder was interested only in sinking the vessel and not in taking the lives of the crew as well. So while the Royal Navy gunners waited in hiding at their stations, the *Prince Charles*'s merchant crewmen went through motions of abandoning their ship in panic.

Meanwhile the enemy was rapidly approaching. At a range of 600 yards the submarine slowed and commenced a concentrated fire. Lieutenant Wardlaw was learning that the Q-ship captain's most crucial decision lay in gauging the exact moment to drop his disguise. The closer he was able to entice his prey, the surer he would be of destroying it. Yet all the time he hesitated, his ship was forced to endure an increasingly accurate storm of shellfire. It was not that he feared losing the Q-ship—these were usually the oldest and most expendable vessels that could be found; but if he hesitated too long he might be sunk before he was able to get off his first shot.

Wardlaw now decided that the U-boat was not going to move closer, and he emitted a loud, shrill whistle. At this signal his crew pushed over the flimsy screens around their guns and opened fire. Although the *Prince Charles* was carrying comparatively weak armament—a 3-pounder and a 6-pounder—the effect of her first round of fire on the U-boat men was devastating. They deserted their guns and fled into the conning tower just as a shell hit the sub about 20 feet abaft of the tower.

A British seaplane drops a bomb in the direction of an innocent-looking sailboat, sending the vessel—actually a U-boat in disguise—crash-diving for its life. A number of submarine commanders concocted such camouflage, with the extended periscope serving for a mast.

She tried to dive to safety but had been injured too badly to succeed. As her stern sank and the British fire continued, the German sailors, realizing that the submarine was lost, came back onto the deck. Then her bow reared out of the water and the *U-36* went under in a sudden plunge, leaving the water strewn with the struggling crew. The *Prince Charles* managed to rescue 15 of the 33 men who had been aboard.

The idea of the Q-ship had at last been proved sound. In a fair fight— the U-boat had been using a 14-pound deck gun—the little collier had destroyed one of the most sophisticated warships in the world. If her tactics had been somewhat unorthodox, they were all the more suited to the occasion for being so. As one of the most experienced Q-ship captains put it, "Submarine warfare had ended the tradition where you hoisted your biggest ensign and challenged your opponent to bloody conflict. A submarine torpedoes you below the belt without any warning and without hoisting colors. So we were equally entitled to employ the same tactics which the enemy had been employing against defenseless passenger steamers, and we tried to get in our attack first."

In the months that followed the *Prince Charles*'s victory over the *U-36*, several more old colliers and freighters were commandeered by the Navy and converted into decoy ships, and eventually the Q-service included everything from large ocean liners to sail-driven fishing boats. Each of them was used in its own way; obviously, a passenger liner nosing around inland waters far from the liner lanes would arouse as much suspicion as a Red Sea dhow in the Firth of Forth. For this reason, the most favored and the most successful Q-ships were the ones most appropriate to the waters in which U-boats preferred to operate—the middistant reaches of the northwest Atlantic approaches off the west coast of Ireland, and the southwest Atlantic approaches, leading from the Bay of Biscay. Here the most common ship was the smallish nondescript collier or tramp—scruffy, dirty and innocuous.

Any Q-ship had to be able to modify her appearance with ease—every night if possible—when she was patrolling a U-boat hunting ground. During the hours of darkness, the Q-ship's men were usually busy painting their ship a different color, adding a dummy funnel, or in one way or another altering her disguise to delude a prowling U-boat into believing that the harmless merchant ship that at dusk had steamed by too far away to attack was not the same one espied going the opposite way the following dawn (pages 46-47).

The most crucial part of the disguise was the fake deck structures that hid the guns. They had to be instantly collapsible and yet sufficiently realistic to stand up to the close scrutiny of an approaching U-boat. Here the British displayed a fiendish ingenuity. Lifeboats were sawed apart at the waist; the two sections could then be whisked apart to uncover the gun. The sides of fake deckhouses were hinged to drop outward, revealing the large 12-pounders that most of the Q-ships carried. And the lath and wire hen coops that frequently graced the boat deck of merchant ships made an excellent nest for rapid-firing Maxim guns, covered with a light tarpaulin.

It was a basic assumption on board a Q-ship that a U-boat's periscope might be watching at any time during the hours of daylight. The appear-

A Q-ship's quick-change artistry

Of the many vessels that the Royal Navy outfitted as sub-fighting Q-ships—including seagoing freighters, coasters, fishing trawlers, schooners and colliers—the most popular was the common tramp cargo steamer. Its assets were numerous. The usual cargo steamer's profile of three raised islands—bow, stern and midships superstructure—was so ordinary that it lulled suspicions. These freighters traveled at little more than eight knots, a torpid pace that made them easy targets for U-boats. They carried enough fuel to stay at sea for up to 24 days. And, with a cargo capacity of up to 10,000 tons, they could carry the stage props and costume changes essential to successful decoy work.

Because U-boat men would be suspicious of a vessel they saw loitering in one area for several days, Q-ships were forced to undergo frequent metamorphoses. Booms, rigging and ships' antennae could be readily altered, and lumber or crates could be brought topside to serve as fake deck cargo. False funnels and ventilators also could be added or removed, enabling a Q-ship to take on new identities overnight, assuming guises as different as those on these pages.

Below, cutaway sections outlined in red reveal the armament carried by the cargo steamer—in this case, garbed as a lumber-laden British vessel. The Q-ship carries depth charges in concealed racks at her stern and is fitted with 14-inch torpedo tubes just beneath the charges. A 4-inch gun is mounted in a collapsible deckhouse on the poop. This structure is masquerading as the housing for a steering engine; to complete the illusion, the fake house can emit puffs of steam, piped aft by the real steering engine amidships. The stern walls and sidewalls of the house are hinged to fall away, so the gun can go into action in seconds.

Amidships, two 12-pounders have been placed on each side of the ship behind hinged plates that can be flung open in a trice to blast an approaching U-boat. Completing the basic armament is a 200-pound bomb thrower that can be moved on tracks into hiding under the fo'c's'le deck.

A little paint and some alterations in components change the black and ocher British steamer with its single funnel into what appears to be a twin-stacked Dutch freighter wearing the blue, white and yellow house colors of the Van Nievelt, Goudriaan and Company *(top right)*. Canvas that is stretched tight along the forward and after wells hides the three-island configuration, giving the impression of a flush deck. The deception is assisted by the addition of several fake ventilators, awning frames at the bow and the stern house, and a large Dutch flag painted on the hull, matching the pennant at the masthead. Before going into action, the fraudulent pennant would be dropped and the hull panel covered with canvas.

Converted hastily to an American tramp *(middle right)*, the Q-ship dons a coat of white paint, the *B* monogram of the A. H. Bull and Company, and an American flag on her hull. One mast has been removed, a crow's-nest added to the foremast, and the fake funnel and some ventilators eliminated. The canvas well covers and dummy cargo of lumber are also gone.

In her final disguise *(bottom right)*—again aided by paint and well covers, but this time abetted also by stubby masts and a canvas screen on top of the bridge—the protean Q-ship wears a Norwegian flag and flies Norway's pennant.

Great care had to be exercised to make each change utterly convincing, because many German submariners had been merchant seamen, some of them pilots in the English Channel. "It was no use," said leading Q-ship Captain Gordon Campbell, "pretending to be something you were not unless you attended to every detail."

THE BASIC Q-SHIP CUT AWAY TO SHOW WEAPONS

THE Q-SHIP AS A DUTCH MERCHANTMAN

THE Q-SHIP AS AN AMERICAN TRAMP

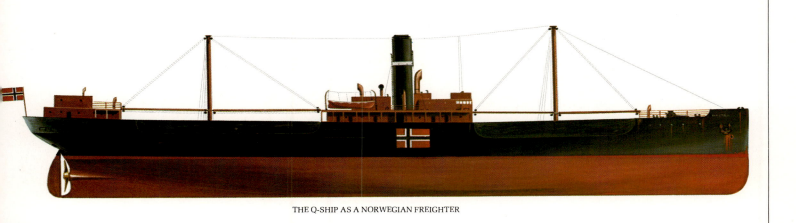

THE Q-SHIP AS A NORWEGIAN FREIGHTER

ance of the crew was therefore a vital factor in the overall deception; the well-drilled Royal Navy crews had to assume the role of easygoing, slovenly merchant sailors. Captain Gordon Campbell of the Q-ship *Farnborough* wore a rig consisting of a reefer and a peaked black cap embellished with a bit of gold lace taken from a pair of fancy-dress uniform trousers. His first officer shaved only one day in every four and dressed in a threadbare coat and a pair of trousers whose seat had been torn out by a bad-tempered dog.

Q-ship crewmen maintained their disguises even in home ports, where the presence of foreign agents always had to be expected. Sometimes this total commitment to disguise caused unforeseen embarrassments. Women refused to go out with the Q-ship men because they wore civvies. Overly patriotic ladies, who made it a practice in wartime England to give white feathers, emblems of cowardice, to men of service age who were not in uniform, frequently bestowed their gifts on Q-ship men. Q-ship captains on land had to live as outcasts from their own service, shun the usual haunts of Navy officers and learn to accept the disdain of subordinates who took them to be humble skippers of lowly tramps.

At sea, Q-ship men were encouraged to lounge about the vessel with an air of nonchalance, to spit on the deck, smoke on duty, and generally to behave in an informal and even disorderly manner.

All this was abovedecks. Below, the quaintly garbed Q-ship men resumed the character of a first-class Navy crew. In the living spaces and out-of-sight gunhouses, the Q-ship was run like a British man-of-war: orders were carried out on the double, and any infringement of regulations that might adversely affect the fighting efficiency of the ship was handled with the utmost severity. Without benefit of uniforms, the distinction between officer and men had to be reinforced by extra-strict discipline—while abovedecks all hands gave the appearance of having no discipline at all.

Nowhere was the uniquely schizoid quality of service aboard a Q-ship more evident than in the panic party, the centerpiece of the Q-ship's stratagem to deceive a U-boat into believing that her victim had been completely abandoned and that it was safe to come in close.

On an average Q-ship the panic party was equal in size to the complement of a normal tramp steamer, some 30 or so men. They were positioned around the ship where a normal crew would be, while the remaining 40 or 50 crew members remained concealed at their posts. When the captain judged that the moment had come to sound the alarm bell for "abandon ship," the dummy engine-room staff would stream up from below, hatless and coatless and wearing greasy clothes. Other panic men would scramble toward the lifeboats, shouting, shoving and clumsily wrestling with the ropes, letting one end down at a precipitous angle, then the other, until the boats plopped violently into the sea. Then, with the idea of creating as much delay as possible and giving the U-boat time to draw close, various men would rush below again to retrieve some precious possession that had been forgotten in the rush (on Gordon Campbell's *Farnborough*, this was usually a stuffed parrot in a beautiful green cage). "Never in Naval warfare," commented Lieutenant Commander Harold Auten, a Q-ship skipper, "had such apparent rabble served His Majesty. It was a triumph of training over training."

Finally, the fake captain would sadly leave the bridge and tumble down into one of the lifeboats, carrying a loose bundle that purported to be the ship's papers. Then, pulling wildly, the panic party would make for a prearranged spot from which they could lure the U-boat into the most vulnerable position. When the submarine surfaced, the panic party's job was to pull back toward the ship as if to reboard her. This generally infuriated the U-boat commander, who was anxious to lay his hands on the ship's papers, since they were best evidence of the vessel and kind of cargo he had destroyed. As often as not, he was maneuvered into following the panic boats closer. This was always a dangerous moment: The U-boat would sometimes loose a burst of machine-gun fire at the panic party to bring them to heel.

As perilous and nerve-racking as Q-ship duty could be, there was no end of volunteers. Yachtsmen, trawlermen, young bloods from the Grand Fleet looking for action, retired admirals prepared to disguise themselves as roughhewn skippers of little tramp steamers, and officers and men from the merchant marine all came forward to man the Q-ships. They were, to a man, exceedingly courageous and possessed of a high sense of gamesmanship.

Typical of their coolness under fire was the behavior of a black cook on Lieutenant Commander Auten's *Stock Force*; he had been specially picked for the crew because Auten believed that a black man would provide a realistic touch for the panic party. This cook had sailed aboard three ships torpedoed by U-boats before he entered Q-ship service, and on his first Q-cruise a U-boat let loose two more torpedoes at his ship. "Just after the second torpedo had missed us, I happened to look down into the little deck forward of the bridge," Auten said. "There I saw the black cook, whose station in action was to lean over the rails smoking his pipe, until the time came for the abandon ship's party to go away. He had been there for four hours, and had watched two torpedoes miss us by inches, knowing full well that if either of them had struck he would have lost his life. He might well have reasoned that in the darkness his leaning over the side smoking a pipe was unnecessary, but he had received his orders, and he would have remained there until he dropped."

For all their courage and their occasional spectacular successes, the Q-ship men were not the most significant factor affecting the course of the U-boat war; the indecisiveness of the German government was. After September 1915, when the U-boats were recalled from their devastating offensive against Britain, Germany spent about a year and a half trying to decide just how to use her extraordinary new weapon. Twice the U-boats were called home and twice sent forth again. At the heart of this indecision was an argument between the German high command, which pressed for full and unrestricted deployment of the U-boats, and the politicians, whose delicate diplomatic dealings would be made much easier by not having to account for these vessels. Always in the background lay the shadow of the United States, with its vast industrial capability and huge reservoir of manpower. Germany had no wish to anger this neutral giant—and she knew that every American inadver-

A chestful of medals attests to the bravery of Gordon Campbell, a vice admiral in this photograph but a Q-ship skipper earlier in his career. Showing the stiffest of upper lips, Campbell once radioed his commanding officer, "Q-5 slowly sinking respectfully wishes you goodbye." In fact his torpedoed decoy ship floated until a rescue ship arrived.

tently killed in a U-boat attack (and there had been many) brought the United States one step closer to joining the Allies.

Early in 1916 the politicians yielded to pressure from the military and unleashed the U-boats once again in waters off Great Britain; but attacks were restricted to armed merchant vessels. Two months later, after loud protests from neutral countries—President Wilson threatened "to sever diplomatic relations with the Germans altogether"—Germany grew cautious and in May 1916 called the U-boats home once more.

For a time the Atlantic and North Sea were empty of the dreaded U-boats, but the lull lasted only for the summer. That fall, the high command won permission for another offensive—again restricted to armed vessels—after convincing the Kaiser that the United States would be unlikely to enter the War. The new campaign was stunningly successful. The U-boat navy now totaled 134 submarines, of which 87 were operational. Among them were the new UC type, equipped for laying mines, and the new UB type, called the tadpole for its diminutive size and designed for coastal defense.

The expanded U-boat fleet dealt the British the worst loss figures since the War had begun, 154 British merchant ships, totaling 487,000 tons, during the last four months of 1916. The Commander in Chief of the Grand Fleet, Admiral Sir John Jellicoe, warned that, if the U-boat war continued to expand unchecked, Britain would be forced to sue for peace by the summer of 1917.

That was just what the Germans had in mind. At the beginning of 1917, the Kaiser gave his approval for the resumption of an all-out, unrestricted U-boat campaign, in spite of the risk of running afoul of the United States. The outcome of the War and the fate of Germany were thus to be entrusted to the U-boats—a turn of events unimaginable in 1914. The German Navy's arguments in favor of the campaign neatly coincided with Admiral Jellicoe's bleak prediction: They were based on a set of statistical calculations showing that if 600,000 tons of British shipping were sunk each month, and the shipping of neutral nations was frightened away from British ports, the British supply system would collapse and the War would be over within six months because Britain would no longer be able to get the raw materials necessary to continue it. "Our object," declared the German Naval command, "is to cut England off from traffic by sea."

In February 1917, 86 British merchant ships totaling 256,000 tons went down. In March the figures soared to 103 ships of 284,000 tons. The U-boat crews worked to their utmost capacity and surpassed all previous performances. One out of every four ships leaving British ports was now lost, including clearly marked and brilliantly illuminated hospital ships. In the bitter wintry weather, the death toll mounted. Of the six lifeboats from the torpedoed Union Castle liner *Alnwick Castle*, for example, two were never seen again, and others were found full of dead and dying and people too weak to stir.

In April 1917 the situation became calamitous. No fewer than 155 British ships, totaling 516,394 tons, went to the bottom. At this rate it was a mathematical certainty that by the end of the year the Allies would lose the War. The Royal Navy's antisubmarine division had no new

A nasty surprise under sail

By the outbreak of World War I, sailing vessels had become oddities among British fighting ships. But the very improbability of a sailing craft being a warship made such vessels almost irresistible targets for U-boats—and therefore likely candidates for the Royal Navy's masquerading Q-ship fleet.

The best-known of the sailing decoys was the three-masted schooner *Prize*. Under the command of Lieutenant W. E. Sanders, the *Prize* won dubious fame for a single encounter. Late in the day of April 30, 1917, off the southwest coast of Ireland, she caught the eye of a U-boat commander with the beguiling name of Baron Spiegel von und zu Peckelsheim. His 235-foot, 18-torpedo *U-93* had just sunk 11 freighters and the baron was now hastening home to watch two of his horses run in the Berlin races.

Naturally, he halted to take the schooner on. But in a perfectly executed Q-ship maneuver *(below)* the *Prize* lured the *U-93* into range, then dropped her

1. The U-93 attacks the Prize—not suspecting her to be a British Q-ship—while a panic party pretends to abandon ship.

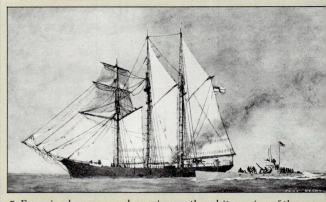

3. Exposing her guns and running up the white ensign of the Royal Navy, the Prize returns fire on the gulled U-boat.

disguise and blasted the submarine with a barrage of shellfire. When the smoke cleared, the U-boat had vanished, but the baron and two of his crew were spotted treading water where the submarine had been. Fished from the sea, they were taken back to England and clapped into prison.

The baron had manners befitting his ancient title. In prison, he lost no time in writing letters of condolence to the next of kin of all his departed crewmen—only to learn subsequently that the place most of them had departed for was home. It turned out the *U-93* had gone under just far enough to wash the baron and a gun crew off the deck. The *Prize*'s fire had shot away her conning tower, punched eight gaping holes in her hull and killed two crewmen, but the U-boat had nonetheless escaped in the gathering darkness and managed a perilous 2,000-mile surface run back to the fatherland, where, after a jubilant reception honoring her heroic getaway, she was refitted for further duty.

Shells from the U-93 crash into the Prize's hull as hidden gun crews stoically wait for the right moment to strike back.

As darkness falls, the Prize gunners let fly a last round of shots before giving up the U-93 for finished and sailing for home.

answers. Only the Q-ships posed any aggressive threat to the U-boats, for only they stood a reasonable chance of locating them.

During the two years since the little collier *Prince Charles* had defeated the *U-36* in early 1915, six more U-boats had been destroyed by Q-ships, and the German submarine captains had learned to regard lone, innocent-looking merchant vessels with profound suspicion. Off western Ireland on March 22, 1916, Captain Gordon Campbell's Q-ship *Farnborough* had encountered one of Germany's latest U-boats—the 17-knot, 11-torpedo *U-68*. Taking the Q-ship for a harmless tramp, the *U-68* then put a shell across her bow to make her stop. After Captain Campbell's panic party had abandoned ship in brilliant confusion, the U-boat approached to within 800 yards, whereupon the *Farnborough* suddenly opened fire on her, holing her so badly that she went under. For good measure, the *Farnborough* then dropped two depth charges on the spot where the U-boat had disappeared. Moments later, the stricken submarine, totally out of control, broke surface, her bow rearing vertically in the air. Five more shells from the *Farnborough* now struck her in the base of the conning tower, and the *U-68* went down for good.

By the spring of 1917, when England was on the verge of succumbing to the German U-boat campaign, the Q-ship service was expanded to 78 vessels. The indomitable Captain Campbell received a new command, the Q-ship *Pargust*. On June 7, 1917, he was once again under torpedo fire, but once again he fooled his attacker with the Q-ship's drastic ruse, and although his own ship was destroyed in the engagement, he sent the *UC-29* to the bottom with a salvo of 38 shells. For this action, two of Campbell's crew got the Victoria Cross, and Campbell a new ship, in which he went forth to fight one of the most heroic—if ultimately fruitless—battles of the War.

Captain Campbell's new Q-ship was the *Dunraven*, a 3,000-ton collier disguised as a defensively armed British tramp steamer. She was specially fitted with six concealed guns, two torpedoes that could be launched from the deck, an armored bridge, a dummy deck cargo confected out of wood and canvas, and an arrangement of perforated piping from which clouds of steam could be blown to convince the enemy that the ship was seriously damaged. On August 4, 1917, the *Dunraven* set sail from Plymouth in the guise of a steamer of the Blue Funnel Line. During the next three days, the ship received radio reports warning that a U-boat was lurking in the Bay of Biscay, and at 10:58 a.m. on August 8, some 130 miles west of Ushant, this U-boat was sighted off the *Dunraven*'s starboard beam, steering toward the ship.

Campbell immediately ordered decoy routine. The *Dunraven* pretended to keep a bad lookout and did nothing but continue to chug along on the same zigzag course. The U-boat rapidly drew nearer and at 11:17, after checking the *Dunraven*'s speed and mean course, dived, resurfacing 26 minutes later dead astern at a distance of about 5,000 yards. The radio reports received by the *Dunraven* had indicated that the U-boat commander preferred to dispose of his victims by long-range gunfire. Sure enough, the U-boat—the *UC-71* under the direction of Lieutenant Reinhold Saltzwedel—promptly opened fire on the *Dunraven* with the submarine's big 105-mm. gun.

Campbell concentrated every effort on tricking the U-boat into drawing closer. He hoisted the red ensign of the British merchant service over the *Dunraven* and opened up on the submarine with his "legitimate" after gun—a small 2½-pound piece common on wartime merchantmen—but he deliberately dropped its rounds short. At the same time, while pretending to be trying to make an escape, he actually reduced the *Dunraven's* speed by one knot.

At 12:10, having shelled the *Dunraven* for half an hour without hitting her, the submarine steamed in close at high speed and at 1,000 yards turned broadside on her and reopened fire. The shelling was now much more accurate; after 15 minutes Campbell considered that the time had come to put into operation the next phase of the deception. He gave the order to abandon ship, the panic party rushed about in pandemonium and "accidentally" upset one of the lifeboats, and the perforated steam pipe was turned on, enveloping the waist of the vessel in a dense pall of steam, giving the impression that the U-boat had scored a hit in the *Dunraven's* engine room.

The U-boat closed rapidly. Three more shells whistled toward the *Dunraven.* The first blew up a depth charge in the stern; the second and third landed nearby and set fire to the poop, which contained the powder magazine. Campbell was now in a considerable dilemma. The poop was on fire and giving off thick clouds of black smoke, and a concealed 4-inch gun and its crew were on top of the poop—in fact directly over the magazine. "I knew for a certainty that the poop would blow up, and with it the gun's crew," Campbell wrote afterward. "I couldn't order the crew to leave the gun, as the ship was 'abandoned' and the boats away. On the other hand, the submarine each second was getting more obscured by the smoke. If I opened fire I would save the men on the poop, but would we get the submarine? I doubted it."

So Campbell made an extraordinary decision. His priority was to sink U-boats, irrespective of the casualties suffered in achieving this end. Campbell therefore chose to wait until the U-boat had come through the smoke close enough to be hit by the *Dunraven's* guns. His decision condemned the crew of the poop gun to remain lying flat on their faces on the deck of the burning poop until they were blown up by the huge store of explosives underneath them. To lie there as the minutes ticked by and the fire spread required a very rare kind of courage. But the gun crew stayed at their posts while the deck grew hot and the fumes became so thick that they had to stuff their mouths with pieces of a torn-up shirt to keep from being asphyxiated.

Finally, at 12:58, when the U-boat had neared to a range of only 400 yards, there was a loud boom. The entire stern of the Q-ship was blown out, exploding cordite and shells rained down all over the ship, and the

Crewmen abandon the fatally stricken Q-ship Dunraven as her attacker, the UC-71, submerges to safety. Q-ships operated at tremendous risk: their job was to lure the enemy in close, and they often suffered the consequences, as shown in this re-creation. The Dunraven was sunk by her intended victim just outside the Bay of Biscay on August 10, 1917.

poop gun and its crew were tossed into the air like toys. Miraculously, all but one survived this ordeal, though most were wounded. One man was saved by falling into the sea, others by landing on the make-believe railway trucks, which softened their fall.

But by breaking cover, even if through no fault of their own, they had given the game away. Lieutenant Charles George Bonner crawled onto the bridge with a bleeding head and burned hands and reported to Captain Campbell: "I am sorry, sir, for leaving my gun without orders. I think I must have been blown up." The explosion had set the alarm bells ringing for "open fire" and the U-boat dived at once. The Q-ship raised the white ensign, fired off a few shots at the vanishing conning tower, and coolly awaited the torpedo strike that was sure to come. There was no thought of flight.

"At 1:20," Campbell wrote, "just over 20 minutes since the submarine had submerged, a torpedo was seen approaching from the starboard side. We watched its approach, and as this was the fifth time we had watched the same thing (there were only one or two men on board who hadn't been torpedoed before) it left us rather cold. It hit us with a crash, just abaft the engine-room: the hatches were blown about the place, and the bulkhead was started between the hold and the engine-room."

Campbell now ordered, "Q abandon ship," and another group of men began a second panic party. Only 34 men were now left on board the *Dunraven*, including the crews of two guns, one torpedo crew, and Campbell and three others on the bridge. Incredibly, with the ship's stern blown away and a gaping hole in her side, Campbell still hoped the U-boat could be lured into a Q-trap. But the submarine commander was a canny one. For nearly an hour he slowly circled the stricken *Dunraven*, examining it minutely through his periscope while the fire in the poop was still raging, the cordite and shells in the magazine were going off most disconcertingly every few minutes, the sea was flooding into the ship and the boilers were dying.

At 2:30 the U-boat came up dead astern a few hundred yards away and opened fire almost as soon as the gun had cleared the surface. The first shell burst on the bridge and removed the helmsman's cap. The second struck nearby, and a large splinter from it passed between the helmsman's legs. The U-boat's position dead astern made it impossible to bring any guns to bear. For 20 minutes the U-boat raked the *Dunraven* with explosive shells. It was, Campbell noted in a vast understatement, "extremely unpleasant." The strain on the men left on board, who had been under fire for nearly three hours, was so great that a member of one gun crew sent a message to the captain asking for permission to take off his boots, as he would rather not die with them on.

Not until the U-boat submerged for another tour of inspection was Campbell able to let fly his two torpedoes. The first missed. The second grazed the submarine's deck but failed to explode, and the U-boat promptly dived. In expectation of the *coup de grâce*, Campbell arranged for a third panic party, leaving only one gun crew on board. But the blow never came. Saltzwedel's U-boat, having used all its torpedoes, broke off the engagement and departed. As the men on board the battered, slowly sinking Q-ship emerged from their concealed quarters, their shipmates bobbing about in the panic boats raised a great cheer, for they thought that no one could have survived the U-boat's bombardment. "It had been a fair and square fight and I had lost," Captain Campbell reported. "As for my crew, words can't say what I think—not a man failed, not a man could have done more."

The U-boat had got away, and the only thing left to do was to try to save the *Dunraven*. An American armed yacht removed the wounded crewmen, and a British destroyer took the ship in tow. But the water in the engine and boiler rooms was gaining faster than it could be pumped out, and the stern was steadily sinking beneath the surface. By the following evening two thirds of the *Dunraven* was underwater and large seas were breaking over her. With the sea rising all around them, the last of the Q-ship's crew were taken off, and in the dark hours of August 10, 1917, the shattered *Dunraven* went down. So ended the most gallant Q-ship engagement of the War.

The *Dunraven* had lost the battle but had won the admiration of the Allied navies. The Admiralty awarded a special £300 grant to the ship's crew and the King presented Victoria Crosses to Lieutenant Bonner and to the petty officer in charge of the after gun, Ernest Pitcher. Other bravery medals went to the rest of the crew. (Campbell already possessed a Victoria Cross for sinking the *U-83* in February 1917.) Rear Admiral William Sims, Commander of the United States Navy in European waters, afterward wrote to Campbell:

"Long after we are dust and ashes, the story of this fight will be an invaluable inspiration to British and American Naval officers and men. I know nothing finer in naval history than the conduct of the after gun crew or, indeed, of the entire crew of the *Dunraven*."

But for Captain Campbell and the members of his crew—who now had four Victoria Crosses among them, an unprecedented concentration—it was the end of the road. Their commander in chief, Admiral Sir Lewis Bayly, had decided they had been through enough. So the most illustrious Q-ship captain of the War was withdrawn from the Q-service to become Bayly's own flag captain aboard the light cruiser *Active*. The heyday of the Q-ship was over.

Altogether more than 180 motley vessels had served in the decoy service. Only 10 of these ever sank a German submarine (four sank two U-boats apiece), but the value of Q-ships extended well beyond their modest record of submarines destroyed. In a sense, they embodied the pluck and ingenuity of the British nation as a whole. They boosted the morale of the Royal Navy antisubmarine forces at a time when little else was being achieved against the U-boats, and the check they exerted on the U-boat commanders' freedom of action in attacking merchant shipping was considerable.

But in spite of the seaman-like skills and tremendous courage of their crews, the Q-ships were not a sufficient answer to the massive onslaught let loose on Allied shipping by the unrestricted U-boat campaign. To defeat that onslaught, the Allies needed to acquire vast new resources and adopt radically new tactics. In April 1917—Britain's blackest month—the Allies gained the first of these essentials when, partly in reaction to the U-boat campaigns, America joined the War.

Chapter 3

Final blows of the first U-boat war

On April 2, 1917, the President of the United States, Woodrow Wilson, appeared before a special joint session of Congress held in the House of Representatives. The House was packed. Congressmen, senators, Cabinet members, Supreme Court justices and other distinguished visitors crowded the chamber. As the President approached the rostrum, a tense and expectant hush fell over the crowd. Everyone knew that the legislators were about to be asked to make a momentous decision.

The President adjusted his pince-nez and began his address. The German submarine campaign, he told them, was a wanton rampage against mankind. Armed neutrality was no longer sufficient to protect American interests and lives. The United States had no option but to "accept the status of belligerency which has been thrust upon it by the actions of Imperial Germany and her associates." In order to make the world safe for democracy—and the world's sea-lanes safe for peaceful passage—America would now have to play its full part in the conflict. "Civilization itself seems in the balance," the somber-voiced Wilson declared.

Enthusiastic applause greeted the President's speech. The votes of both Houses of Congress on April 6 were overwhelmingly in favor of war. But Woodrow Wilson himself felt mostly sadness; he commented later that his speech was "a message of death for our young men."

And so, nearly three years after the conflict had erupted in Europe, the United States declared war on Germany. The reasons for doing so were various and complex; the U-boat offensive, although it was taking a growing toll in American lives, was not the sole cause of the United States's abandoning its long-avowed intention of avoiding entanglement in European wars. But it was a powerful contributory factor. The U-boats' manner of making war had provoked a fiery anger in the American public, and every congressman listening to President Wilson's address could feel that anger's heat.

America's intervention brought no immediate relief to the beleaguered British, since men and weapons were not yet available in sufficient quantity to throw into the battle. In vain, Admiral William Sims, commanding United States Navy forces in Europe, warned that Britain was in imminent danger of collapse under the U-boat onslaught and he urged that every available antisubmarine vessel be sent at once. Walter Hines Page, the United States Ambassador in London, shared Sims's fears. "What we are witnessing," Page declared, "is the defeat of Britain." As the U-boat attacks went on—549,987 tons were sunk in May 1917—the Admiralty forecast that the War would be lost by November.

In early May, six American destroyers arrived in Queenstown, Ireland. They were a help, but they were not the answer. What American belliger-

Fishermen wave from their trawler as six American destroyers steam into Queenstown, Ireland, on May 4, 1917, to reinforce the beleaguered Allies. By the end of June, 37 of these destroyers were based in Queenstown to guard the western approaches against U-boat penetration.

ency really signified in those dark and uncertain days was the future promise of the United States's truly astonishing industrial productivity. The Bethlehem Steel Company, for example, would soon be able to build a large destroyer in only six weeks, while British yards required no less than 18 months to construct a similar vessel. The British were not slow in trying to tap this industrial cornucopia: They presented their new ally with a shopping list that included 55 destroyers for convoy escort, 41 convoy cruisers, four battleships, more than 100 aircraft, 100,000 mines and 250 small minelaying craft to establish a huge barrage across the North Sea, as well as an unspecified number of merchant ships and miscellaneous antisubmarine patrol vessels.

It would take time to fulfill the British Admiralty's seemingly boundless requirements, let alone America's own, and a large proportion of the naval hardware manufactured in the United States did not come out of the industrial pipeline until after the War was over. But America's support was enough to effect one major change: It gave Britain the confidence to introduce the convoy system at last.

Convoys were not new to war. England had used them during her wars against France in the early 19th Century. In the present war, small-scale convoys—coal traffic from France across the English Channel, timber traffic from Sweden across the North Sea—had been running for some time. But their introduction on a large scale had been persistently vetoed by the Admiralty and the merchant marine alike. The Admiralty feared that the shortage of escorts would enable the U-boats to destroy the concentrations of merchant ships wholesale. The merchant marine, having sacrificed its most experienced officers and engineers to the ever-expanding Royal Navy, feared that the considerable difficulties of station keeping by ships of different speeds and sizes in tightly packed convoys, especially when zigzagging and at night, would be insuperable for inexperienced crews and would lead to many collisions and disasters at sea. Far better, they argued, for a ship to sail independently and take its chances of giving the U-boats the slip in the vastness of the ocean—a fallacy that only time and experience could disprove.

The entry of America into the War emboldened the Admiralty to pull ships for convoy protection from British Naval squadrons far and wide, in the confidence that any losses of these escorts would eventually be made good. The first long-haul convoy, 17 ships from Gibraltar, reached Britain on May 20, 1917, followed soon after by another convoy of 12 ships from America; both arrived without loss. By August, all Britain-bound ships in the Atlantic with a speed of less than 12 knots were being convoyed; subsequently, faster ships were also convoyed. Schedules were arranged so that escorts could shepherd one convoy out to the limit of their protective territory, turn it over to other escorts and then pick up an inward-bound convoy.

In spite of all misgivings, the system worked. At the end of August, only 2 ships in 100 were being sunk when in convoy, compared with 1 in 10 ships sailing alone. By October, more than 1,500 merchant ships in almost 100 convoys had been brought into port with the loss of only 24 vessels, only 10 of which had been sunk while in convoy; the loss rate thus was less than 1 in 100. November's monthly total of

59

Explosive barriers across the North Sea

Allied minefields (blue areas) lie athwart the routes used by German submarines cruising the North Sea. By the end of 1918, Allied warships had laid more than 165,000 mines. Though few U-boats were actually blown up by them, before war's end, some crews were beginning to balk at orders to pass through the mine barriers.

lost tonnage was down to 259,521—less than half the figure for April.

At the same time that the convoying system deprived submarines of convenient targets, the Allies labored to deny U-boats access to the open sea. A new and deadly mine known as Mark H2—a copy of the basic German mine—became the principal ingredient of vast barrages that were used to seal off the U-boat bases. The mine barrier between Folkestone and Cape Gris-Nez, laid in November 1917, proved so effective that U-boats were virtually unable to enter the Channel from the North Sea. Another barrage, stretching across the whole of the Heligoland Bight from the Danish to the Dutch borders, was strewn with more than 25,000 mines to block the U-boats' passage from the north German bases. And still farther north, an immense 240-mile barrage of 70,000 mines eventually spanned the North Sea from Norway to the Orkneys (page 59).

An even more feared antisubmarine weapon was the depth charge, which claimed its first U-boat in July 1916, and soon increasing numbers of U-boat men were forced to endure the terrors of depth-charge attacks: the concussive blows of the underwater explosions, the violent rocking, the lights going out, instruments shattering, water spurting from cracked pipes and valves. Even though most depth charges fell wide of the mark, they shared credit with mines for sinking more U-boats than any other Allied weapon: 35 apiece.

In the last year or so of the U-boat war, Allied air power became

another crucial factor in the struggle. Airports, seaplane stations and airship bases for antisubmarine work sprang up all around the coast of Britain. Flying boats pounced out of the sun on unwary U-boats, ultimately sinking seven and damaging 40. Four hundred blimps, some with 50-hour endurance, were put into service as convoy air escorts and U-boat spotters in the western approaches, the Channel and the North Sea, and they eventually patrolled a total of 2,250,000 miles. Of the 312 ships torpedoed in convoy from April 1917 to the end of the War, only two were hit while an air escort was present.

In one way and another, the world became an unfriendly place for the German submariner. At the peak of U-boat effectiveness, 70 freighters were sunk for every U-boat lost. By July 1917 the ratio had fallen to only 16 freighters for every U-boat lost. And the U-boat mortality rate would grow far worse. Of 55 U-boats actually at sea in May 1918—the highest total at any one time during the War—16 were lost, making that month the most disastrous in the U-boat's history. Though U-boat production was increased, it was countered by crash shipbuilding programs in Britain and America. During the second quarter of 1918, ship production overtook losses. The vital statistics of the U-boat campaign thus clinically revealed the impending defeat of the U-boat navy.

As more and more German submarines were destroyed by one Allied weapon or another, the U-boat campaign became more bloody and bru-

As the North Atlantic waters foam over the deck, officers and crew of the U-58 line up to surrender after their sub was damaged by depth charges from American destroyers on November 17, 1917. While assembling, the Germans opened the sea cocks and the U-boat went down minutes after this picture was taken.

tal. From the start, some commanders had taken their orders for unrestricted warfare as a license to kill indiscriminately. One case was that of Lieutenant Wilhelm Werner of the *U-55,* who torpedoed the steamer *Torrington* 150 miles southwest of the Scilly Isles on April 8, 1917. The *Torrington's* captain and 20 of the crew from one of the ship's two lifeboats were ordered on board the U-boat. The captain was sent below, and the rest of the crew were lined up on the deck and their life jackets were taken away from them. Then Werner gave the order to dive, and the U-boat submerged with the sailors still standing on the deck. There were no survivors. Four days later, Werner disposed of some of the crew of the steamer *Toro* in the same way and, at the end of July 1917, Lieutenant Paul Wagenführ of the *U-44* gave the same treatment to men from the steamer *Belgian Prince.*

Early in 1918 a number of clearly marked Allied hospital ships came under U-boat attack, even though the German government had publicly stated that hospital ships would not be harmed. Again Werner was foremost among the offenders. On January 4 his *U-55* torpedoed the hospital ship *Rewa* in the Bristol Channel. Four crewmen on the *Rewa* were killed, but all 279 patients aboard the ship were removed before she sank. On February 26 another U-boat sank the hospital ship *Glenart Castle* off southwest England with the loss of 153 lives. In the same area the hospital ship *Guildford Castle* barely escaped destruction on March 10 by turning to evade a U-boat's torpedo. The torpedo scraped along the vessel's side but did not explode.

Perhaps the most callous atrocity of the War was that perpetrated by Lieutenant Helmut Patzig of the *U-86* against the crew and medical staff of the hospital ship *Llandovery Castle* on the night of June 27, 1918. Torpedoed 116 miles west of Fastnet Rock, off southern Ireland, the clearly lighted converted liner—which fortunately had no wounded on board—filled rapidly and sank within 10 minutes. As the lifeboats pulled clear, the U-boat surfaced, and the *Llandovery Castle's* master, Captain R. A. Sylvester, was ordered to come alongside. Patzig questioned him about eight American airmen who he alleged had been on board. Sylvester denied the claim, pointing out that his vessel was a hospital ship and that his staff included seven Canadian medical officers who perhaps had been mistaken for Americans.

Patzig turned away, then approached the other lifeboats at high speed and demoniacally began to run them down, hurling the submarine this way and that as he smashed them like matchwood. Only the master's boat was spared. In the darkness the men in this boat heard the *U-86* open fire on the people who had been thrown into the water. Then the U-boat melted away into the night. The 24 survivors in the master's boat were eventually picked up by another ship. Of the other 234 people from the *Llandovery Castle,* including 14 nurses, no trace was ever found.

For this crime, Patzig and his lieutenants, John Boldt and Ludwig Dittmar, were arraigned for trial in Leipzig after the War. Patzig went into hiding and never showed up. His two lieutenants were found guilty and were sentenced to four years' imprisonment each, but shortly after the trial they escaped.

Still, for every barbarous U-boat act a chivalrous one could be cited.

Certain commanders were as consistently merciful toward their victims as others were callous. Lieutenant Hans Rose, who gained a reputation as one of the most humane U-boat captains of the War, sometimes towed a torpedoed ship's lifeboats shoreward until they were in sight of land. In the southwest approaches on December 6, 1917, Rose torpedoed the United States Navy destroyer *Jacob Jones*, the first American destroyer to be sunk by a U-boat in the War. After watching her crew take to their boats in the wintry waste of the ocean, Rose felt compelled, at great risk to himself, to send a radio signal to the British naval base at Queenstown giving the latitude and longitude of the survivors and asking for help to be sent to them. Then he made off as fast as he could.

So effective were the Allied antisubmarine measures that by mid-1918 U-boat attacks against convoys were rare. The climax of the U-boat war on shipping had passed—though the Allies could not be entirely certain of this at the time. Secretly, the German war leaders had lost faith in U-boats as a war-winning weapon. The Russian collapse had freed whole German armies from the Eastern Front, and the leaders now reasoned that, if the War could be won, it would be won on land—in a great new offensive by a hugely reinforced army on the Western Front.

U-boats still passed down the Channel on their way to their hunting grounds in the western approaches. But week by week, running the

From the open cockpit of a blimp, a Royal Navy airman keeps watch over a convoy steaming below. Blimps were excellent antisubmarine sentinels; observers in World War I blimps spotted 49 U-boats and led surface attacks on 27.

gantlet of the Channel mine barrages proved more difficult and dangerous. And if the U-boats squeezed through the mines, what then? Lying in wait for them was a hostile world of enemy warships, submarines, Q-ships and aircraft. Even out in the comparative safety of the open ocean, the U-boat men were tormented by the knowledge that to return home they had to run the whole gantlet in reverse.

By the summer of 1918, the U-boat flotilla based in Flanders was losing one submarine every week, and the average life of a U-boat was reckoned at no more than six cruises. To maximize the fighting potential of the beleaguered force, the time devoted to repairs, refits and routine maintenance was shortened. The strain began to tell on the U-boat men. Commanders aged prematurely. A few men became mentally ill. Morale declined, and there was an increase in cases of feigned sickness and overstayed leave.

Meanwhile, two million American troops flooded across the Atlantic to Europe, where they swelled the Allied land forces. Only three troop transports were ever sunk by the U-boats.

Germany's leaders woke up belatedly to the full implications of America's involvement in the War. Clearly, something had to be done to come to grips with this new and powerful enemy. Somehow the War would have to be carried to the United States itself in order to interrupt the flow of American troops and munitions to the battlefields and draw American Naval forces away from European waters. Searching for an answer, the Germans turned to a new class of war submarine: the U-cruisers. These giant U-boats were the one exception to the U-boat navy's general decline. U-cruisers were to be the vanguard of a new submarine offensive that would reach to the most distant Atlantic shipping lanes—southward beyond the Equator, and eventually across the ocean to the East Coast of the United States.

Only nine of these U-cruisers ever went into action, although the submarine-building program of 1917 and 1918 aimed to produce a great many more for long-distance raiding in the following two years. Seven of the nine were originally meant to function as mercantile submarines and only later were converted into cruisers. But the other two were designed from the keel up as war vessels. Displacing nearly 2,500 tons submerged, 311 feet in length, and armed with six torpedo tubes and a minimum of two 5.9-inch guns, these last two were the largest U-boats commissioned in World War I.

First to set off on a trial war patrol was the *U-155*, one of the converted cargo subs. Leaving Kiel on May 24, 1917, she cruised for 10,220 miles in 105 days, sank 19 ships and bombarded the Azores in an attempt to impress the world with Germany's new might. In September another former cargo U-boat, the *U-151*, also set course south toward the Azores at the start of one of the longest cruises ever made by a submarine up to that time. The *U-151* traveled more than 12,000 miles and sank 13 ships without once coming under attack herself. Other U-cruisers followed, to Madeira and the Canary Islands, the Spanish Sahara and Liberian coast. They remained unmolested until one day in May 1918 when the *U-154*, returning home from West African waters, was blown to bits by a torpedo fired from a British submarine, the *E-35*, lurking in ambush off Cape St. Vincent, Portugal. But by then, having acquired experience in long-range operations, the U-cruisers were turning to remoter and more hostile seas. Earlier that spring, several of Germany's largest submarines had been readied for raids against shipping along the American coast.

The pioneer this time was the *U-151*, under Lieutenant Commander Heinrich von Nostitz und Jänckendorff. With a hand-picked crew of eight officers and 65 men and provisions for a five-month cruise, the *U-151* left Kiel on April 14, 1918, and headed north across the Baltic on a remarkable voyage. Under cover of fog the *U-151* slipped through the British blockade on the surface and reached the open Atlantic.

The *U-151*'s task in American waters was not simply to sink ships but to lay mines along the main routes taken by munitions ships on their way to Europe. A first batch was to be laid in Chesapeake Bay to catch the ships coming out of Baltimore, America's biggest war port. A second batch was intended for Delaware Bay and ships outward-bound from Philadelphia and other inland ports. The U-boat made landfall off Virginia and headed up the coast. At first it dodged and dived amid the heavy traffic of steamers, warships and sailing craft, and then resorted to lying on the bottom during the day and surfacing to continue the voyage at night.

When they set about laying their deadly cargo of mines in the entrance to Baltimore Harbor on the night of May 21, the U-boat men were afraid of being run down in the dark. But they were helped by the Americans themselves. "Far from the scenes of the War," Lieutenant Frederick Körner later remembered, "they blissfully kept their ships' lights burning, just as in the days of peace." In the bright moonlight the U-boat must have been clearly visible from land. But apparently no one was on watch. By 9:30 p.m., half of the *U-151*'s mines had been laid. On the radio news broadcast for ships at sea from Arlington, Virginia, after the weather reports, iceberg warnings, stock exchange quotations and baseball results, came a reassuring bulletin: "No submarine. No war warning."

On her way up the coast to Delaware Bay that night, the *U-151* fell in with three schooners and ordered them to stop. The 26 men in their crews were taken on board the U-boat as prisoners and their fresh food taken for provisions before charges of TNT were exploded on the vessels—the U-cruiser's first victims in American waters. Then, after laying the rest of the mines across Delaware Bay, the *U-151* headed off through a heavy sea fog, coolly using its own high-pitched siren to clear a passage down the main shipping lane to the open sea.

On May 28 the *U-151* arrived off New York. "That night," Körner related, "we had our first sight of the bright lights of Broadway, the great glow that hangs over New York City after dark. The splendor of the Western metropolis filled us with a restless longing. A wild idea came of stealing into the harbor and up the Hudson, of landing at some obscure place and taking a night off along the Great White Way. Fire Island Beach was also a temptation, with its pretty houses, long beach and white surf. But there would be no welcome there for us."

For three days, the *U-151* cruised up and down, dragging along the seabed a long line with a cable-cutting mechanism attached to the end.

"SPURLOS VERSENKT"
(Sunk Without a Trace)

On June 27, 1918, the *Llandovery Castle*—a British hospital ship plainly marked with the Red Cross—was torpedoed by the Hun.

Determined to "sink without a trace" the U-boat commander shelled the lifeboats and shot nurses as they struggled in the water.

But Germany can never hide the damning evidence of her hideous crimes. The cries of the women and wounded men, murdered in the dead of night, come echoing across the waves:

"Wipe out this THING that strikes in the dark, this assassin of helpless men and defenceless women!"

Buy MORE Bonds. Buy with all the money you have and pledge all you can save in the months to come.

LIBERTY LOAN COMMITTEE, THIRD FEDERAL RESERVE DISTRICT
LINCOLN BUILDING, PHILADELPHIA

In a German painting of 1917 (above), a U-boat crewman prepares to toss a line to survivors of a sinking Allied ship. Such chivalrous deeds did occur—and so did acts of brutality. One of the most notorious was the incident depicted in the United States war-bond poster at left: the 1918 sinking of an unarmed hospital ship off southern Ireland and the shooting of many of her medical staff and crew.

She severed two telegraph cables in this way. With her special tasks accomplished, the U-boat now set about sinking as much shipping as possible. It was Commander von Nostitz' plan to continue on north to Boston and raise havoc along the coast of New England. But the boat soon ran into dense fog, and when the American radio predicted that there would be even worse weather farther north, the U-151 turned southward and headed for the sun.

The 26 prisoners were still on board. They had been well treated, fed the same food as the U-boat men and kept amused with American phonograph records—which the Germans had brought along on their mission for amusement. But the guests could hardly be said to have enjoyed themselves. Endless crash dives and occasional emergencies provoked panic among the prisoners. One of the captured schooner captains told the U-boat men that he had sailed the seas for many years but that submarine life was too much of a strain for him; his heart was pounding like a trip hammer.

His enforced stay was almost at an end, however. On June 2 a bright sun was shining, the sea was calm, and Nostitz had a field day; he sank six ships between dawn and twilight—three sailing ships and three steamers. He transferred the 26 prisoners into the lifeboats of one of the steamers, confident that they would be able to make their way safely to shore, a distance of only a few miles. By the time the day's work was over, there would be 448 people bobbing about in boats off the coast of New Jersey. Not one person had lost his life so far.

Some of the ships' survivors were to give a vivid description of their encounter with the U-boat. The captain of one of the steamers told of being boarded by Körner: "The German officer came right up to the bridge and extended his hand. It was certainly a funny way to capture a boat, but he looked friendly and I shook hands with him. But I was in for more shocks yet, when he said in excellent English, 'I'm sorry to have to do this, captain, but this is war, you know. Get your men off as quickly as possible. We are going to sink your ship.' He seemed to be apologizing for capturing me and I got the impression that he was ashamed that he had gotten only a little freighter instead of a transport."

The U-151's sudden, devastating emergence into the open shattered American complacency. But it was the sinking of the liner *Carolina* on her way from Puerto Rico to New York that caused the greatest sensation. The first intimation that the *Carolina* was in trouble was a distress signal picked up just after 6 p.m. on June 2 by radio operators at Cape May, New Jersey, the Brooklyn Navy Yard, and Arlington. The message read: SOS. STEAMSHIP CAROLINA BEING GUNNED BY GERMAN SUBMARINE. Cape May answered at once, requesting the position of the ship. But there was no reply. The *Carolina* was known to have more than 300 people on board, and Coast Guard stations were warned by telephone to look out for both the submarine and the survivors.

At 6 o'clock that evening, the *Carolina* had been steaming 60 miles due east of Cape May. A Mrs. Westbrook of New York, one of the few passengers who had not gone belowdecks for supper, first spied a low-lying hull on the surface of the sea less than two miles away. "Why," she said to a lady near her, "there comes a submarine." A minute later a 6-

inch shell whistled past the stern of the steamer. The SOS had barely been sent when Cape May's signal asking for the ship's position was received. But then the U-boat's radio operator broke in on the receiving frequency and warned: YOU DON'T WIRELESS—WE DON'T SHOOT. When the ship's operator began sending another SOS, three more shells splashed nearby. The *Carolina's* captain, T.R.D. Barbour, ordered the operator not to transmit their position.

The *Carolina* hove to and, on command from the *U-151*, abandoned ship in good order but "with a great wailing of women's voices," Körner remembered. According to Captain Barbour, one of the German officers addressed his American victims in impeccable English. "Is everybody off your ship?" he shouted through a megaphone. "I'm going to shell her." When he was told yes, he added: "Pull for the shore." The *Carolina's* 10 boats headed west in two groups. With dusk falling and the wind rising, the *U-151* circled the abandoned ship and fired three shells into her port side, then three into her starboard side. The *Carolina* upended, her stern in the air. After hanging vertically in the water for 10 minutes, the ship went down at exactly 8:15.

The sinking was to bring about the first loss of life on the *U-151's* voyage. When a great storm blew up in the night, one lifeboat capsized; it was righted again, but by then 13 of its occupants had drowned in the dark waters. At 1 o'clock the next afternoon, the British freighter *Appleby* rescued the 19 survivors in that boat. The next afternoon the last of the *Carolina's* boats finally approached land at Atlantic City. A parade of the Knights of the Mystic Shrine was passing along the boardwalk and hundreds of bathers were romping in the breakers. No one saw the little boat row in until it was at the seaward end of the piers. Flying pathetically from the end of an oar was a distress signal—a white shirt. The discovery electrified the crowd. An eyewitness reported:

"The band that had been playing 'Where Do We Go from Here' swung, as if on signal, into 'The Star Spangled Banner,' halted in its tracks and faced the sea. Pleasure-seeking hundreds on the boardwalk stopped, looked, then started with a rush for the beach. Bathers stopped romping. They gazed, spellbound for an instant, then took up the shouts of welcome that burst from the crowd. Beach guards launched their boats and bent their backs to cut the combers towards the yawl. Excited Shriners, in the full regalia of their order, rushed waist deep into the surf.

"The guards swept alongside the craft, lifted out two women who had collapsed and started back to the shore. Others transferred some of the passengers into their boat and leaped into the yawl and tore the oars from the hands of the exhausted men and pulled the others into shallow water. As the yawl shot up on the sand under the powerful drive of the life guards, the strains of the music swept out with renewed vigor. Men and women stood with bared heads. A little girl, not more than 12 or 13, was first lifted ashore. She was dripping wet, but smiling and she blew a kiss to the crowds that cheered her as she was carried into the hospital tent. A big six-foot Shriner peeled off a green velvet coat that topped off his brilliant raiment, and flung it about her shoulders. Two frail women were carried in. They were dressed in heavy blue overalls and jumpers. One fainted as a sudden blast from the band carried the strains of the

Wearing borrowed clothes, weary survivors of the steamer Carolina, sunk by the U-151, gather in June 1918 in Atlantic City, New Jersey, after a 48-hour ordeal in a lifeboat. This German foray to the very shores of the United States greatly alarmed Americans; 3,000 New Yorkers volunteered for the Navy the day after the story ran in the newspapers.

anthem to her. 'We're saved,' the other said simply, and then fell unconscious into the arms of a physician.''

War had come to America, and the shock was felt up and down the coast. In New York, steamship companies were besieged by the relatives of missing people. Ports were closed, sailings were canceled, freight rates rose and insurance premiums soared. The Navy took over coastal shipping, organized convoys, enjoined radio silence at sea. Blackouts plunged the skyscrapers of Manhattan into unfamiliar darkness every night. Panic sightings of U-boats were reported everywhere, but though United States seaplanes and patrol boats scoured coastal waters, they found nothing—for by now the *U-151* was miles away.

The U-cruiser continued southward, sinking more ships and dodging more destroyers. Her 13th victim, the Norwegian steamer *Vindeggen*, presented some problems. A woman and her two-year-old baby daughter were on board, and the sea was too rough for them to be placed in the lifeboats. Moreover, the ship was loaded with 2,000 tons of copper, a very scarce metal in wartime Germany that was desperately needed in the manufacture of shells. Nostitz decided to take the woman and child on board and to replace the U-boat's iron ballast with as many of the copper ingots from the *Vindeggen* as the submarine could carry. The *Vindeggen*'s master, given a course by his captors, steered toward an empty quarter of the ocean with the *U-151* trailing behind. Some 150 miles out from the American coast, the two vessels stopped, and for the next two days the copper was transshipped to the U-boat. When the laborious task was completed on June 10, the crew of the *Vindeggen* were placed in lifeboats, the woman and child were brought aboard the submarine, and the ship was blown up with explosive charges.

When the *Vindeggen* went down, the Norwegian flag fluttering proudly from the masthead, her old captain stood rigidly at attention in his lifeboat. On the submarine the woman cried and the little girl clapped her hands with glee at the strange sight. The tiny tot, Eva Ugland, soon became the U-boat's darling. The cook prepared cakes, candies and dishes of canned fruits and whipped cream specially for her. The sailors fed the delicacies to the child with an unflagging delight.

To cheer everyone up as the U-boat headed for land, towing the *Vindeggen*'s lifeboats behind her, the *U-151*'s crew got out on deck and sang old songs to the accompaniment of a guitar and mandolin. At about 5 p.m. that day, another Norwegian steamer, the *Henrik Lund*, was sighted. The Germans set the *Vindeggen*'s boats adrift, sank the *Henrik Lund* and then took the lifeboats from both ships in tow. Soon after dark a patrol boat was sighted. The *U-151* cast off the boats—after placing little Eva Ugland and her mother in one of them—and steered away, staying on the surface to make sure that the boats' occupants were safely picked up. The people in the boats began to make a tremendous noise to attract the patrol vessel's attention, waving lanterns and setting off rockets. Under the guns of the U-boat, just 300 yards off, the patrol boat drew up and took the whole crowd on board. Only then did the *U-151* depart.

Fuel was now running low and the American waters were suddenly empty of ships. After two days of fruitless hunting, the U-cruiser headed for home. Six weeks later, at 9:30 a.m. on July 20, 1918, the *U-151* made fast to the pier at Kiel at the end of her historic raid. The boat had covered the prodigious distance of 10,915 miles in 94 days, had sunk 23 ships totaling 61,000 tons and had been responsible for the loss of four more sunk by the mines she had laid. More importantly, as Lieutenant Körner pointed out afterward, "we had shown a skeptical world that even the wide expanse of the Atlantic was not enough to keep us from a superraid to the coast of far-off America. Surely this is a warning of what later wars may bring. For the day will come when submarines will think no more of a voyage across the Atlantic than they do now of a raid across the North Sea. America's isolation is now a thing of the past."

The success of the *U-151*'s raid encouraged the Germans to send more giant U-cruisers to America. The *U-140*, the *U-156* and the *U-117* were active off the American coast through the summer and early fall. But they found the Americans better prepared this time, and consequently they accomplished less. On her way home, the *U-156* ran into the vast Northern Barrage 130 miles west of Bergen and was lost with all hands when she struck a mine on September 25. By then, the *U-155*, the *U-152* and the *U-139* also had set off for American waters. But they would not

With binoculars at the ready, young watch officer Karl Dönitz stands on the deck of the U-39 in 1917. Dönitz, master architect of Germany's submarine warfare in World War II, wrote of the original U-boat corps: "Every submariner felt himself to be as rich as a king and would trade places with no man."

have time to achieve their goals. Despite the *U-151's* success, Germany's war efforts in general, at sea and on land, were fast collapsing.

In the Mediterranean the U-boat war was nearly over. By September 1918, the monthly total of shipping sunk there had fallen to 49,000 tons. But the U-boats put up a bitter fight until the very end.

One of the last U-boat actions in the Mediterranean involved a relative newcomer, a cool and determined 27-year-old submarine commander whose name was destined to be linked inseparably with the history of the U-boat: Karl Dönitz. Lieutenant Dönitz had learned his work on the *U-39*, commanded by the second highest scoring U-boat ace of World War I, Lieutenant Walther Forstmann. Later Dönitz had been promoted to commands of his own, first to the Mediterranean minelayer *UC-25*, then to a large U-boat, the *UB-68*. The early hours of October 4, 1918, found Dönitz in his new boat lying in wait off Cape Passero, on the south coast of Sicily, and at 1 a.m. a British convoy of fully laden ships from India and the Far East came in sight en route to Malta.

Making a fast surface attack, Dönitz broke through the convoy's escorts and managed to torpedo one of the steamers before a destroyer charged at him and forced him to dive. By the time he caught up with the convoy again, dawn was breaking and it was too light for another surface attack. So Dönitz dived a second time. He was just maneuvering into an attack position at periscope depth when his chief engineer found he could no longer keep proper trim. Bow heavy, the *UB-68* suddenly stood on its head and plunged out of control into the depths. Dönitz at once ordered all tanks to be blown and both engines set full astern. Then the lights went out. His watch officer in the conning tower produced a flashlight, and together the two men watched in horror as the needle of the depth gauge fell swiftly past 230 feet—at that time a U-boat's maximum permitted depth. At 260 feet they heard the hull begin to creak from the water pressure. At 302 feet the needle quivered and stopped, then suddenly began to rise. Clearly the tanks had blown after all; now the U-boat was shooting up through the sea like a stick that had been forced down under water and then released. A shudder ran through the boat as she burst above the surface and fell back.

Dönitz put his head out of the conning-tower hatch, then quickly withdrew it. The *UB-68* had come up in the very middle of the convoy, and every ship on the sea seemed to be firing at him. He cried out: "Dive! Dive!" But his chief reported back: "We've no more compressed air left." A U-boat that dived without compressed air could never resurface again. But if the *UB-68* was unable to dive, she could not hope to survive long on the surface either, for the gunfire directed at her was intense. There was only one thing left to do. "Abandon ship!" Dönitz shouted.

The U-boat soon sank, and Dönitz had difficulty keeping himself afloat until he discarded his heavy leather clothing and sea boots. By the time a boat from the Royal Navy sloop *Snapdragon* fished him out of the sea, the future chief of the German Navy and head of the German Reich was clad in nothing more than a shirt, a pair of underpants and one sock. "Now we are quits, captain," the English commander said to him as he climbed on board. "You blew up a steamer under my nose last night, and now I've sunk you." Six of the *UB-68's* crew were missing. The survivors

"Ash cans" that shattered the U-boats' sanctuary

At the opening of the War, British ships could ram or shell a surfaced U-boat, but had no weapons to use if the U-boat dived. One day in 1915, Admiral Sir Charles Madden, a Grand Fleet staff officer, listened to a report of a U-boat's easy escape from a British cruiser by diving, then commented to Admiral Sir John Jellicoe: "Wouldn't it have been fine if they had had a mine that when dropped overboard exploded when it reached the depth at which the submarine was lying?"

"That remark gave us the germinal idea of the depth charge," wrote Jellicoe later. "I asked the Admiralty to produce a 'mine' that would act in the way that Admiral Madden suggested. It proved to be very simple."

The device was an ash can-shaped steel drum filled with 300 pounds of TNT and equipped with a pressure-sensitive firing apparatus preset for a certain depth. At first, depth charges were rolled off racks at the stern of surface warships, but in 1918 throwers (*right, top*) capable of hurling them 75 yards were introduced. An exploding charge could destroy a U-boat 25 feet away and damage one 50 feet away. Even explosions that did no harm to their target could cause trauma akin to shell shock in U-boat crews. Wrote United States Rear Admiral William Sims, "The hardiest underwater sailor did not care to go through such frightful moments a second time."

The depth-charge thrower used a powder charge to hurl its missile toward a U-boat. A yank on the lanyard set off a blast to the firing chamber; the resulting hot gases, expanding into the mortar-like projector tube, ejected the cradle— called an arbor—and the depth charge it held. As the depth charge arced toward its target, the arbor fell away.

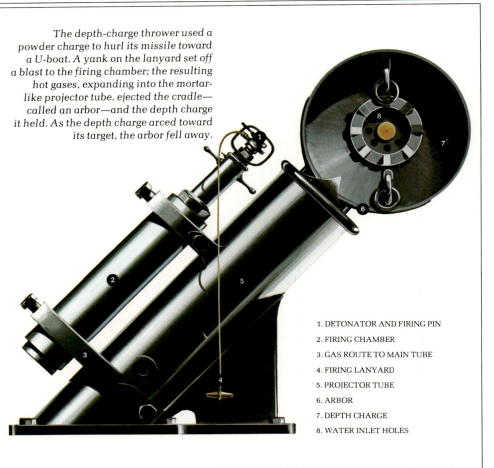

1. DETONATOR AND FIRING PIN
2. FIRING CHAMBER
3. GAS ROUTE TO MAIN TUBE
4. FIRING LANYARD
5. PROJECTOR TUBE
6. ARBOR
7. DEPTH CHARGE
8. WATER INLET HOLES

The level at which a depth charge exploded was controlled by the rate of water flow through a preset valve at one end of a charge. After filling a pistol bellows chamber, the water drove the detonator against the primer, causing it to explode and set off the main charge.

1. WATER INLET VALVE AND
   PISTOL BELLOWS CHAMBER
2. DETONATOR
3. PRIMER

4. FILLING HOLE FOR EXPLOSIVE
5. LIFTING RING
6. MAIN CHARGE
7. OUTER CASING

gave three cheers for the Kaiser and then were led below as prisoners of war. A hot bath was run for Dönitz, and the commander's white tennis clothes were laid out for him to put on. Thus sportingly attired, Lieutenant Dönitz was conveyed to the British naval base at Malta.

The U-boat war did not long outlive Dönitz' capture (indeed, Germany had proposed an armistice with the Allies on the very day he was taken prisoner). With the Central Powers crumbling on all fronts, the German U-boats covering the Mediterranean could no longer count on secure bases. It was decided that the Mediterranean submarines should attempt to return to Kiel. Thirteen U-boats set course westward to run the gantlet of massed antisubmarine forces at the Strait of Gibraltar. Groping along beneath the surface, the hum of hostile warship propellers everywhere, all of them succeeded in getting through into the Atlantic, and then headed for Germany via the north of Scotland.

Other U-boats were coming home as well. The Flanders U-boat base had virtually ceased to function because of the barrages in the Strait of Dover and across the Heligoland Bight, and the advance of the Allied armies on the Western Front now made it imperative to shut down the base entirely. By October 20 no U-boats remained on the Flanders coast.

Far out at sea, the big U-cruisers on their long patrols to America received recall orders. At 6:30 a.m. on October 22, 1918, in the middle of the North Atlantic, Lieutenant Adolf Franz of the *U-152* was handed this message by his radio operator: COMMENCE RETURN CRUISE IMMEDIATELY. BECAUSE OF CURRENT NEGOTIATIONS, ALL MANNER OF MERCHANT WARFARE FORBIDDEN. U-BOATS ALREADY RETURNING. ATTACK WARSHIPS ONLY BY DAY. ADMIRALTY STAFF OF THE NAVY, BERLIN. The new German Chancellor, Prince Maximilian of Baden, had ordered the U-boat campaign against merchant shipping suspended in anticipation of the forthcoming Armistice talks.

The final sinking of an enemy ship by a U-cruiser had taken place 21 days earlier. The protagonist was none other than Lieutenant Lothar von Arnauld de la Perière, who had made his reputation as the greatest ace of all on the *U-35* in the Mediterranean. In command of the big *U-139*, the irrepressible Arnauld launched a series of persistent attacks against a well-defended convoy of 10 British ships in the Bay of Biscay. Despite fierce gunfire and depth charging from the convoy escorts, he succeeded in torpedoing one ship before being forced to dive for cover.

"Less than a minute later," Arnauld recounted, "there was a terrible crash overhead and our boat shook from stem to stern as if it had been cracked open by a giant blow. The lights went out. Water rushed in from above. The boat listed to one side." In a chance in a million, the ship he had just sunk had settled on top of the *U-139* and was carrying her down to the ocean floor. Only by blowing all tanks was the U-boat able to force its way out of the freighter's death grip and return to the surface, where its crew patched the torn hull with cement.

Another of the last U-boat engagements of the War was stranger still, perhaps the strangest of the whole conflict, because it pitted a U-boat not against Allied ships but against vessels of Germany's own Navy. No shots were fired, but the confrontation was as serious and potentially as deadly as any previous one.

The U-boat commander involved was Johannes Spiess, who, after years of toiling away in the old prewar *U-19*, had just been awarded command of the *U-135*, the fastest, most sophisticated submarine in the German Navy. Spiess was justly proud of his new command and anxious to give it its baptism of fire in the final struggle. But before he could take the *U-135* to sea against the enemy, he was caught up in events that were traumatizing his country.

As the war effort disintegrated that October, discontent smoldered in Germany. After a year of worsening hunger and hardship caused by the British naval blockade, the population was disillusioned with both the War and Germany's leaders. None were more discontented than the sailors of the High Seas Fleet, who with their ships had been sitting in north German bases for most of the last two and a half years, ever since their inconclusive foray against the British Grand Fleet at the Battle of Jutland. On October 29, 1918, they began to mutiny in large numbers.

On the morning of October 31, Spiess was summoned before the U-boat flotilla commander at Wilhelmshaven, Commodore Andreas Michelsen. The commodore's first question took him aback. "Are you," he asked, "absolutely sure of your men?" Almost mechanically Spiess answered: "Certainly, commodore." He was then informed that the crews of the battleships *Thüringen* and *Helgoland* had mutinied, and he was ordered to move the *U-135* out to the ships' anchorages and thereafter act upon the orders of the Naval command. The implication was plain: the *U-135* was to attack and sink the mutinous German battleships if called upon to do so. Written orders to this effect were refused him. Immediately Spiess sailed his new boat toward the dreadnoughts. He was joined by two loyal harbor vessels, plus a steamer carrying a boarding party of 200 marines.

The *U-135* took up a position near the *Thüringen*, ready to fire guns and torpedoes. With fixed bayonets, the marines boarded the battleship and sealed off the upper decks and hatches, while the ringleaders of the mutiny sought refuge in the forecastle. The mutineers were given two minutes to surrender—two minutes too long in Spiess's opinion; at the end of that time, the marines, and the U-boat if necessary, would open fire. The mutineers capitulated. Meanwhile Spiess had noticed something odd happening on the other renegade ship, the *Helgoland*. "First one and then another of the 15-cm. casemate guns were trained on the *U-135*," Spiess recalled. "Soon all the guns were trained on us. Very unpleasant. The distance was about 550 yards. One hit would have sufficed to finish us." With the *Helgoland*'s entire broadside battery trained on the U-boat, and the U-boat's bow torpedoes pointed at the *Thüringen*, the tension was almost unbearable. But it was a last effort at resistance. A signal called the *U-135* over to the *Thüringen* and hundreds of mutineers were taken into custody.

In Spiess's view, a golden opportunity had been lost. If he had torpedoed the battleships, he believed, the mutiny in the fleet would have been stifled once and for all. Instead, it spread, and its leaders no longer proclaimed disobedience, but revolution. By November 4 most battleships were flying the red flag and were under the control of revolutionary committees. The Mediterranean U-boats, nearly home after their long retreat, received the news in a Norwegian fjord. Lieutenant Adolf

Franz on board the *U-152* heard it off the Faroe Islands in a shattering series of radio messages on November 6: TO ALL U-BOATS: FIRE WITHOUT WARNING ON SHIPS WITH RED FLAG. ALL OF KIEL HOSTILE; OCCUPY OPENING OF KIEL BAY. CLOSE KIEL OFF COMPLETELY; LET NO SHIP DOCK OR DEPART. BREAK RESISTANCE BY ALL MEANS. OPERATIONAL BOATS STEAM TO BORKUM ROADS IMMEDIATELY, SCOUT BOATS STEAM TO HELIGOLAND AS SOON AS POSSIBLE.

Chaos mounted. Another order directed U-boats and torpedo boats in Kiel and Wilhelmshaven to seek sanctuary in Heligoland. But even in Heligoland revolution had broken out, and vessels loyal to the government were unwelcome. The U-boat navy had not a refuge in the world.

The German submariners, unbeaten by the enemy and loyal and disciplined to the last, were thus defeated by their own comrades in arms, the sailors of the surface warships. On November 9 the U-boats were ordered back to their bases to submit to the ignominy of capitulating to the mutineers. "On November 9," wrote General Erich Ludendorff, "Germany collapsed like a house of cards. All that we had bled four long years to maintain was gone. Order in state and society vanished. All authority disappeared. Chaos, Bolshevism, terror made their entry into the German fatherland." Late that night the Kaiser signed his abdication and fled into exile in Holland. At 5:40 a.m. on Monday, November 11, Germany signed the Armistice, and at 11 o'clock that morning the guns ceased to fire.

The surrender of all U-boats at ports designated by the Allies was a crucial condition of the Armistice agreement. If the Germans attempted to scuttle their submarines, the Allies warned, Heligoland would be placed under permanent Allied military occupation. The port chosen for surrender was Harwich, on England's east coast. On November 20, as the dawn mist cleared from the sea 20 miles out, the long low shapes of 20 German U-boats could be seen being marshaled into captivity by Royal Navy warships. British crews boarded the U-boats and took over from the German crews, and as they entered Harwich the British white ensign was hoisted above the German flag. In the days that followed, the humiliation was repeated over and over. Counting those that were interned in other ports, 176 U-boats finally entered captivity. Rusting in German shipyards lay 224 more U-boats in various stages of construction for a great submarine offensive that would never take place.

The British reception of the surrendering U-boats was less than worthy of the occasion. As soon as the vessels were moored in the estuary of the Rivers Orwell and Stour, the officers and men of the Harwich naval station launched an orgy of looting. Swarming over the water at night in every kind of small craft (even duck punts), they ransacked the U-boats for valuable instruments and any other movable objects. No less a personage than one of the Lords of the Admiralty in London sent a message that a German chronometer was to be obtained for him, but by then there was little loose to be found on board, and illicit naval parties were even cutting up the periscopes with hack saws to get at the prisms.

With the end of the first submarine campaign in history came the dreadful reckoning. Germany had started the War with 20 operational U-boats, had built 345, and had lost 178 through enemy action. Of the 13,000 officers and men who had served in U-boats, 515 officers and

4,849 men had lost their lives, a mortality rate of more than 40 per cent.

But this was nothing compared with the casualties the U-boats had inflicted. They had sunk nearly 5,000 ships, totaling a colossal 11 million tons of shipping—the greatest part of it British. More than 15,000 British civilians had died as a result of U-boat attacks. The U-boat had proved to be one of the most formidable weapons of modern war, bringing Britain to within a hair's breadth of collapse. But the very savagery of the U-boats' onslaught had in the end drawn the United States into the War and ensured Germany's ultimate defeat.

Peace did little to reconcile the British people to their former enemies. Arriving at Southampton as a prisoner of war, Karl Dönitz and his U-boat crew were hissed by an angry crowd of women dockers. In the prisoner-of-war camp at Redmires, near Sheffield, where 600 other German officers were held, Dönitz read newspaper headlines proclaiming: "HANG THE KAISER, HANG THE U-BOAT COMMANDERS!"

The recrimination was not confined to the British. Among Dönitz' fellow officers in the prisoner-of-war camp, among the former admirals and generals of the high command in Germany, among the defeated soldiery, the defected sailors, the near-starving civilian populace of the shattered fatherland, the debate raged endlessly—why had they lost the War? For Grand Admiral Alfred von Tirpitz there was a simple answer: "The German people did not understand the sea."

Young Karl Dönitz, contemplating the lessons of the U-boat war in the

enforced leisure of his prison camp, arrived at the same conclusion. "The blame for the defeat," he was to write many years later, "lay in the Continental mindedness of our government, our Army leadership and the entire German people." Germany had been victorious in the past because her opponents were Continental countries and the fighting was done by armies. "Now our political and strategic position had been fundamentally altered," Dönitz continued. "For the first time, 1914 was a sea contest, and the greatest sea power was on the side of our opponent, whom we could fight with any hope of success only in the Atlantic. And this we did not understand."

He understood it now. In the years after his return to Germany in July 1919—the bitter years of crushing war reparations and national impoverishment, of political anarchy and civil violence, of raging inflation and military impotence—Dönitz knew that if ever there was another war it would be a continuation of the first, waged in much the same way and against much the same enemies. If Germany was to win the next war, Dönitz concluded, the issue would be decided in the Atlantic—and by U-boats. But if U-boats were to determine the outcome of a second war, they would have to be used in a new way—in overwhelming strength, in packs working in concert, in ruthless onslaughts at night in a totally unrestricted campaign. This much he had worked out from his experiences of the last U-boat campaign. If these lessons were applied, Germany could win the next war at sea.

Ominous even in captivity, rows of German submarines awaiting their final disposition lie in the harbor at Harwich, England, in December 1918. Within a few years the Allies were to scrap most of the U-boats—not foreseeing that these destructive vessels still had a major role to play in naval warfare.

A clandestine crop of subs for the next round

World War I had been over barely 15 years before Adolf Hitler became Chancellor of Germany and began planning to throw off the "shackles of Versailles"—the terms of the peace treaty that restricted German armament to minimal self-defense and proscribed the building of U-boats altogether. German military strength would expand, Hitler pledged to the heads of his armed forces; in particular, the Navy would have a fleet of U-boats.

The Navy was already one jump ahead of the Führer, thanks to the uncanny foresight and intricate maneuvers of Gustav Krupp, head of the mammoth industrial empire that bore his name. The Krupp family, armorers for Europe's warriors for well over 100 years, had ties to royal families and heads of state everywhere. Checked in Germany, they had only to carry their armaments enterprises abroad.

Gustav Krupp had lost no time in doing that. In 1922 he dispatched the first of 40 German engineers to a Dutch company at The Hague, where they found employment drafting U-boat blueprints. The company was to pass through a number of reorganizations, eventually becoming known as the Ingenieurskantoor voor Scheepsbouw, or Engineering Office for Shipbuilding. But from the start it was financed by Krupp capital—and directed by Krupp genius. Soon it was selling U-boat blueprints—and construction expertise—to Japan, Spain, Finland, Turkey and Holland. The first of the company's U-boats was built for Turkey under German supervision in Holland in 1927.

Having shown foreign shipbuilders how to produce submarines, Krupp began ordering diesel engines, electric batteries, periscopes and other vital U-boat elements from those firms. These parts were secretly shipped to Germany and stockpiled. In March 1935, when the Führer publicly repudiated the Versailles Treaty, the Krupps—with their thriving shipyard operations all over the world and their stockpile of parts at home in Germany—were ready to conjure up U-boats as if by sorcery. Before the year was out, 14 U-boats had materialized at the German Navy yard at Kiel.

By the summer of 1939 the German Navy had a U-boat arm of 57 vessels and more than 1,000 well-trained officers and men, all under the command of Commodore Karl Dönitz, the brilliant U-boat officer who had formulated the principles of U-boat warfare as Krupp had devised their production. In the third week of August, 40 of those vessels were dispatched to their war stations around Britain—ready to strike the moment that Hitler gave the nod.

Five trim new U-boats line up at Kiel harbor in 1935—primed in advance, like an earlier generation of U-boats in 1914 (page 18), for war with Britain. The vessels, part of a training flotilla commanded by Commodore Karl Dönitz, were inspected by Adolf Hitler (emerging from a forward hatch, inset) that same year.

Chapter 4

A daredevil thrust at the Royal Navy's heart

All through the daylight hours on Friday, October 13, 1939, the German submarine *U-47* lay silently on the floor of the sea, east of the Orkney Islands. At a depth of 300 feet the U-boat was immune to all effects of waves and weather, and only occasionally was her trim disturbed as underwater currents gently raised and lowered the steel hull.

World War II had begun six weeks before. German Panzers had already overrun Poland in the east and were biding their time in the west before smashing into the Low Countries and France. The German Navy, meanwhile, had commenced an offensive against the Navy and the merchant shipping—the very life line—of Great Britain. A German U-boat, the *U-29*, had just scored an astonishing success in sinking the aircraft carrier *Courageous*, off the west coast of England, on September 17 *(pages 80-81)*. And now the *U-47* was about to strike an even bolder blow.

For the past five days, ever since the *U-47* had slipped out of Kiel at the start of Special Operation *P,* her crew had reversed the normal rhythm of life, sleeping submerged during the day to avoid detection, and surfacing at night to resume course. On October 13 the U-boat had dived at 4:37 a.m. and she was not due to resurface till after 7:00 p.m. The crew, comprising some 40 men, had almost 15 hours to wait—a period of inactivity that many of them found almost unbearable penance.

In order to stretch out the U-boat's limited supply of electricity and air, Lieutenant Günther Prien, the boat's captain—known to his friends as Prüntje (Little Prien) and to his crew as der Alte (the Old Man)—had ordered all unnecessary lights and auxiliary equipment to be switched off and all crew members not on duty to turn in; a man lying down, doing nothing, consumed appreciably less precious oxygen than a man standing up, doing work.

But it was not easy to sleep. A submarine lying deep for a prolonged period, with its electric heaters switched off, grew painfully cold and clammy inside. In the unfamiliar silence on board the *U-47*, every odd sound from outside and inside the U-boat was magnified and startling. As the crew lay in their narrow bunks in the semi-darkness of the congested hull, they listened to the steady drip of condensed moisture off the pipes and plates and the subdued voices of the skeleton watch in the control room, checking the boat's trim and air supply—even to the breathing of their fellow crewmen. Yet none of this, by itself, was enough to ruin a trained U-boat crew's repose. What made their rest so fitful was not so much the exterior noises around them as their own interior tumult. For their commander had just briefed them on the purpose of their awesome mission. They were going into Scapa Flow!

There was not a man in the German Navy for whom the name Scapa Flow did not have a very special meaning. Scapa Flow, a 50-square-mile expanse of almost landlocked deep water in the Orkney Islands, north of Scotland, was the finest natural roadstead in the British Isles. Strategically it was one of the most important anchorages in the world, guarding the approaches from the North Sea to the Atlantic and hence the main exit route of the German Navy from German ports.

In World War I Scapa Flow had been used as a main anchorage by the Royal Navy. From there the Grand Fleet had sailed to fight the

Günther Prien, commander of the U-47's audacious strike on Scapa Flow in October 1939, smiles inscrutably aboard his submarine. Described by a German Naval staff officer as "a clear thinker not given to complex pondering," Prien was perfectly suited to the unpredictable hazards of U-boat combat operations.

German High Seas Fleet at Jutland in 1916—the greatest naval engagement of the War—and it was there that the interned German surface fleet scuttled itself in 1919, an event burned deep in the psyche of every German sailor ever after.

Twenty years had passed, and Scapa Flow was once again the base of the British fleet, once again the pivot of Britain's mastery of the seas. To the British Admiralty, the harbor seemed impregnable to attack by sea, its sheltering islands festooned with guns, its entrances barred with antisubmarine booms, nets, cables, blockships and patrol vessels. Scapa was Britannia's maw. Even if an enemy could manage to penetrate this sanctuary of British Naval power, the chances of safe escape were thought to be infinitesimal.

There were two precedents in World War I to demonstrate the point. In November 1914 the *U-18* tried to enter Scapa Flow by following along in the wake of a British supply ship that had been let through the boom; the U-boat was quickly detected, rammed and sunk. In October 1918 the *UB-116* tried the same trick, but was also spotted and was blown up by mines that were detonated by remote control from the shore.

Now, in a new war against an old enemy, the young crew of the *U-47* learned that they were to try where their predecessors had so signally failed. At a crowded general stand-to of officers and crew in the white-

A powerful hunter that fell victim to her quarry

British sailors scramble down the sides of the torpedoed aircraft carrier Courageous. Nearby vessels picked up almost 700 survivors.

painted torpedo room forward, Prien had finally divulged the secret of his boat's special mission. Once they were inside, they would wreak havoc. "First we're going to sink aircraft carriers, then battleships and cruisers, and all we can get."

The high command, Prien told them, was sure that the boat would be able to get in, not so sure it would be able to get out. If the *U-47* did not achieve its objective within the allocated time, it would be trapped inside the Flow by the torrential tide. "But I am determined to get in and do what we have to do," Prien declared, "and I am more determined to get you all out again and back home."

Nobody spoke. The idea was too much to take in at once. All by themselves, they were going to take on the biggest battle fleet of any nation engaged in the War. If they succeeded they would strike the most devastating individual blow ever delivered in submarine warfare, achieve perhaps one of the greatest feats of arms in naval history. It would be not only a tactical triumph but a strategic victory that could radically change the balance of power at sea.

And if they failed? Everyone knew about the fate of the *U-18* and the *UB-116*. Everyone was anxious and full of foreboding. But they were young and felt themselves immortal. And they trusted the Old Man. From the exalted commander of U-boats, Commodore Karl Dönitz, to the

The War had scarcely begun before Karl Dönitz' U-boats demonstrated the inadequacy of the antisubmarine tactics of the Royal Navy. On September 17, 1939, the 22,500-ton aircraft carrier *Courageous*, accompanied by four destroyer escorts, was zigzagging back and forth off the coast of Ireland in the western approaches to the English Channel. The huge warship was on antisubmarine patrol and the members of her crew were in high spirits. Only three days before, a similar force, led by the carrier *Ark Royal*, had detected and sunk the *U-39*. Hunting U-boats looked like easy sport.

But that was an illusion. Only a few miles from the *Courageous*, the *U-29*, under the direction of Lieutenant Otto Schuhart, was traveling at periscope depth, undetected by either the carrier's planes or the escorts' various listening devices. Otto Schuhart was not trying to escape from the British vessel; he was stalking her, watching for an opportunity to launch the U-boat's torpedoes.

So far the zigzagging carrier had not presented Schuhart with a promising target, and he knew that if the *Courageous* steamed away he would never catch her. She was capable of 25 knots, while the *U-29* could make only eight knots submerged.

Then suddenly, before Schuhart's incredulous eyes, the carrier changed her course and was exposed broadside to the U-boat. "The vast size of the target upset all normal calculations," Schuhart later recalled. The looming side of the ship was too big to miss, and Schuhart quickly fired three torpedos without even waiting for an exact range reading. He then took the *U-29* down to 250 feet to await the outcome. The submarine's deep dive was barely under way before she was rocked by the concussion from two tremendous explosions.

A pair of torpedoes had struck the *Courageous* amidships, throwing aircraft from the flight deck and littering the sea with wreckage. The projecting deck of the carrier was split asunder and tongues of flame shot out from the black smoke of burning fuel oil.

Minutes later the ship began to capsize, and hundreds of panic-stricken crewmen leaped into the frigid water, only to find themselves thrashing in a film of poisonous oil. Within 15 minutes after being torpedoed, the *Courageous* capsized and disappeared. Of the 1,200 officers and men on board, 518 were lost, among them Captain W. T. Makeig-Jones.

The aircraft carrier's escort vessels scurried futilely about, making blind depth-charge attacks. Captain Schuhart and the crew of the *U-29* quietly eased along underwater until the bombardment ceased, then surfaced and ran for home, with the distinction of being the first Germans to sink a major British warship in World War II.

greenest control-room hand on the *U-47*, everyone believed in Prien.

The Old Man—of medium height and stocky frame, fair-haired, square-jawed and handsome in a boyish way—was 31 years of age. To his crew, most of whom were in their late teens and early twenties, this made him a seasoned veteran. He had been in service for seven years and there was little he did not know about U-boats. He had been born in 1908 in the Baltic port of Lübeck, son of a judge. His parents had separated before he was 10 and he was brought up in Leipzig by his mother.

In the smoke, grime and poverty of that industrial city, he resolved early to make his career on the sea, where a man could breathe clean air. At 16 he served on a square-rigger as deck boy and then progressed to seaman on a freighter. He became an officer in the German merchant service and at 24 passed the examination for his master's ticket.

In 1933 Prien learned that the German Navy was looking for officer candidates, and he left the merchant service to begin training. By 1935 he had graduated from U-boat school in Kiel and was commissioned as watchkeeping officer aboard the *U-26*. He had seen active service in the Spanish Civil War, had captained the *U-47* for nearly a year now, and on his first wartime patrol in September had sunk three ships and been awarded the Iron Cross, Second Class. His merchant service inspired a well-placed confidence in his seamanship, and as a naval officer he had proved himself courageous, clever and cool under pressure.

"Prien was all that a man should be," his commanding officer, Karl Dönitz, wrote later, "a great personality, full of zest and the joy of life, wholly dedicated to his service and an example to all who served under him. Typical of the man and his outlook is a remark he made before the War when he said: 'I get more fun out of a really good convoy exercise than out of any leave!' I held him in great affection and esteem."

None of his long years of preparation helped Prien get to sleep as he waited for night to come and for the *U-47* to start her singlehanded assault on the assembled might of the British Navy. The responsibility for the operation was entirely his. For security reasons he was maintaining complete radio silence, so he could not consult U-boat headquarters in Germany if his mission ran into problems. He lay on his bunk in what was fancifully called his cabin—a minute space, with a tip-up wash basin and a miniature desk, to the left of the U-boat's central passageway immediately forward of the control room—and pulled the green curtain shut for privacy. He had memorized the chart of Scapa Flow, and now he kept going over and over it in his head—the route in, the British fleet anchorages, the known defenses, the route out. He tried several times to fall asleep but he could not. At last he got up from his bunk and began to pace restlessly through the boat.

Prien could be proud of his Type VII-B submarine, the *U-47*. Type VII was destined to become the classic U-boat of World War II. It was only a refinement of its World War I predecessors, not a radical new design. Even so, by the standards of its time it was a formidable combat submarine and an ideal model for mass production. Type VII-B was 218 feet long, displaced 753 tons, made 16 to 17 knots on the surface and was a quick diver. Powerfully armed with four bow torpedo tubes and another at the stern, an 88-mm. gun forward of the conning tower, and a 20-mm. antiaircraft gun on the deck behind it, Type VII-B had a range of 8,700 sea miles at 10 knots—sufficient for a prolonged patrol around the British Isles or into the western approaches beyond.

Though there was precious little room for human beings amid the machinery and specialized equipment that filled the cigar-shaped steel tube of the hull, the interior of the *U-47* seemed to Prien infinitely spacious in the gloom. The control room, normally so cramped and full of bustle, looked vast in the dim light, with only a few crewmen on watch. At the illuminated chart table, Prien saw the navigator, Wilhelm Spahr, bent over the hydrographic chart of Scapa Flow.

"Hello!" Prien whispered. "What are you doing here?"

"I'm just having another look at the charts," Spahr whispered back.

"But it's time for you to lie down," Prien told him, concerned that his navigator might suffer from lack of sleep when the action started.

Like Prien, Spahr had been unable to sleep. He had got up to study the chart again, trying to fix in his mind every important navigational feature, because he knew that once the U-boat had surfaced the captain would have no chance even to glance at it.

Prien turned back to his cabin and pulled the green curtain fast behind him again. Shortly afterward someone went past a little too noisily.

"Quiet!" hissed the radio operator, resting in his cubicle opposite the captain's cabin. "The Old Man's sleeping."

From behind the green partition came Prien's cheerful, amused voice: "The Old Man never sleeps. He just rests his eyes."

So the interminable day passed. The air, fetid with diesel fumes and body odor, grew staler, the metalwork colder and clammier. Men stirred fitfully in bunks like coffins, each alone with his thoughts. Where would they be this time tomorrow? Would they be prisoners of the British? They had planned to scuttle the boat if escape proved to be impossible. But would the British Navy even let them surrender? Would they lie trapped in the U-boat's hull at the bottom of the Flow? What would it be like to die in this steel tomb?

Commodore Karl Dönitz, commander of the U-boat arm, had got them into this predicament. The attack on Scapa Flow was his idea.

Toward the end of World War I Dönitz had been interned in a British prisoner-of-war camp. A confirmed submariner, profoundly fascinated by the independence and comradeship of submarine life on the high seas, he had remained in Naval service on his return, in the hope that Germany might one day possess U-boats again—even though the victorious powers had decreed in the Treaty of Versailles that Germany would never be allowed such weapons. For the next 16 years Dönitz was a surface sailor, rising to command the training cruiser *Emden*. And for most of that time the German Admiralty had been secretly engaged in submarine development *(pages 76-77)*.

When Hitler officially repudiated the Versailles Treaty in 1935 and began to rearm for war, his shipyards started assembling U-boat parts. By the end of the year more than two dozen submarines were under construction. Some of these new U-boats were assigned to the submarine-training flotilla, the rest to Germany's first operational flotilla. To command the new U-boat arm, Grand Admiral Erich Raeder, Commander in Chief of the German Navy, chose Commodore Karl Dönitz.

Dönitz was free to create his new command in any image he chose. He aimed to build an elite force, composed of specially selected men, trained to perfection and inculcated with a suitably aggressive spirit for their essentially offensive role in war. The six-month training schedule was rigorous in the extreme, demanding complete familiarity with U-boats under all conditions. Every submarine crew had to make 66 dry-run surface attacks and 66 mock attacks submerged before it even went on to its first torpedo-firing practice. The result of all this training was a small but formidable force of first-class underwater fighting men.

Almost alone among senior officers in Germany, Dönitz believed that the next war would inevitably involve Britain. Not even Hitler subscribed to this view. Hitler hoped to form an alliance with Britain that would leave him free to carry out his real war aim—the expansion of German territory by military conquest in the east. But traditionally Britain had always opposed any nation that waxed too powerful in Europe. Dönitz correctly foresaw that any aggrandizement of Germany by military conquest would inevitably result in Britain's becoming not an ally but an enemy. He further foresaw that, in any war with Britain, Germany's key weapon would be the U-boat. In 1917 U-boats had come close to defeating Britain by almost severing the country's shipping life line. Dönitz was convinced that, properly handled, U-boats could starve and beggar Britain into defeat in any future war.

Yet Hitler had little comprehension of naval affairs. He was proud of Germany's big, bold, capital warships like the *Bismarck* and the *Tirpitz*, which he saw as symbols of Nazi power. He was correspondingly uninterested in the furtive little U-boats. Thus, in the period leading up to the outbreak of war, the German Navy concentrated on the construction of surface warships as the principal means of destroying enemy merchant shipping—in the unlikely event of war with Britain. Dönitz had calculated that he needed a force of 300 U-boats to ensure victory in the Atlantic. But he had only 57 submarines at his disposal when war finally came; of these, barely half were deep-sea boats capable of extended operations in the North Atlantic.

As he considered his position, Dönitz felt no jubilation in the message he sent his commanders on the afternoon of September 3, 1939: COMMENCE HOSTILITIES AGAINST BRITAIN FORTHWITH. Without the means for a swift victory, he knew what a long, bloody siege was in the offing. He warned his officers: THIS WAR MUST BE TAKEN VERY SERIOUSLY. MAKE NO MISTAKE ABOUT IT— IT MAY WELL LAST FOR SEVEN YEARS, AND WE SHALL PROBABLY BE ONLY TOO HAPPY TO SEE IT END THEN IN A PEACE BY NEGOTIATION.

Dönitz faced a second problem, every bit as distressing to him as his weakness in numbers. From the outset he had planned a campaign of unrestricted U-boat warfare. He meant to sink British ships where he found them, and without warning. But the Führer vetoed the plan. Hitler insisted that the U-boat arm must operate in accordance with the conditions of the Prize Regulations. This was a prewar international code of conduct for naval warfare, which restricted raiders to sinking only those merchant ships that were directly assisting an enemy war effort—and even then, only after stopping them, examining their papers and arranging for the safety of their crews.

Hitler was not in the least motivated by humanitarian considerations. He wished only to avoid offending neutral nations, particularly the United States, and he still hoped to reach a quick settlement with Britain, which would free him to pursue his grand design against Russia.

Dönitz' cause was not enhanced when on the very first day of the War one of his U-boats—the *U-30,* under Lieutenant Fritz-Julius Lemp—mistook the British liner *Athenia,* with more than 1,400 civilian passengers on board, for a troopship and torpedoed her without warning. The *Athenia* sank, and 118 passengers died—22 of them United States citizens. The British were enraged, the Americans alarmed, Hitler furious, and Dönitz deeply embarrassed. Ever fearful of involving America in the War, the Germans denied that a U-boat had sunk the *Athenia;* all reference to the sinking was deleted from the *U-30's* log, and Lemp and his crew were sworn to silence.

It was in these circumstances that Dönitz conceived the attack on Scapa Flow. To recoup from the *Athenia* blunder and advance the claims of the U-boat arm, he needed to strike a spectacular blow against a legitimate enemy target—the Royal Navy. Within a day or two of the outbreak of the War and the *Athenia* debacle, he resurrected an idea that

In Wilhelmshaven to review U-boat crews in September 1939, Adolf Hitler talks with the Commander in Chief of the German Navy, Grand Admiral Erich Raeder (left), and the commander of the U-boats, Commodore Karl Dönitz. The Führer's visit was intended to convince U-boat enlisted men, such as those standing rigidly at attention here, that they were part of an elite organization.

he had long toyed with: a U-boat sortie into Scapa Flow to deal the British a swift, reeling blow and make the U-boats the toast of Germany.

Dönitz was not a man to procrastinate. He immediately ordered all existing German intelligence reports on Scapa Flow to be sent to him at his headquarters in Wilhelmshaven. On September 6, only three days after the start of the War, the Luftwaffe sent a Heinkel bomber over Scapa Flow to take aerial photographs, and Dönitz dispatched a U-boat to cruise the approaches and report on tides and currents. The air photos revealed a whole fleet of light and heavy warships at anchor in the Flow. A second aerial reconnaissance provided precise details of all the obstacles guarding the various entrances.

There were seven entrances to the Flow—three main ones at the western end, which were closed with antisubmarine booms, and four narrower ones at the eastern end, which were guarded with blockships. From a close examination of the air photos, Dönitz decided that there was one possible route into the anchorage. This was by way of Kirk Sound, the most northerly of the entrances on the east side of the Flow. Three blockships were sunk across Kirk Sound. They had not been sunk bow to stern in a continuous line but lay overlapping, so that a small vessel could steer a zigzag course between them.

Dönitz also saw that between the southernmost blockship and the land there was a narrow but navigable channel about 50 feet wide and 20 feet deep. Between the northernmost and middle blockships there was a similar channel, a little wider but shallower than the southern one. Dönitz noted in the *U-boat Command War Diary:* "Here, I think, it would certainly be possible to penetrate—by night, on the surface at slack water. The main difficulties will be navigational."

Dönitz had no difficulty in choosing the commander for this dangerous mission. Günther Prien had all the right professional and personal qualities, the proper mixture of dash and caution to push it through. A few weeks after Prien returned in glory from his successful first patrol, he was summoned to a meeting with Dönitz on board the U-boat depot ship in Kiel harbor. It was Sunday, October 1. Dönitz was standing by a big round table covered with charts, and the first thing Prien's eyes settled on as he went in, he recalled later, was the topmost chart with the words "Bay of Scapa Flow" printed in large letters on it. Dönitz explained why he had summoned him. He outlined his plan, pointed out the difficulties, indicated the British fleet anchorages, the defenses, the proposed way in and out.

"Do you believe a determined commander could get his boat inside Scapa Flow," Dönitz asked, "and attack the enemy forces lying there?"

Before Prien could answer he was told to think it over for 48 hours and report back on Tuesday. If he felt he could not carry out the mission, nothing would be held against him. He was sent away with the entire file on Scapa Flow to study, including all the air photos and charts. At home, after Sunday supper with his wife, Prien began to work through the problem: the British defenses, the risk of detection, above all the violence of the rip tides, which could flow at 10 knots. It was all a tremendous gamble. But if properly calculated it could perhaps be done.

Prien did not wait the full 48 hours. At 2 p.m. on Monday, October 2, he presented himself in Dönitz' cabin again. Dönitz addressed him bluntly: "Yes, or no?"

"Yes, sir!" Prien replied.

"Well, make the necessary arrangements then." And that, for the moment, was that. They shook hands and parted.

Six days later, without ceremony, Prien's *U-47* slipped out of the Kiel Canal and set a course for Scapa Flow.

At last the interminable waiting at the bottom of the North Sea was nearly over. At 2:00 p.m., Friedrich Walz, the cook, made his way aft. Before long, a variety of kitchen noises issued from the galley, where an electric stove, a 50-quart electric pot, a sink and cupboards were squeezed into a space the size of a closet. Here the cook had to prepare dinner for 40 men. But by 4:00 dinner was ready. The word was passed along, and the men swung their legs over the sides of their bunks and sat down to what would certainly be their last meal for a long time—and might be their last meal forever.

It was a gala feast, the best the Navy could provide on combat patrol: soup, roast ribs of salt pork, potatoes, green cabbage and gravy, washed down with very strong, sweet coffee. The men called it a "hangman's dinner" and ate with a hearty appetite, chaffing one another and cracking jokes with an exaggerated jocularity.

When they had finished they began to clear the U-boat for battle stations. They washed the dishes and stowed them away. They raised the bunks and lashed them to the side. They uncovered the spare torpedoes beneath the deck plates and lowered the loading beam to lift them into the rapid loading position by tubes 1 and 2. They got out the explosive charges and time fuses with which to scuttle the boat if the need arose. They dismantled the radio encoding machine and placed the radio logbook, signal book and secret papers in a heap, with an explosive charge on top. They checked the escape apparatus and filled the emergency food pouches with cigarettes and chocolate. Finally, they tore the flotilla identification name off the ribbons round their caps so as not to reveal their unit if they fell into British hands. They never stopped joking about going off to pick potatoes in Scotland as prisoners of the British. It was too real a possibility to take seriously. Prien noted in the U-boat log: "Crew's morale splendid."

Toward 7:15, by which time it was after dark on the surface, Prien's metallic voice rasped through the intercom to all stations in the U-boat: "To diving stations!"

The bridge watch mustered beneath the lower hatch in the control room, pulling their oilskins over their submariner's leathers and fidgeting with their binoculars. The chief engineer took up his position behind the two hydroplane operators in the control room, where he could correct the trim and watch the two depth gauges and the fine depth indicator called the Papenberg, resembling a large thermometer, which showed the boat's depth to the nearest three inches and was used for depth keeping during periscope observation.

"Pump ballast to sea," the chief ordered, and slowly the boat began to rise from the bottom.

This German cartoon, published after the sinking of the British passenger liner Athenia, accuses Winston Churchill of destroying his own ship and shows him being brought to justice for his crime. The clumsy lie was an attempt to hide the fact that the vessel had been mistakenly torpedoed by the U-30's overeager captain.

"Fore planes hard a-rise, after planes up five!" the chief instructed the two planesmen seated at their push-button controls. The *U-47* lurched and groaned. The depth-gauge needle trembled. The electric motors began to hum as the boat planed slowly upward. There was total silence in the control room. The chief stared intently at the depth-gauge needles turning counterclockwise.

"Boat rising," the chief said; "200 feet . . . 160 feet. . . ."

At 80 feet Prien ordered a hydrophone search. The hydrophone operator could hear no surface sound. At periscope depth—some 45 feet down—Prien took a quick look around the surface. All was clear.

"Ready to surface!" the chief reported.

"Surface!" Prien ordered, mounting the metal ladder that led from the control room through the lower hatch to the conning tower.

"Blow all main ballast tanks!" the chief ordered. The control room petty officer opened the main valves on the blowing panel. Compressed air hissed into the tanks, and at once the craft began to get lighter.

"Surfaced!" the chief called out. The *U-47* was already rocking with the motion of the sea. The noise of the waves slapping along the steel skin of the U-boat's exterior could occasionally be heard above the din in the control room.

"Equalize pressure!" Prien ordered. "Opening upper lid—now!"

Fresh, chill air streamed into the boat's interior as Prien clambered up the ladder from the conning tower through the upper hatch to the bridge. The watch climbed up after the captain.

"Blow to full buoyancy with diesel!" Prien commanded. "And stand by main engines!"

The submarine had become a surface warship again. Suddenly the engine-room telegraph rang. The boat gave a shudder as the diesel engines were clutched in, the gentle rocking motion gave way to a forward surge and the rhythmical beat of the diesels grew to a roar. As the U-boat's bow nosed through the North Sea swell, the men were struck in the face by a cold wind and drenched by showers of spray. The *U-47* turned toward the dark mass of the enemy coast ahead. The final phase of Special Operation P had begun.

Prien was not at all happy with what he saw from the bridge. It was not the dark night he had reckoned on. Although the moon was new, the narrow crescent was unexpectedly bright. Even worse—and quite unforeseen—the entire northern horizon was glowing with the northern lights, great billows of atmospheric radiance surging backward and forward in long undulating streams. Prien cursed them, even thought of postponing the attack for 24 hours, but decided to proceed.

The submarine was now following the tide on a northwesterly course toward Holm Sound, at the southeastern end of Scapa Flow, into fierce currents of swirling water so strong that a boat would be swept through even with its engines dead. The *U-47* clearly ran the grave risk of ripping open its thin-walled fuel and ballast tanks on the rocks or the sunken blockships. So any attempt to penetrate into Scapa Flow should be made on slack water, after full tide, when the current was minimal. Navigation here was difficult even in daylight; at night, and in wartime, it would be hazardous in the extreme.

Wearing oilskins against the incessant spray sweeping over their long, low craft, crewmen on the conning tower of the U-552 scan the horizon with their powerful binoculars, in search of an enemy. The grueling four-hour watches, wrote one man who endured them, "can seem an eternity. Every sea gull will turn into an attacking plane, every scrap of cloud will look like a trail of smoke."

Even getting to Kirk Sound, the entrance chosen by Dönitz, proved to be perilous for Prien and the *U-47*. Shortly after 11 p.m., approaching Rose Ness, at the entrance to Holm Sound, Prien spotted a shadow, a darkened merchant ship in his vicinity, and was forced to submerge until the shadow had vanished into the night. Just before midnight, after fixing his position by the Rose Ness lighthouse, darkened but still dimly visible 650 yards away on the starboard bow, Prien gave a course change to 270 degrees—and brought the *U-47* into the wrong sound.

Momentarily he was nonplused. Nothing looked as he had expected. Instead of two blockships there was only one, and there was only one opening, not the two that the air photos had indicated. From the control room below came a warning shout from Spahr, the navigator, who had been working out the U-boat's course on the chart by dead reckoning and had monitored the sonic depth finder after Prien's course change. Spotting the error, Spahr gave Prien a new course of 30 degrees hard astarboard, and Prien at once altered course to avoid being swept aground by the current that here was still running hard into the Flow.

A few minutes later Kirk Sound was clearly visible. "It is a very eerie sight," Prien noted in the U-boat log. "On land everything is dark, and high in the sky are the flickering northern lights, so that the bay, surrounded by fairly high mountains, is directly lit up from above. The blockships lie in the sound, ghostly as the wings of a theater."

Lieutenant Engelbert Endrass, Prien's first officer of the watch, who was responsible for torpedo firing on the *U-47*, turned to his commander and remarked: "What about it? Lovely night for shooting!"

Prien was too preoccupied to answer. The *U-47* was now entering Kirk Sound. The tide was past high water, but not quite slack. There was still a strong but navigable current running behind the boat. Everything began to happen very fast. The northern passage looked the most promising—it was twice the width of the deeper southern channel. Prien ordered hard aport and signaled the loud, rumbling diesel engines to be turned off and the quietly humming electric motors to be switched on in their place. Keeping close to the lee shore, the *U-47* eased past the sunken hulk of a two-masted bark with 15 yards to spare. But at slow ahead in the swirling current it was difficult to gain any purchase with the rudder. So Prien ordered the submarine to starboard so it could hug the shore, where the water appeared calmer.

Ahead, where the channel narrowed, loomed the blockships *Thames* and *Soriano*, their masts cut down and only their bridge superstructure above water. The British Admiralty—unable to rig up a continuous antisubmarine boom because the force of the current would have swept it away—had filled these vessels with concrete, sunk them and linked them together with a rope 12 inches in diameter and several wire cables six and seven inches in diameter.

On the bridge of the *U-47*, Prien ordered a course of 270 degrees and nosed forward between the hulks. Whenever he wanted to change direction now he called out the rudder angles, not the course bearing, to the helmsman down in the conning tower. There appeared to be a gap of more than 100 feet between the blockships. Prien eased past the south-facing stern of the blockship *Thames*, and then straight ahead saw the huge rope and other cables connecting it to the *Soriano* sloping down into the water. He could see the cables quite clearly because of the white water swirling around them, and he steered for the center of the gap between the *Thames* and the *Soriano*, with the hope that there would be a belly in the cables over which he could ride. But suddenly the current took hold of the U-boat, pushing it to starboard, and at the critical moment the rudder failed to respond. The submarine drifted uncontrollably into the antisubmarine defense.

Only Prien and the four members of the watch on the bridge knew what was going on. The rest of the crew, immured within the hull, could only imagine the submarine's maneuverings. The men in the forward torpedo room and the aft engine and motor rooms were beginning to get worried. Their stations were so far from the control-room escape hatch that their chances of getting out alive were slight if disaster suddenly struck the U-boat. So when they first heard the heavy metallic rattle of the cables fouling the keel they grew alarmed, many men believing they had struck a mine mooring and would at any moment blow up.

"Contact!" someone shouted up from the control room.

"Acknowledged!" came Prien's calm reply from the bridge. The cables were sliding under the boat. But in riding over the barrier, the U-boat had slewed around toward the shore. Suddenly the boat struck bottom and grounded. Prien had to act swiftly. The current was still moving fast. Every second could drive the U-boat more firmly aground. And if the boat could not get off, the dawn would reveal it to the British.

To force the boat's head to port, back into the channel and away from the shore, Prien ordered the port engine stopped, the starboard engine slow ahead, the rudder hard aport. When that proved insufficient, he ordered the diving tanks to be blown, in order to lighten the boat and increase its clearance (the tanks had been partially flooded to lower the boat and reduce the amount of silhouette visible above water). The boat slipped clear at once and floated free in the turbulent water. Prien fought to bring it around to port, calling for a series of rapid rudder changes as the boat threatened to ground once again. But finally the *U-47* steadied and kept a straight course head on. The blockships fell astern, the narrows opened out to reveal a wide mass of dark water, and at 27 minutes past midnight, on the morning of Saturday, October 14, 1939, Günther Prien called down to his crew: "We're in!" Before him stretched a marvelous view of Scapa Flow.

"It is," Prien noted in the U-boat's log, "disgustingly light. The whole bay is lit up." But that did not dampen his jubilation. He had taken into Scapa Flow the first U-boat ever to penetrate the British redoubt undetected. He turned to a seaman and remarked: "We're in for a big thing tonight!" Then, with the crew at battle stations for an imminent torpedo strike, the *U-47* headed west in search of the British fleet.

For a moment, as Prien eased out of the inlet, the *U-47* was caught in the headlights of a car driving along on the road near the village of St. Mary's. The German U-boat men stared in horror as the whole starboard side of their craft was illuminated. They were so close to shore they could see parked trucks and sentries. But the light passed and nothing happened. The *U-47* pressed on, into the heart of the British Home Fleet anchorage. But what Prien found there was a bitter disappointment.

"To the south there is nothing," he noted in the U-boat log. "I go farther in. To port I recognize the Hoxa Sound coast guard, to which in the next few minutes the boat must present itself as a target. In that event all would be lost; at present no ships are to be seen, although visibility is extremely good. We proceed north by the coast."

The British fleet was not where it was supposed to be, not where the air photos had indicated a mass of warships at anchor a few days before. Prien had cruised for nearly three and a half miles, anxiety mounting with every beat of the diesels, which by now had been restarted. And he had not seen a single vessel of any description. So he turned to port, completed a wide circle, recrossed his own tracks and headed north toward the island called Mainland.

For more than a mile the *U-47* proceeded slowly across Scapa Flow, but no battleships, no aircraft carriers, no cruisers, not so much as a launch came into view. Where had the British gone?

More than half an hour had passed since the *U-47* entered Scapa Flow. And now at last, in the far northeast corner of the Flow, Prien detected through his night binoculars a faint shadow across the water. As he drew nearer, the shadow grew larger and clearer, until he saw before him, clearly silhouetted against the sky, the unmistakable superstructure, tripod mainmast, and huge gun turrets of a British battleship. Prien crept closer. "Here," he said to Endrass, passing the glasses, "take a peep at that. There's another one behind her." To westward, about a mile beyond, lay a second ship, all but her bow hidden from view by the hull in front. Prien took them both to be battleships. In fact one was the battleship *Royal Oak*, the other H.M.S. *Pegasus*, an old seaplane tender of 6,900 tons converted into a seaplane transport.

The *U-47* crept closer still, then Prien ordered the engines cut off. Lieutenant Endrass stood hunched over the master sight, working out his torpedo attack. He planned to fire a salvo of three torpedoes in a fan—the first aimed at the bow of the more distant ship, the others at the starboard side of the nearer ship. The farther ship was a difficult shot at some three miles, but it ought to be impossible to miss the nearer one.

"Flood tubes for surface firing!" he ordered.

"Tubes flooded!" the report came back from the forward torpedo room. The tubes were now ready for the outer doors to be opened and the torpedoes launched with a blast of compressed air. Then they would be on their own, propelled toward the target by their own electrical power.

Endrass lined up the cross hairs of the torpedo aimer on the two ships.

"Open outer doors!" he ordered.

Next he pressed his firing lever. Simultaneously, as insurance against electrical failure, a crewman belowdecks pressed a manual firing switch. The first one-and-a-half-ton torpedo, carrying 800 pounds of TNT, was impelled from its tube. The U-boat bounced. Two seconds later the second torpedo was launched, then the third.

"Torpedoes on their way!" reported the hydrophone operator, who could hear their propellers underwater. Navigator Spahr stared at his stop watch, counting the time to impact. In silence the 40 Germans on board the *U-47* waited for the first explosion.

On October 10, as Prien was making his way to Scapa Flow, most of the British Home Fleet, returning from an abortive operation in the North Sea, had been diverted from Scapa to another anchorage. Fearing—correctly—that the Flow was insufficiently secure against submarine attack, Admiral Sir Charles Forbes, the fleet commander in chief, had ordered the vessels to Loch Ewe, a haven on the west coast of Scotland. Only a few auxiliary ships and the *Royal Oak* had been left behind. The *Royal Oak* was repairing minor damage from a recent voyage, and was scheduled to leave Scapa Flow on October 14. The battleship, displacing 29,000 tons, was a World War I vessel that boasted eight enormous 15-inch guns and armor plating up to 13 inches thick. She was still a fine ship but she was too slow to keep up with the rest of the fleet, although she had been to sea several times since the outbreak of the War.

Shortly after 1 o'clock the crewmen on board the *Royal Oak* were surprised to hear an explosion in the bow of the ship. Almost immediately afterward the anchor cables began to run out with a terrific rumbling roar, and a large amount of water was seen to fall onto the bow deck. In the forward spaces the impact was heavy enough for some men to be pitched out of their hammocks and for cockroaches to fall from the overheads. But amidships it sounded no louder or more serious, according to one witness, than "a large zinc bath dropping on to the deck of the wardroom bathroom." Many of the men turned over in their hammocks

A British Navy launch is dwarfed by the great bulk of the battleship Royal Oak, anchored off Weymouth, England, on June 27, 1938. When attacked by Günther Prien's U-47 in Scapa Flow, the 22-year-old Royal Oak was flagship of the 2nd Battle Squadron of the Home Fleet.

and went to sleep again. To most, the explosion seemed a rather subdued and puzzling affair, and there was little general alarm. Only to the men sleeping near the bow did it seem particularly violent.

Some men thought it was a bomb from a German airplane. Others thought the ship had swung onto a drifting mine. The smoke and evil-smelling fumes evident belowdecks forward suggested to some that an internal explosion might have occurred in the paint shop, or that a carbon-dioxide bottle had blown up in the refrigerating section. The master-at-arms was heard going around the ship forward, reassuring the men: "It's only a CO_2 bottle gone up. Away you go, lads; it's nothing startling, turn in." For many minutes after the explosion, no one took particular alarm. The lights were still on; the ship's broadcasting system still worked. But when the chief shipwright found that the air pipes were venting air under considerable pressure from the bow spaces below-decks, he realized at once that the ship was holed and taking water.

Even this was not a cause for undue concern. The bow compartments were small and sealed off by watertight bulkheads; they could flood without affecting the trim of the ship. There was no evidence that the Royal Oak was listing or going down by the bow. Captain William Gordon Benn, asleep in his cabin at the time of the explosion, came on deck soon after, along with other senior officers. But no orders were given summoning the ship's company to action stations. No one on board had any idea that a huge hole, big enough for a double-decker bus to drive through, had been punched in the stem and keel of the ship near the paint store. The crew of the battleship was thus tragically unprepared for what happened next.

Back on the U-47, Prien was under the impression that the first torpedo had hit the more distant ship, the Pegasus. He thought the second and third, aimed at the Royal Oak, had missed. Since neither ship appeared to be sinking, Prien ordered the U-boat turned about and he fired the stern torpedo at the Royal Oak. That, too, missed. Prien attributed these frustrating misses to faults of course, speed and drift.

Puzzled but undaunted, Prien withdrew while two more torpedoes were loaded in the bow tubes, making a total of three ready for firing. The U-47 made another approach, closer this time. Again the sub was pointed at the motionless silhouette of the Royal Oak; again Endrass bent over the aimer sight on the bridge. "Fire!" The three torpedoes were launched broadside in rapid succession.

Now on board the Royal Oak there was no mistaking what was happening. At 1:16, 12 minutes after the first explosion, came a second, amidships, which sent up a huge column of white spray as high as the spotting top and shook the ship so violently that the steel bulkheads wobbled as if made of cardboard. Almost immediately afterward there was another explosion amidships, just forward of the mainmast; this was more violent even than the previous explosion, and it sent up a thick, black cloud of smoke. With a gaping hole in the starboard engine room, the Royal Oak began to heel quickly over to starboard. As it did so, still another tremendous explosion, under the Marines' mess deck, seemed to lift the great ship out of the sea.

This final explosion put out the lights, plunging the ship into dark-

ness belowdecks. It destroyed the broadcasting system, so that the senior officers were unable to give any orders, even "Abandon ship." Worse still, it set a magazine on fire aft and sent burning cordite—the explosive propellant for the shells—raging through the vents.

"It was like looking into the muzzle of a blow lamp," one Marine recounted. "The flame was bright orange outside and an intense blue inside." Men ran around screaming in the dark with their clothing on fire and their blackened flesh curling off like paper from a wall.

The force of the last explosion had blown a huge hole in the deck plating of the aft section, amidships, and it seemed that the whole starboard side was melting and collapsing. As the ship rolled farther and farther over, men began to slide down toward the hole, dropping into the fires still raging in the magazine beneath. Belowdecks, survivors, dazed with horror, groped their way about in the dark, looking for a way of escaping into the open. Already the Royal Oak had listed so far over that it was clear to all on board that she had only a few minutes more to live.

Most of the 1,200 crew members were belowdecks when the ship was hit. The greater proportion of them were trapped inside. Some men,

U-47 crew members watch as a cloud of spray rises from a torpedo hit on the British battleship Royal Oak. This artist's rendering, faithfully repeating the U-boat commander's error, shows the battle cruiser Repulse anchored beyond the stricken ship; in fact, it was the seaplane transport Pegasus. A third British ship, in the background at left, is purely the artist's fancy.

believing that the ship was under air attack, lost any chance of survival by actually moving deep down into the ship to gain the cover of the protective deck armor overhead. Some never even found the ladders but blundered about, lost in the dark, till the end. Others found the ladders but could not open power-operated armored hatches because the electricity had failed. Two sailors were sliced in half at the waist when a manually operated steel hatch suddenly slid shut under its own weight as the angle of heel increased; as their bloody lower halves fell, they knocked the men below them off the ladder. Many men were trapped, pinned down by heavy gear sliding across the sloping decks.

By now the ship had heeled over to an angle of 45 degrees. The spotting top on the tripod mast began to sheer, and the guns swung around their turrets and pointed down into the water. The starboard portholes, which were covered only with plywood blackout screens while in port, had already dipped into the sea, and the water flowed freely through them. The portholes on the port side now pointed skyward, and through these the last men to escape from inside the doomed ship wriggled their way out. Once through, they could either climb up the ship's side to the deck or slither down to the sea.

The temperature of the sea was 48° F. Immersed in such cold water, the average man could not expect to survive for long. The chances of survival for the men of the *Royal Oak* were reduced still further by a shortage of lifesaving equipment. There had not yet been a general issue of life jackets, and most of the life rafts had been smashed in a storm at sea a few days before. A large liberty launch, capable of carrying hundreds of men, was crushed when the spotting top crashed down on it. Apart from wooden planks and floating wreckage, only a picketboat and a Navy-contracted fishing drifter called *Daisy II*—both boats tied up amidships on the port side—offered survivors any possibility of keeping afloat on the water. Power failure had made it impossible to use the ship's wireless or signal lamp to send an SOS, and neither from the shore nor from the *Pegasus* was there any apparent sign that the disaster overwhelming the *Royal Oak* had been observed. In fact, sailors aboard the seaplane transport had felt the force of the explosions. They were too far away to see what was happening and were not yet aware that the *Royal Oak* had suffered an enemy attack. They launched two boats to investigate, but undertook no serious rescue operation until some time later. Only a few of the *Royal Oak's* sailors were eventually saved by the launches from the *Pegasus*.

The men who boarded the *Daisy* while she was still tied up to the battleship did so initially in an extraordinarily orderly manner, having been organized into a file to go down the ship's ladder by a junior duty officer, who exhorted the men with fairground cries: "Roll, bowl, or pitch, every time a coconut, form a queue here, my lucky lads!" But the *Daisy* was being slowly dragged out of the water by the *Royal Oak's* roll, and was forced to cast off. After that it was every man for himself. Many sailors jumped off the dying ship, bouncing off the side as they fell. The men scrambling over the ship's barnacle-encrusted bottom as the port side reared up lacerated themselves horribly. Both the *Royal Oak's* Captain Benn and the ship's second-in-command, Captain R. F. Nichols, managed to take to the water. But Rear Admiral Henry Blagrove of the 2nd Battle Squadron, who happened to be on board as a passenger, was not so lucky. He was last seen on the quarter-deck by the engineer commander, who survived. "What caused those explosions, Engineer Commander?" the admiral had asked.

"Torpedoes, Sir." The engineer commander had no doubt, after the second explosion, about what had hit the ship.

"My God!" the admiral exclaimed. He was never seen again.

The ship's angle was now approaching 90 degrees. Suddenly she gave a great lurch, and turned turtle. "The thing which struck me most," one survivor recalled, "was the tremendous noise; it was like a huge tin full of nuts and bolts, slowly turning over. Racks of shells must have been coming loose, and other gear, so that anybody still inside had no hope. It must have been an absolute nightmare." More than 800 men remained trapped inside the hull as the *Royal Oak* turned upside down. Half a dozen were left standing on top of the inverted ship's bottom, and as she slowly sank beneath them they waded off into the water as if from a beach. The time was about 1:33—less than 29 minutes after the first of the *U-47*'s torpedoes had struck the *Royal Oak*, and 17 minutes or so after the last. With a great gasping sound, the battleship disappeared in the waters of Scapa Flow.

But the tragedy was not quite played out. The picketboat was so overloaded that it soon capsized and sank, drowning a number of men. The fishing boat *Daisy II* began pulling survivors aboard. There were several hundred men in the water. Those who could not swim thrashed about, crying out for help, while some who could swim burst out singing: "Roll out the Barrel," "South of the Border" and "Daisy." Many men were so thickly covered in black oil that had seeped out of the battleship's fuel bunkers that they were almost invisible. Some were so badly burned that it was difficult to haul them out of the water without causing further injury and pain. One sailor was burned so terribly that the flesh ran off his hands and face like water. "He was holding them in front of him like downward pointing claws," one of the survivors observed, "and the flesh was dripping off them."

About 50 men struck out for the rocky cliffs half a mile away. The cold was intense, as one swimmer recalled: "It got past my flesh until I could feel my own skeleton. I was aware of every bone in my body." More than 30 of these swimmers succumbed to the cold and drowned. A number of those who made it to the rocky shore were so exhausted that they collapsed and died there. But three men had enough strength left to walk two miles to the village of Scapa and raise the alarm, while another man, who swam off in the opposite direction, managed to reach the *Pegasus* after nearly three hours in the water.

The *Daisy* had pulled up to the seaplane transport just a few minutes before. She had picked up 386 men—the greater part of the final total of survivors. These cold, shocked, injured, oil-covered men were given blankets, hot baths, cocoa, whisky and medical care according to their needs. By the time the sun rose, it was clear that there was no one else left alive in the waters of Scapa Flow. Twenty-four officers and 809 men had died in the attack.

The intrepid raider's route to glory

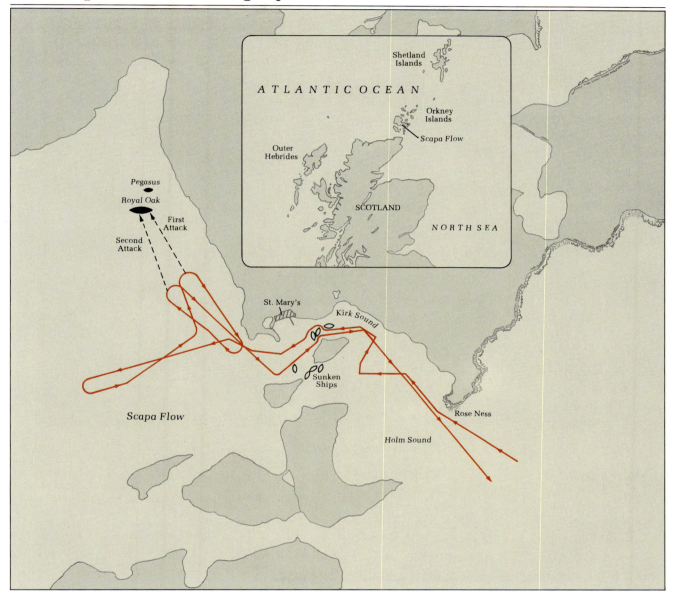

Entering Holm Sound, the U-47 maneuvered past three sunken ships and traveled west. Finding the waters of Scapa Flow deserted, the submarine made a loop and headed north, sighted the Royal Oak and the Pegasus, and delivered a first attack. After doubling back to reload, the U-47 attacked again, then swung southeast for Holm Sound.

By then Günther Prien and the crew of the *U-47* were no longer in the vicinity. The explosions made by the four torpedoes had been clearly heard by the men in the U-boat and clearly seen by the men on the bridge. There was a great feeling of relief and pride among Prien's crew, and everyone grinned and shook hands.

Although there were still five torpedoes left, Prien decided to break off the attack in Scapa Flow and withdraw as quickly as possible. In a controversial entry in his U-boat log, presumably written with his commanding officer in mind, Prien justified his precipitate retreat on the grounds that there were signs that the expected British counterattack was already under way and that for a variety of reasons he could no longer carry on undetected by the enemy. "The harbor springs to life,"

he wrote. "Destroyers are lit up, signaling starts on every side, and on land, 2,000 meters away, cars roar along the roads. All tubes are empty. I decide to withdraw because: (1) With my periscopes I cannot conduct night attacks while submerged. (2) On a bright night I cannot maneuver unobserved in a calm sea. (3) I must assume that I was observed by the driver of a car that stopped opposite us, turned around and drove off toward Scapa at top speed. (4) Nor can I go farther north, for there, well hidden from my sight, lie the destroyers that were previously dimly distinguishable."

In fact, there were no British destroyers; there was no response from the British whatsoever. Not for an hour and a half after the sinking did Captain Benn's message reach Admiral Sir Wilfrid French, in command of Orkney and Shetland. This was the first official suggestion that enemy action had taken place. If there had been any other worthwhile targets, Prien could have stayed on in Scapa Flow and inflicted further damage with impunity. As it was, the change of the tide alone gave him every rationale for pulling out. Prien's log entry here is odd, as well. He had decided to go out through Kirk Sound by the narrower but deeper southern channel rather than the shallower but broader northern channel, through which he had entered. "It is now low tide," he wrote. "The current is against us. Engines at slow and dead slow, I attempt to get away. Things are difficult. Course 058, slow—10 knots. I make no prog-

Survivors of the Royal Oak, garbed in hand-me-downs and canvas gym shoes, carry a floral wreath to a mass funeral on October 16, 1939, for shipmates lost in Scapa Flow when their battleship was sunk by Günther Prien's U-47.

ress." Prien was correct about the tide, but the strong ebbing current was behind, not against, the *U-47*, as the tide tables for that morning clearly show. Prien should have known this but, as his boat was buffeted by the tumultuous swirls and cross eddies of the racing current, it may have seemed that he was butting into the tide.

There were no cables or ropes across the southern channel. It twisted past the broken-up remains of an old World War I blockship called the *Minich*. "At high speed," Prien recorded, "I pass the southern blockship with nothing to spare. The helmsman does magnificently. High speed ahead both, finally three-quarter speed and full ahead all out. Free of the blockship. But then: ahead—a breakwater! Hard over and again about. And at 2:15 a.m. we are once more outside."

Almost two hours after entering Scapa Flow, the *U-47* had escaped unscathed into the safety of the North Sea. Prien told his crew: "One battleship is sunk, another ship is damaged, and we got away."

Everyone burst out cheering; they embraced one another and toasted themselves with beer specially brought out for the occasion. "The glow from Scapa is still visible for a long time," Prien wrote, in another bizarre entry in the log. "Apparently they are still dropping depth charges." In fact, there was no glow, for there were no longer any fires. And there were no depth charges. No one yet knew for certain that a U-boat had been there at all, and the *Royal Oak's* survivors were still being picked up.

At the British Admiralty in London it was announced, during the course of the morning, that the battleship *Royal Oak* had been lost—"believed by U-boat action." The following day a group of Navy divers went down to investigate.

The wreck presented a ghastly spectacle. There were bodies stuck half out of portholes, bodies crushed by fallen gear, bodies bobbing up and down in upright positions on the seabed. Some divers were said to have come up crazed with the horror of what they had seen. Their reports confirmed the worst: The *Royal Oak* had been sunk by torpedoes. There were huge holes below the water line, where the ship's steel plating had been blown inboard. In addition, the divers brought up part of the afterbody of a torpedo. No further evidence was needed.

In the meantime, Günther Prien made a safe and uneventful return voyage across the North Sea. The British Admiralty announcement, broadcast by the BBC news, had been picked up and jubilantly rebroadcast throughout Germany. From German high command bulletins sent out by radio, Prien knew that the ship he had sunk was the *Royal Oak*. He was therefore not altogether unprepared for the reception that was laid on for him when he finally tied up at Wilhelmshaven on the morning of October 17. Brass bands were playing on the jetty, and there were cheering crowds and hundreds of sailors lining every ship to cheer the triumphant heroes on their return.

The German Navy's most senior officers had come down to the dock en masse to meet Prien and his crew in person: not only their commanding officer, Karl Dönitz, who had recently been promoted to rear admiral, but the commander of Navy Group West and even Grand Admiral Erich Raeder. Dönitz clambered onto the narrow deck of the *U-47* and shook hands with every member of the crew. On Prien he conferred the Iron Cross, First Class, and on all of the others the Iron Cross, Second Class. It was a rapturous time for them all. "We had a drink," one of the *U-47* crewmen recalled later, "and another drink, and in the end we were all quite drunk."

That afternoon Prien and the rest of the crew flew via Kiel to Berlin to meet the Führer. On the following day, Hitler decorated the heroic captain with the Knight's Cross of the Iron Cross. The German radio had already announced that it was Prien's U-boat that had sunk the *Royal Oak* and his name was on everybody's lips. A nation at war needs heroes. To Dr. Joseph Goebbels' Ministry of Propaganda and Popular Enlightenment, Prien filled the bill admirably. But his deeds would have to be enlarged and embellished for popular consumption. In fact, the papers had already begun the process. "Victorious U-Boat Returns Home," proclaimed the Nazi paper *Der Angriff.* "*Royal Oak* and *Repulse* Torpedoed in the Bay of the Scapa Flow."

On the afternoon of the 18th, Prien was taken to tea at the Propaganda Ministry and introduced to reporters by Hitler's press chief, Dr. Otto Dietrich. One American correspondent who was there, William Shirer, noted in his diary: "Prien is clean-cut, cocky, a fanatical Nazi, and obviously capable." In the evening, commander and crew were invited to the Wintergarten Theater, where they were joined by Dr. Goebbels himself and Prien was forced by the adoring audience to make a speech. In the

Straight and steely as a periscope, Günther Prien accepts congratulations from Adolf Hitler on receiving the Knight's Cross of the Iron Cross on October 18, 1939. The coveted award was bestowed on Prien for his raid on Scapa Flow—a feat Hitler pronounced "the proudest deed that a German U-boat could possibly carry out."

Slipping past the cruiser Emden and her cheering crew, the U-47 glides into Kiel harbor on October 23, 1939. So overwhelming were the accolades heaped upon Günther Prien and his men following their sinking of the Royal Oak that Prien groused to a friend, "I am an officer, not a film star."

days that followed, Prien was idolized like a film star, while the popular press blew his exploits into the very stuff of legend.

The Scapa Flow raid not only made Günther Prien the first German naval hero of World War II, but also gave Germany a tremendous psychological victory and caused Hitler and his military advisers to turn to U-boats as the foremost weapon in the war against the British. As autumn turned into winter and prospects dwindled for the quick peace that Hitler sought, the U-boat campaign escalated toward a total siege of Britain. "The more ruthlessly economic warfare is waged," declared Admiral Raeder, "the sooner the War will end." Hitler concurred: "A concentrated attempt must be made to cut Britain off." And to his tiny U-boat navy Dönitz reiterated the lesson of Scapa Flow: "Attack and keep on attacking . . . we must be hard in this War."

So a steady stream of brilliant and single-minded U-boat commanders put out to sea in Günther Prien's wake to press a new submarine offensive against Britain, and the fortunes of the Third Reich became bound up with the 2,000 or so U-boat men in their steel tubes, circling the coast of the British Isles.

Durance vile in the belly of a submarine

"The heat. The stench of oil. Lead in my skull from the engine fumes," wrote German war photographer Lothar-Günther Buchheim, recalling fragmentary images of his voyage aboard the *U-96* in 1941. "I feel like Jonah inside some huge shellfish whose vulnerable parts are sheathed in armor." Impressions like Buchheim's were an everyday experience for the 40,000 men of the German U-boat fleet. Their lives at sea bore little relation to the notions of glamor and high adventure their heroics inspired in the public mind. The submarines were cramped, odoriferous, unsanitary, and claustrophobic to the point of inducing madness.

Living accommodations were squeezed in wherever machinery and weapons allowed. In a typical U-boat the bow compartment, a tapering section only 12 feet across at its widest point, housed, slept and fed about half the vessel's complement, some 25 men who shared their living space with an arsenal of torpedoes, loading carriages and other U-boat gear. Six bunks were stacked in tiers on each side of that small compartment. The bunks were used in shifts, men returning from one stint of duty climbing into beds that were still warm from the bodies of other men who had just risen for their watches.

Toilets were the scarcest amenity of all. The typical U-boat had two for about 50 men, but at the outset of a patrol—when the vessel was provisioned for a mission that might last several weeks—one of the heads sometimes served as a food locker. And neither could be used whenever the U-boat descended below 80 feet, because at that level the pumps that flushed the toilets into the sea could not function against the water pressure outside the hull.

U-boat men generally endured their tribulations in good humor. "The word 'hygiene,'" observed Buchheim, "is greeted by U-boat crews like a comedy routine." And they cheerfully referred to their black underwear—dyed that color because it would not look dirty even though it went unlaundered—as "whores' undies."

But humor sometimes failed in the face of routines repeated ad nauseam under glaring electric lights that obscured all distinction between night and day. Buchheim recalled his own method of trying to cope with the ennui: "I try to go limp, to extinguish all thought. Am I asleep or awake?" In the world of a U-boat on patrol, it was sometimes hard to tell.

Framed by torpedoes suspended from loading carriages, seamen in a U-boat's bow compartment inspect reserve torpedoes stored beneath the deck plates. The prospect of spending the weapons in battle was something "the men actually look forward to," wrote one U-boat diarist; "at least it clears a space."

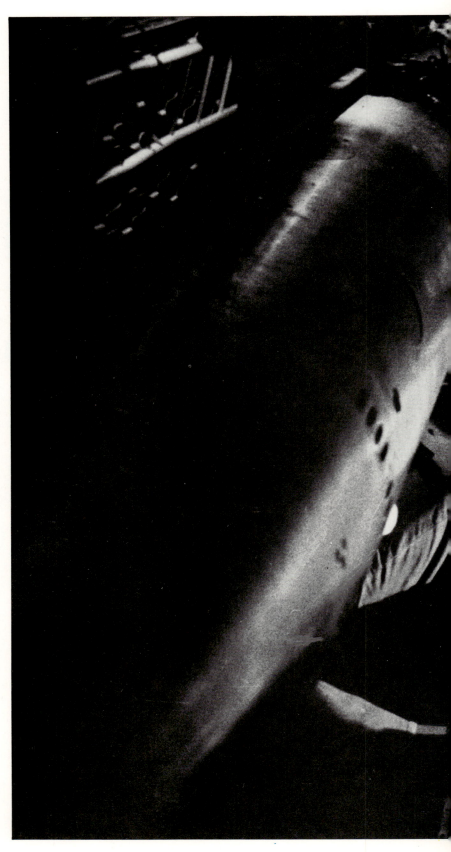

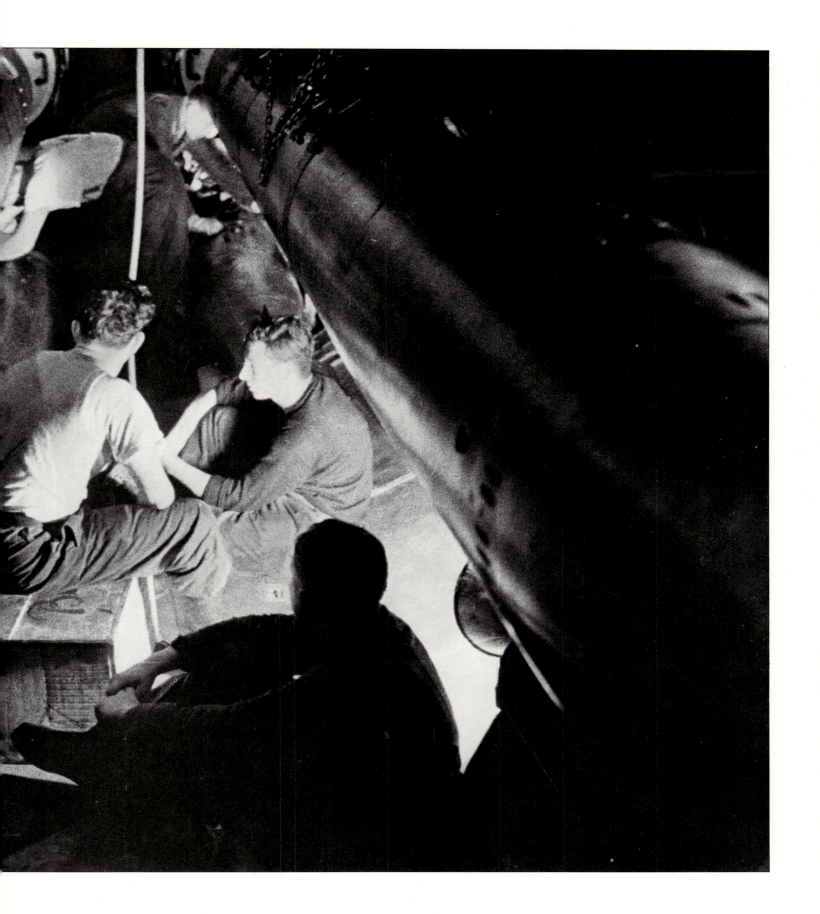

In a tiny galley equipped with two hot plates, a cook stirs up a
meal while a steward looks on. "The very food tasted of U-boat,"
recalled a submariner. "Diesel oil with a flavor of mold."

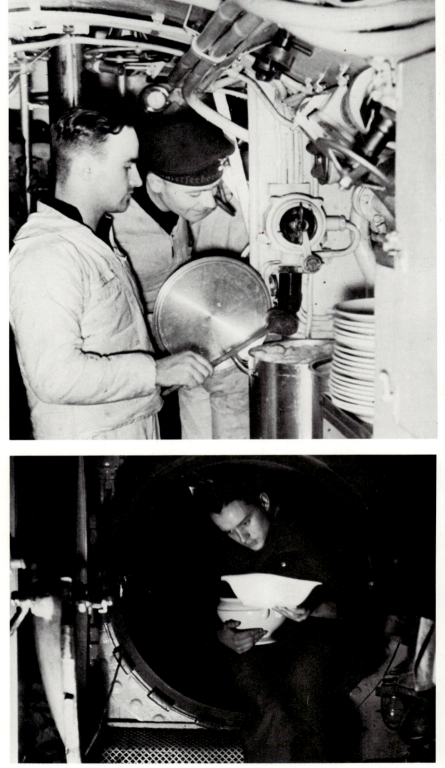

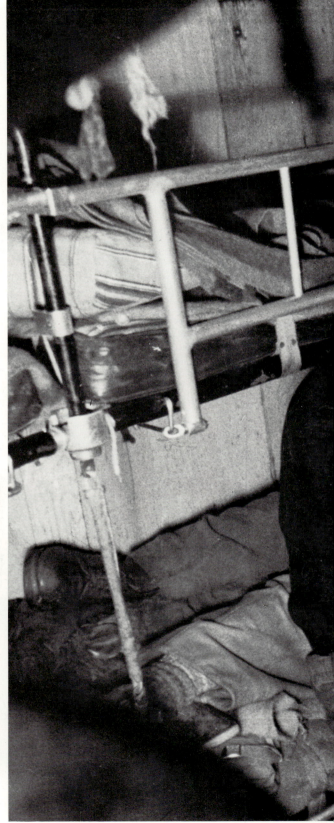

Laden with crockery for a mess table, a steward squeezes
through a circular doorway. U-boat crewmen were always having
to stoop, step up or slip sideways to get past an obstacle.

With eyes as empty as the used dishes on the drop-leaf table before him, an exhausted sub crewman slumps after taking his meal on the edge of a bunk in which a shipmate is napping.

Off-duty crewmen play cards in the bow compartment of their U-boat. To maintain morale, Naval authorities encouraged card games, chess matches, songfests and painting contests.

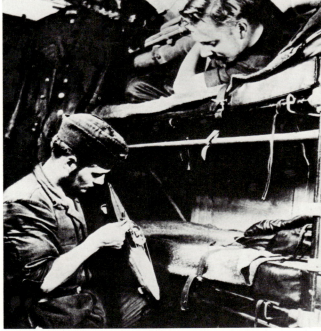

Under a shipmate's scrutiny, a seaman assembles a model U-boat. "No chance for privacy," noted one man; "every idiosyncrasy was served up for our companions to observe."

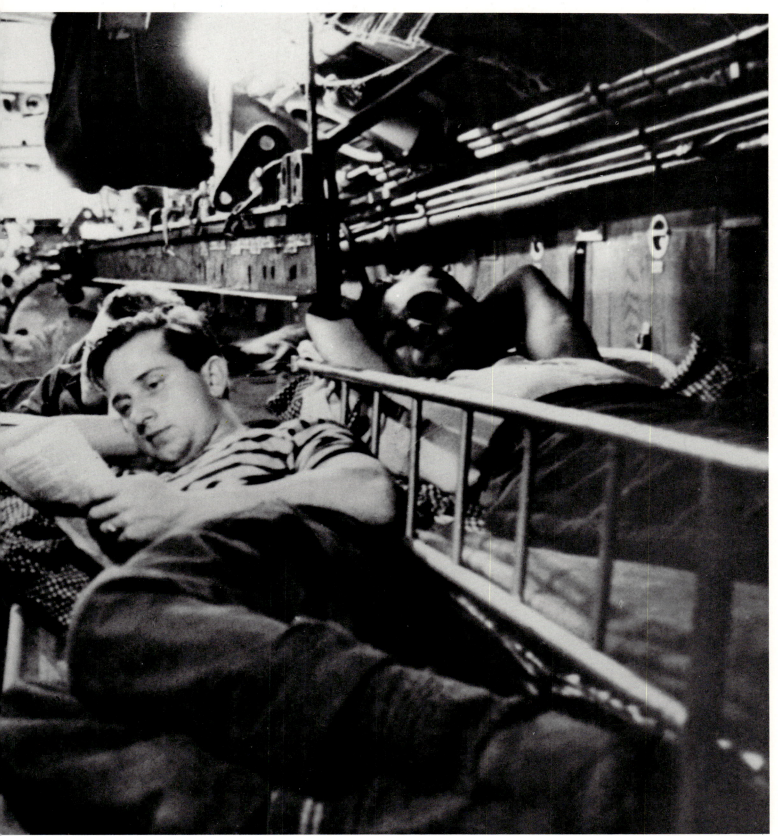

Three wakeful U-boat men lie in their bunks as the hours tick away. Sleep, one poetic submariner recalled, "is a cobweb veil, which the slightest sound will tear to shreds."

Chapter 5

The gray wolves' Happy Time

F irmly gripping the periscope handles, peering intently into the eyepiece, Lieutenant Commander Victor Öhrn guided the *U-37* in the stalking of a freighter. He observed to an officer making notes for the log: "The distance is narrowing. The steamship draws in quickly." If his voice betrayed any excitement, there was good reason. The hunt was a treat for Öhrn, who spent much of his time at U-boat headquarters serving as staff-operations officer to U-boat Commander in Chief Karl Dönitz. He was at sea now—on May 27, 1940—only because Dönitz had chosen him to initiate a new offensive.

Since early 1940, some of the U-boat pressure on Britain's maritime supply lines—brought to bear in the wake of Günther Prien's daring raid on Scapa Flow in October 1939—had lifted. For three months that spring, no German submarines were even in Britain's vicinity, all having been diverted to support the invasion of Norway. That operation over, Hitler had agreed three days ago to unleash Dönitz' gray wolves in a new "unrestricted" campaign against shipping around Britain. Until then, none but British ships could be sunk without warning; now the only vessels that were to be spared the U-boats' predations were those of the United States and the so-called friendly neutrals: Italy, Russia and Japan. Admiral Dönitz had dispatched the *U-37* on May 15, so Öhrn was already approaching his hunting ground at the western end of the English Channel when the Führer approved the new campaign, and the ex-staff officer had in his sights a target with which he could mark the occasion.

Despite the new leeway in choice of victims, Öhrn expressed some concern—but not a lot—about the freighter's eligibility. He looked for a flag or markings to ascertain her nationality, or for armament indicating belligerency. "I cannot see the stern yet," he said. "Tube ready. Shall I or not?" He studied the target. "On the side a yellow cross in a small square, dark blue ground. Swedish? Presumably not. I raise the periscope a little." Then he saw what he was looking for: "Hurrah," he said exultantly, "a stern gun, perhaps an antiaircraft gun. Fire! It cannot miss."

It did not. The torpedo struck home and the ship went to the bottom.

The ease of the kill was a portent of sorts. It inaugurated a ship-shooting spree that would surpass the most optimistic U-boat man's dreams. During his four-week patrol, Öhrn was to sink 11 ships totaling more than 43,000 tons—an astonishing score, but one that would soon be bettered by other commanders. By summer the U-boats seemed to be sinking Allied ships at will, with few losses to themselves. The following months were so full of heady success—with enemy ships exploding and sinking in droves; with crowds, kisses, roses and medals awaiting

With a brassy send-off from a shoreside band, a U-boat glides from the German submarine base at Lorient, France, to patrol the North Atlantic. In the fall of 1940, at the pinnacle of their success, the submariners were seen off with fanfare, and upon their return from a mission were regaled by their countrymen with champagne and garlands of flowers.

the submariners coming home from patrol—that U-boat men would always remember the period as *die Glückliche Zeit,* "the Happy Time."

Like most eras that profoundly color human emotions, the Happy Time had no clear-cut beginning and end, and dating it depends largely on the inward eye of the recollector. Even historians differ in the dates they assign to it. But for all practical purposes the Happy Time can be said to have lasted from the summer of 1940, when the campaign initiated in May by Öhrn went into high gear and U-boats began sinking Allied merchant ships at the overwhelming rate of eight per sub per month, until the spring of 1941, when the Allies managed to stem the onslaught and bring down the ratio of U-boat kills to two ships per sub per month.

Even then, the battle was far from done. Long after the Happy Time had ended, the British faced a dismal, bitter test of not only their material capacity to survive, but their deepest resources of fortitude. At times they were so short of the supplies sustaining their island nation, and of the shipping that carried those supplies, that the War's outcome seemed to depend solely on national will. Well into 1943, control of the Atlantic remained in doubt, and ultimate U-boat victory a real possibility.

It was not that the Allies ignored the grim lessons of World War I. They knew what they needed to do; they simply lacked the means to do it effectively. Britain adopted the convoy system almost as soon as World War II began, but for the first 18 months of the War the convoys were poorly protected. Few escort ships were available, and hardly any of them had sufficient fuel capacity to accompany outbound convoys farther than about long. 15° W., roughly 200 miles off the west coast of Ireland. Beyond that point the convoys sailed virtually alone, while the escorts waited to pick up inward-bound convoys. Furthermore, the Allies lacked adequate intelligence on U-boat movements and effective means to detect and destroy the submarines. British scientists between the wars had developed an underwater echo-location device, asdic, but it did not work as well as had been hoped *(pages 110-111).* Ship's radar was still in a primitive state of development. Aircraft, later the U-boats' most dreaded enemy, were still few in number, short in range and inadequately armed—and they could not provide escort cover at night.

To some extent, the Allies had their own faulty security to blame for their troubles. For a large part of the U-boat war, Dönitz was remarkably well informed about Allied convoy movements, mainly because a special German Navy department called B-Dienst was decoding British naval signals. But he had another source of information that represented a truly incredible security lapse by the United States. After the War began in Europe, American shipping insurance firms continued the normal business practice of sharing risks with European underwriters. The United States companies freely cabled their European partners information about the insured cargoes—including war matériel for Britain—together with names of ships, sailing dates and destinations.

It so happened that one recipient of all this information was a major Swiss underwriter in Zurich, which had joint arrangements with a Munich insurer. The Swiss company routinely relayed its shipping information to its associate in Munich, whence it became readily available to

A hearing aid for sub hunters

Hunting submerged U-boats in World War I was a frustrating guessing game for the British, who usually learned of an enemy submarine's presence only when the U-boat scored a torpedo hit. But by the outbreak of World War II the British had put into use an electronic eye that, according to a secret report, "removes from the submarine that cloak of invisibility which was its principal source of strength in the late war."

The Royal Navy's optimism rested on a secret U-boat tracking instrument dubbed asdic—an acronym for Anti Submarine Detection Investigation Committee, an Anglo-French scientific group that had spent 20 years developing the device. To the United States Navy, the instrument became known as sonar, for sound navigation ranging, and truly it was more ear than eye.

The apparatus consisted of an electronic sound-transmitting and -receiving unit, encased in a metal dome and fitted to the bottom of a patrol ship's hull. The transmitter sent out high-frequency impulses—audible pings—that bounced back when they struck an object. These echoes, picked up by the receiver, were monitored by an operator who wore earphones and watched the fluctuations of a line traced on a moving sheet of paper. The time that elapsed between transmission and reception indicated the range of the object; the pitch revealed whether it was approaching or moving away.

The British loftily proclaimed that with asdic "one

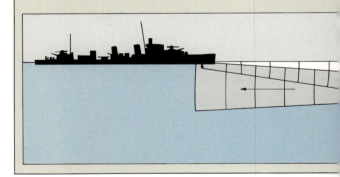

destroyer could do the work of a whole flotilla.'' But under the conditions of naval warfare, asdic quickly displayed serious limitations. It supplied only the bearing of a U-boat, not its submerged depth. The echoes bouncing off U-boats have a confusing resemblance to those from an array of other underwater objects—rocks, sunken wrecks, schools of fish and whales. Even differences in temperature between layers of water caused sound-wave echoes. Weeks of combat experience and a keen ear were necessary for a seaman to use asdic equipment effectively.

Even with veteran asdic operators, the British still found U-boat detection an exceedingly difficult business. Asdic's useful range was a scant 1,500 yards, and the swath of its transmission resembled a narrow horizontal cone (below). Knowing this, U-boat commanders—who could hear the sound impulses underwater—soon learned to dodge asdic scans by heading in a direction that made the pings sound fainter. The German Navy later developed a counterasdic measure called *Pillenwerfer*, which consisted of chemical pellets that were released into the water. They emitted streams of sound-reflecting bubbles to decoy the asdic operator while the U-boat escaped.

Nevertheless, the British scored a number of U-boat kills using asdic. And at the peak of the Battle of the Atlantic, many a U-boat was deterred from attacking a convoy when its crew heard the pings that signaled enemy hunters groping toward them.

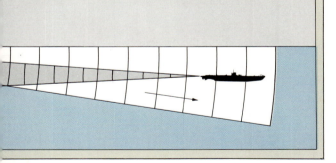

German Naval Intelligence. This meant that U-boat headquarters knew not only the contents of many of the major shipments of matériel bound for British ports, but when and where in the Atlantic to lie in wait. The U-boats thus could hardly fail to score in the summer of 1940.

In 1941 the United States Justice Department learned of the joint underwriting arrangements and took steps to curtail the flow of shipping information. But the practice continued even after the United States entered the War, and not until early 1943 were the insurance companies required, under the Espionage Act, to put their shipping data under wraps. During that time, U-boats set out with virtual road maps and timetables. As a result of the Zurich connection, uncounted tons of shipping went down before it even left American territorial waters.

On the far side of the Atlantic, the Germans were exploiting other successes. After they took France in May 1940, Dönitz installed his submarines in ports along the Bay of Biscay—Brest, La Pallice, Saint-Nazaire, Bordeaux and Lorient. This represented a major strategic transformation of the U-boat war: Instead of wasting time and fuel on the long voyage from bases on the Baltic coast of Germany, through the North Sea and around the coast of Scotland, U-boats could now begin their patrols many hundreds of miles nearer to the operational area—the western approaches, where Atlantic convoy routes converged toward British ports. The submarines therefore not only could get to the operational area much sooner and stay there longer, but could reach out into the Atlantic as far as 25° W., well beyond the range of the British convoy escorts—a powerful factor in the Happy Time.

Admiral Dönitz himself was one of the most important elements contributing to the era of U-boat success. He presided over the slaughter with consummate artistry. In 1941, at 50, Karl Dönitz was in his prime, a strategist without peer in the history of submarine warfare—and a study in human contrasts. Always very stiff, very correct, very cold, he never showed emotion; it was later said that when told of the deaths of his two sons in action at sea, one of them in a U-boat, he showed not a flicker of reaction. But the resolute jut of his chin and the penetrating gaze of his steel-blue eyes gave expression to a sternly independent personality and an exceptionally clear and analytical intelligence. Although he drove his U-boat crews almost to the limits of their endurance, his understanding of their front-line difficulties and his concern for their welfare kept morale surprisingly high and inspired an enduring personal loyalty to the man they called ''Uncle Karl'' or ''the Lion.''

Dönitz ran his vast operation almost singlehandedly. His immediate staff was extraordinarily small: a chief of staff (Rear Admiral Eberhard Godt), two operations officers, a handful of specialists and watchkeeping officers. After the transfer of bases to France, Dönitz moved his own headquarters from a wooden hut in Wilhelmshaven to a country château at Kerneval, near Lorient. He orchestrated the U-boat war from there until 1942, when the Bay of Biscay came under Allied attack and the Führer ordered him first to Paris and later to Berlin.

On the wall of Dönitz' operational command room at Kerneval was an enormous map of the Atlantic Ocean divided into a number of grid squares, each bearing two reference letters; these, in turn, were subdivided into squares with two reference numerals. Thus, for example, if Dönitz wanted the *U-551* to patrol the convoy route from the 48th to the 53rd parallel, some 450 miles east of Newfoundland, he ordered it by radio to proceed to square BC 35.

The German high command took great security precautions. Dönitz had two means of keeping a lid on the destinations of his U-boats. One was to send a U-boat out and then radio instructions in code; the other was to give the commander a sealed envelope with instructions he was not to read until he had sailed 20° west of Biscay. From the moment the commander got his orders, the U-boat remained in radio communication with Dönitz' headquarters, sending back regular situation reports and, whenever necessary, receiving new orders in return. This unceasing flow of radio information accounted for the deadly speed with which the U-boats responded when gathering for a kill.

If, during 1940 and the first months of 1941, Karl Dönitz had had the 300 U-boats he dreamed of and fought for, there is little doubt that his submarines would have brought Britain to defeat. But although work on surface vessels was suspended in 1940 so shipbuilders could concentrate on constructing U-boats, the submarines could be built and manned only so fast. For all the U-boat arm's success, Dönitz was in fact operating on next to nothing during the Happy Time. He spent the War's first winter with no more than 10 and often as few as two U-boats on patrol. But the paucity of boats was more than balanced by the enthusiasm and dedication of the young men who called themselves "the Dönitz Volunteer Corps." Recruiting drives met their goals with ease, and the volunteers distinguished themselves by their aggressive zeal in carrying out Dönitz' standing orders. Those orders were to keep attacking, whatever the enemy did: "Do not let yourself be shaken off; if the boat is temporarily driven away or underwater, follow up in the direction of the convoy, try to get in touch again and once more ATTACK!"

No U-boat man more vividly illustrated the gusto, the boldness and the persistence of Dönitz' men than Lieutenant Otto Kretschmer, the proud son of a Silesian schoolmaster. Kretschmer took the new *U-99* on her first patrol at the end of June 1940. On the sunny afternoon of July 5, he found himself in the path of the 2,053-ton Canadian steamer *Magog* and sent a single torpedo streaking through the long Atlantic swell to break her in two amidships. Two days later a second lone ship came over the horizon. She was the 1,514-ton Swedish ship *Bissen*, and Kretschmer sank her with one torpedo amidships. That night he sighted a convoy heading out from Britain—his first convoy—and quickly maneuvered the *U-99* into its path. Slipping past a destroyer by less than 100 yards, Kretschmer attempted to fire into the heart of the convoy, with torpedoes to right and left. Only one of the torpedoes scored a hit. He dived to slip away from the escorts but soon picked up propeller noises on the hydrophone. "I believe my crew are going to get their baptism of depth charging this time," he was later to write in a present-tense narrative for his official war diary.

The depth charging began almost immediately, the hull-jolting explosions dangerously pummeling the *U-99* even when Kretschmer took her down to 350 feet. After two hours the U-boat's oxygen supply system

Square-jawed and steely-eyed, with medals and badges gleaming on his uniform, a U-boat petty officer stands before his craft in this recruiting poster that trumpets, "Volunteer for the Navy." The glamor of the submarine arm's success was clearly the advertisement's main appeal: the U-boat's pennants announce the sinking of six Allied ships.

failed, and the crew had to resort to emergency breathing masks. Kretschmer commanded them to lie still and avoid any unnecessary exertion. After six hours some were gasping, and the depth-charge pounding continued. After 12 hours the air was foul and visibly yellow, and many of the men feared they were soon to die, either from lack of oxygen, from exploding depth charges or from being crushed by water pressure if the batteries, which kept the vessel moving slowly and therefore prevented it from dropping below its permissible depth, gave out.

Finally, after 14 hours of continuous depth charging, the attackers overhead gave up. But he took no chances. He waited for five more hours before surfacing. After nearly 20 hours below, Kretschmer clawed the hatch open and his crew staggered out to collapse on deck, gulping the cool fresh air. Kretschmer's reaction was not just relief that the experience was over, but satisfaction that it had taken place. "We all felt like school children at Christmas time," he wrote in his diary. "Now we have received all the presents the enemy can give us. We all have fresh confidence in our ship."

Kretschmer immediately resumed the offensive. Before heading for port, he sank three more ships and whimsically ordered a fourth, a small Estonian freighter, to turn herself over to German authorities in Bordeaux as his war prize (the freighter never made it; she was bombed en route in the Bay of Biscay). And on his next voyage, two weeks later, he sank seven ships (a record for a single mission) totaling 65,137 tons, picking off three of them with single torpedo shots from the very midst of a convoy, where he had arrived at night unnoticed by the escorts on the convoy's perimeter. The U-boat's presence there threw the convoy into such confusion that two ships, zigzagging in an effort to evade the U-99, collided and sank; they were not added to Kretschmer's tally but, credited with 44 ships totaling 266,629 tons, he would nonetheless become the highest-scoring U-boat commander of World War II.

Kretschmer was only one of more than a dozen U-boat aces whom the Germans venerated as national heroes during the Happy Time and beyond. Perhaps the most widely known was Günther Prien of Scapa Flow fame, who in June 1940 sank 66,588 tons of shipping in one of the most spectacular patrols of the War. Another was Joachim Schepke of the U-100, who in August torpedoed five ships in three hours.

In style and personality the three aces—Kretschmer, Prien and Schepke—were very different from one another. Kretschmer was probably the most brilliant and respected. A single-minded professional naval officer, he demanded absolute discipline from his men, turning them into the most efficient of all the U-boat crews and earning their complete loyalty and admiration. He was so quiet that he was known in the service as "Otto the Silent." Yet his intensity was legendary. Once, when directing an attack, he struck a subordinate on the back of the neck and shoved the fellow out of the way in his impatience to get to the controls. So intent had Kretschmer been on his objective that he did not even remember the incident when, in a more relaxed moment at a dinner party, the subordinate reminded him of it.

Schepke, by contrast, was easygoing, a handsome, debonair, boisterous, laughing bon viveur with an eye for the ladies and an actor's flair that made it easy for him to play the part of a hero, his captain's cap set at a rakish angle on his head.

Prien was a man of immense determination. He could never wait to return to sea—though he was possessed of sufficient sentiment to go with his wife's mauve scarf around his neck and to save fan mail from children. With torpedo and gun he remorselessly increased his tonnage of sinking, driven by a sense of duty to the Navy, the Reich and the Nazi Party, by a sheer love of the chase, and by a compelling will to excel.

The sinking statistics that they and their comrades together produced were astonishing. In June 1940, with an average of only six U-boats at sea at any given time, Dönitz' force sank one enemy ship per day, for a total of 289,000 tons—without the loss of a single U-boat. Between July and October—the peak of the Happy Time—the U-boats destroyed 217 ships, totaling a staggering 1,111,185 tons.

As the Happy Time continued unabated, the tactics of U-boat warfare began to change. The methods used during World War I and the early months of World War II could no longer be employed. By late 1940 it was risky to hang about on the surface and use the guns to sink shipping—all ships had radios now and could summon help. Asdic, while far from perfect, made underwater attacks perilous. Thus, following Kretschmer's lead with increasing effectiveness, the U-boats turned to making attacks on the surface at night, where their low silhouettes were almost invisible to the naked eye and asdic could not find them.

Partly in response to the stiffening of the Allies' defenses, Dönitz began in September 1940 to experiment with a tactic he had worked out as a result of his experiences in World War I: the wolf-pack attack. Now, instead of sending U-boats on the prowl alone, he sent them in groups of four or five together—with commensurate results. On September 7 a wolf pack with Prien and Kretschmer in the forefront sighted a convoy of 53 ships and sank five of them in one night. Two weeks later, on September 21, a pack of four sank 11 ships in seven hours. On October 18 a quintet of U-boats sighted a convoy of 34 ships, and Otto Kretschmer's war diary tersely recorded the violence and tension of the slaughter that began just before midnight:

"2330. Now attacking the right wing of the last line but one. Bow shot at a large freighter. The vessel zigzagged, with the result that the torpedo passed in front of her and hit her even bigger neighbor. The ship, about 7,000 tons, was hit below the foremast and sank quickly by the bows.

"2358. Bow shot at large freighter approximately 6,000 tons. Range 750 yards. Hit below foremast. The explosion of the torpedo was immediately followed by a high sheet of flame and an explosion that ripped the ship open as far as the bridge and left a cloud of smoke 600 feet high. Ship's forepart apparently shattered. Ship still burning fiercely, with green flames."

Midnight passed, and for the wee hours of October 19, Kretschmer's war diary continued:

"0015. The destroyers are at their wits' end, shooting off star shells the whole time to comfort themselves and one another. Not that that makes much odds in the bright moonlight. I am now beginning to pick them off from astern of the convoy.

Wearing his new Knight's Cross of the Iron Cross, Lieutenant Otto Kretschmer enjoys a beer with members of the crew of his U-99 after their return from a record-breaking patrol on August 5, 1940. It was for this two-week mission, during which he and his crew sank seven ships, that Kretschmer won the prized medal.

U-boat aces Günther Prien (left) and Joachim Schepke use champagne glasses to reenact one of their devastating joint attacks against Allied convoys in the fall of 1940. During the night of October 19-20 a wolf pack of seven U-boats, including Prien's U-47 and Schepke's U-100, sank 12 Allied ships.

"0138. Bow shot on a large, heavily laden freighter of some 6,000 tons. Range 945 yards. Hit below foremast. Ship sank at once.

"0155. Bow shot on the next ship, a large vessel of about 7,000 tons. Range 975 yards. Hit below foremast. Ship sank in 40 seconds."

By 2 a.m. the five-member wolf pack had sunk 17 ships totaling 80,000 tons—half the entire convoy.

For the British, such punishment—repeatedly inflicted throughout these months—was clearly insupportable. "How willingly," Churchill wrote later, "would I have exchanged a full scale attempt at invasion for this shapeless, measureless peril, expressed in charts, curves and statistics." By the end of the year, half of Britain's vital oil imports had been sent up in flames, and before long food imports were cut by half as well. By February 1941, British ships were being sunk at an awesome rate of seven million tons a year, more than three times faster than replacements could be built.

Yet in that same month there began a series of fateful events, involving the three leading U-boat aces, that would signal like the long shadows of approaching evening that the Happy Time would not last forever.

On February 18, 1941, on the eve of a voyage, Prien invited his officers and an old friend, Wolfgang Frank, to a farewell dinner. They drove out of Lorient down the dark wintry lanes of the Brittany countryside until they came to an inn run by an old Breton lady who was famous for her cooking. "We sat on until late," Frank would remember, "over a meal that one could easily have written a poem about. We finished one bottle after another, telling stories of merchant ships and yachts, of battleships and submarines. Prien was in brilliant form and filled with a passionate eagerness to be in action again."

Early next morning, Prien prepared to set out to sea again in the *U-47*. He was impeccably dressed for the occasion. His leather coat had just come back from the cleaner, and it was as stiff and shiny as armor. His cap cover was newly starched and brilliant white. A brass band was playing on the quay, and a large crowd had gathered to see Prien off. A young girl handed him a bunch of fresh camellias, which bloom early in Brittany, and Prien plucked one of the blooms, gave it to the girl and stuck another in his buttonhole.

Kretschmer had come down to say good-by. "Prüntje," said Kretschmer, addressing Prien with the familiarity of an old friend. "I'll be following you in a couple of days. Have a convoy ready."

"Just leave it to Papa's nose to smell something out," Prien replied. "I have a hunch about this trip. I have a feeling it will be a big one for us all." On that note he took his leave.

Three days later Kretschmer left Lorient in the *U-99*. An Army band, playing "The Kretschmer March," specially composed in his honor, followed the boat as far as the harbor entrance on board a commandeered river steamer. The next day Schepke went too, departing in the *U-100*. Germany's three top U-boat aces were out in the Atlantic together.

South of Iceland they were ordered by Dönitz to form an interception line with other U-boats across the probable course of a particularly large convoy, outward-bound from Britain. In the hope of running into the convoy, they steamed eastward in company for a while, and as long as they were in sight they continued to exchange personal and often frivolous semaphore signals with one another. After some days it became obvious that they had missed the convoy, and they spread out to widen the search. Suddenly, on March 7, Prien came upon it; he reported to headquarters: ENEMY IN SIGHT ON NORTHWESTERLY COURSE. SPEED 8 KNOTS.

For the rest of the night and throughout a squally day, Prien shadowed the convoy and transmitted reports of its position, course and speed for the benefit of other U-boats. It was a large convoy, covering many square miles and strongly escorted by destroyers and corvettes. No one knows exactly what happened to Prien in the early hours of March 8, and decades later the details of that morning's events and the vessels involved in them were still being disputed by naval historians. But one widely accepted version is based on the log of the escort destroyer *Wolverine*, commanded by Lieutenant Commander Jim Rowland. It seems that Prien surfaced and ventured too close to the convoy under cover of a rain squall. When the squall suddenly cleared, the *U-47* was almost immediately attacked by the *Wolverine*. Rowland's log tells the story:

"0023. Smoke was seen resembling diesel exhaust and hydrophone

Platefuls of medals for the U-boat elite

**KNIGHT'S CROSS
WITH OAK LEAVES, SWORDS AND DIAMONDS**

Of the 900,000 men in the German Navy during World War II, none were more generously decorated with medals and badges than the 40,000 men of the U-boat corps.

Some of these accolades, such as patrol badges (*page 3 and below*), were bestowed by the thousands. Others, including the coveted orders of the Knight's Cross, were awarded only for exceptional merit.

Of the 318 Knight's Crosses won by the Kriegsmarine, 145—almost half—went to the less than 5 per cent of Navy men who were in the U-boat arm. The highest order (*left*) was given only twice: to *U-181* Lieutenant Commander Wolfgang Lüth and to *U-967* ace Albrecht Brandi.

Most U-boat men only dreamed of such glory. Yet the chance that anyone might be singled out for honor helped sustain what Dönitz called "a spirit of selflessness and readiness to serve."

Lieutenant Jochen Mohr beams over two Knight's Crosses—a homemade one around his neck and an edible one before him. They were presented by the crew of his U-124 before the official ceremony in early 1942, when he received the real medal. Mohr was given the honor for passing the 100,000-ton mark in enemy sinkings during raids off the Eastern Seaboard of the United States.

Submariners receive Iron Crosses (on ribbons) and patrol badges (on tray) from senior officers after returning from a war patrol. The two awards were liberally granted to U-boat men to boost morale.

effect was reported on the same bearing a moment later. Course was altered and speed increased to 18 knots.

"0026. A wake was sighted and *Wolverine* increased to 22 knots. A minute later it was seen to come from a U-boat. At 0029, 'Full speed ahead' was ordered and course altered to keep pointed at the U-boat, which was zigzagging wildly at high speed." When a fellow escort fired a star shell, lighting up the surrounding sea, "the U-boat promptly dived at a range of about seven cables."

The *U-47* was now at its most vulnerable—beneath the surface and slowed almost to a halt. Fifteen minutes after diving, Prien's boat was detected by asdic at 5 degrees off the *Wolverine*'s port bow and was subjected to a depth-charge attack lasting more than an hour. In Prien's experience this was not unusually long, but at least one of the depth charges seems to have come within range of the U-boat, for its fuel tanks apparently sprang a leak.

"At 0320," Rowland continued, "Engineer Officer reported on bridge that he had unmistakably both seen and smelt shale oil (when we shone a 10-inch light on the water)." Around 4 a.m. it was clear from the loud propeller noises in the *Wolverine*'s hydrophones that the U-boat had surfaced and was making off at high speed. "An oil track some 50 feet in width was sighted. Following up we came across a large patch with a narrow track of thick oil leading off to starboard."

The *U-47*, with Prien aboard, vanished. But the *Wolverine* clung doggedly to the chase, and at 5:14, closing rapidly from five miles' distance, the destroyer's hydrophone loudspeakers clearly picked up a harsh metallic rattling from the U-boat. In all probability the earlier depth-charge attack had blown the *U-47*'s propellers out of alignment, and this was causing a loud rumbling from the propeller shaft, with the ever-present danger that the engines would be torn from their mountings.

"At 0519," Rowland wrote, "sighted U-boat and altered a few degrees to port. Increased to 'Full speed,' and passed to all quarters 'Stand by to ram.' At 0522, U-boat submerging and altering to starboard. I at once ordered 'Starboard 30' as the U-boat was being overhauled very rapidly and now considerable cavitation could be seen from her propellers."

Twist and turn as he might, using all the wiles and ruses he had learned in a year and a half of submarine warfare, Prien found his luck running out. In the dim predawn light of a northern March day, his pursuers could peer into the crystal-clear water and see the phosphorescence around the submarine, some 50 feet down. Wrote Rowland: "A rush of bubbles was creating a patch of disturbed water and leading out of it was a V-shaped track, about 20 yards in length. Having served some six years in submarines it is my firm conviction that the latter was caused by air escaping from the bow buoyancy vent and that I could see the bubbles underwater near the point of emission. The large patch gave me the impression of air from the main ballast vents with possibly some phosphorescence around the conning tower."

As the *Wolverine* passed over the bubbles, Rowland gave the order to fire. A pattern of 10 depth charges straddled the approximate position of Prien's boat. At 5:43 the surface of the water was shattered by a tremendous explosion, and the *Wolverine*'s men saw an orange light beneath

A convoy of some 30 Allied ships heels into a sharp emergency turn in this photograph taken from a Royal Air Force Coastal Command antisubmarine plane. Early in the War the Admiralty favored small convoys because they were maneuverable, but by the spring of 1943 it found that convoys of up to 150 ships could operate successfully.

the surface. It continued glowing for 10 seconds—then disappeared.

All through the day that followed, Dönitz called Prien on the radio: U-47, REPORT POSITION, CONDITIONS AND SUCCESS. Again: U-47, REPORT POSITION. There was no reply. That underwater orange glow that the *Wolverine's* men had seen marked, beyond reasonable doubt, the deaths of Günther Prien and his 47 men. Günther Prien—the 33-year-old "Bull of Scapa Flow," Dönitz' favorite U-boat captain, with one battleship and 28 merchant ships totaling 160,935 tons to his tally and the oak leaves to the Knight's Cross of the Iron Cross to his credit—had finally met an end as dreadful as any he had inflicted on countless other seafaring men.

On the same night that Prien met his death, the *U-110*, commanded by Lieutenant Commander Fritz-Julius Lemp, who had sunk the *Athenia* on the first day of the War, sighted another convoy off Iceland. Among the widely scattered U-boats that answered his call to the scene were Schepke's *U-100* and Kretschmer's *U-99*. The remaining two of Germany's top trio of U-boat aces were about to go into action together.

Heavy rain squalls and a fierce east wind held them up, and eight days

Impromptu heraldry that cheered the submariners' spirits

When the *U-47* was charging home after goring the British at Scapa Flow in 1939, a jubilant lieutenant, Engelbert Endrass, seized a can of paint and emblazoned the conning tower of the U-boat with the figure of a snorting bull. The bull, the spontaneous creation of the moment's triumph, endured as the *U-47*'s insignia ever after, and it was one of the first examples of a fashion that spread through the entire U-boat fleet.

Many of the emblems that appeared on German submarines were of obscure origin. The *U-203* assumed the coat of arms of Essen because that city had adopted the crewmen as its special champions. The crew of the *U-558* made a watchword of a phrase from an old folk story—"Wooden Eye, Be Alert"—and used the one-eyed cleric to whom it referred as an emblem. And when the *U-338* slipped prematurely down the ways at its launching, the crew dubbed their vessel the "wild donkey," painting a kicking burro on the conning tower.

In the intimacy forged over months of shared fears and shared triumphs, the U-boat men invested the insignia with highly charged emotional significance. Not only did they persist in painting the devices, they sometimes endowed the figures with a kind of life of their own. The crew of the *U-201* adopted a snowman as a tribute to their esteemed commander, Adalbert Schnee, whose surname is translated as "snow." When Commander Schnee won the Knight's Cross, his men decorated the snowman with a painted cross to match.

U-338: Wild donkey

U-203: Essen coat of arms

U-94: Sea monster and British lion

U-132: Eagle and swastika

U-124: Edelweiss blossom

U-558: One-eyed cleric

U-47: Bull of Scapa Flow

U-201: Schnee's snowman

U-216: Britain pierced by a sword

U-34: Elephant and Churchill

passed before the pack finally gathered around the convoy. This time the U-boats found themselves confronted by an escort handled with skill and an aggressive spirit that they had rarely before encountered.

First, Schepke was chased by two destroyers from a Royal Navy escort group under Commander Donald Macintyre, who was to become one of the leading U-boat killers of the War. The *U-100* dived but suffered depth-charge damage that eventually forced her to the surface—where she had the misfortune to become the first U-boat to be detected in a night attack by ship's radar, up to that time an ineffectual instrument. The two destroyers, *Vanoc* and *Walker,* made a tight, high-speed turn and swept along the radar bearing till the silhouette of the *U-100* came into sight. The *Vanoc* then raced straight at the submarine, aiming her sharp bow at the conning tower. Some of the U-boat men jumped overboard and tried to swim out of the way. Men on the *Vanoc* could hear Schepke's voice quite clearly as he shouted to his crew in German: "Don't panic. They're going to miss us. They'll pass astern."

Schepke's cheering words were in vain. With a terrible crash the *Vanoc's* bows sliced into the U-boat's conning tower, throwing some of the men on the bridge into the sea, severing Schepke's legs at the trunk, and jamming him between the bridge shield and the periscope standard. The destroyer rode right over the U-boat before stopping, then went astern and drew clear with a grinding jolt. As the *U-100* rose into the air, Schepke's legless torso was jerked free and thrown into the sea. Schepke was still alive, still wearing his white-covered commander's cap at a rakish angle on his head. For a few seconds he thrashed wildly about with his arms in the heavy Atlantic swell. Then the sea mercifully closed over his mutilated body. Now only one of the three great aces was left.

Aboard the *U-99,* meanwhile, Otto Kretschmer had been having a tense time of his own. During the attack on the convoy that had killed Prien the week before, Kretschmer had infiltrated the enemy columns, hitting two ships—one of them a 20,000-ton whaling factory ship, the largest of its sort in the world. Forced to dive by two corvettes that bore down out of the rain squall, Kretschmer and his men had been thrown around in the rocking, pitching hull while more than 100 depth charges were dropped on them. At 4:24 a.m., after the *U-99* had finally crept away under cover of the convoy wreckage in the sea above, Kretschmer heard Prien send his last radio report, then listened all day as Dönitz futilely tried to summon his favorite from his grave in the depths.

The *U-99* came up on the other convoy on March 16, the same day that Schepke and the rest of the pack first gathered around it. Kretschmer resorted to his own special tactic, driving into the midst of the enemy and coolly torpedoing six ships. When his supply of torpedoes was exhausted, he prudently headed home on the surface in darkness. But at that point a destroyer was sighted, and instead of making a surface run for safety the officer of the watch ordered the *U-99* to dive. Kretschmer was furious, for in diving the submarine had immediately made its presence known on the destroyer's asdic.

By incalculable mischance for Kretschmer, the destroyer was the *Walker.* In all that vastness of the wild Atlantic, the *U-99* had arrived in almost exactly the same position in which the *U-100* had been sunk just half an hour earlier. The *Walker* was standing by while the *Vanoc* picked up Schepke's surviving crew members, five in all. Commander Macintyre on board the *Walker* was astonished to hear a positive asdic echo from almost directly under the *Vanoc's* stern. While the *Vanoc* slowly withdrew, the *Walker* went straight into the attack, dropping six depth charges, which were all that could be prepared in time. When the *Walker* turned for another run, she received a dramatic signal from the *Vanoc*: U-BOAT SURFACED ASTERN OF ME. Illuminated by the harsh glare of the *Vanoc's* searchlight beam, the *U-99* lay stopped on the water. From her bridge came a signal-lamp message in uncertain English: I AM SUNKING.

The depth bombs had put the *U-99's* engine out of action and so damaged the propellers that the boat, unable to keep speed, had sunk to 720 feet; at that depth the hull had begun to crack, and Kretschmer was forced to blow air into the ballast tanks and shoot nose first to the surface, like a cork. There the *U-99* wallowed, listing, as Macintyre's men wildly fired their guns at her. Kretschmer calmly lit a cigar as he organized the destruction of the secret codes and papers, the escape of the crew and the scuttling of the boat.

He was the last one of the *U-99's* crew to be rescued by the *Walker* from the icy water. Kretschmer hardly fitted his British captors' image of a U-boat commander: Instead of a fanatical Nazi, they found a quiet-voiced, polite, unpolitical, professional officer who spoke good English and was quick to congratulate Macintyre on his success. Taken to Macintyre's after cabin, the leading U-boat ace sat in a leading U-boat killer's armchair and fell into a sleep of utter exhaustion.

Because the loss of three of Germany's most idolized war heroes was certain to have a mournful effect on the nation's morale, the Führer's headquarters at first refused to permit any official announcement. Even Prien's wife was not allowed to know the truth. Kretschmer's and Schepke's fates were not disclosed until near the end of April; Prien's not until May 23, a full 10 weeks after his death. Then, in an Order of the Day, Karl Dönitz issued a valediction of sorrow and defiance:

"Günther Prien, the hero of Scapa Flow, has made his last patrol. We submariners bow our heads with pride and sorrow. Even though the vast ocean hides him, Prien still stands in our midst. No U-boat will go to sea against the West but he will sail with her. No blow against England will be struck by us but his aggressive spirit will guide our hand."

By some reckonings, the loss of the three aces marked the end of the Happy Time. Germans were stunned and baffled. "Had the British introduced new weapons or techniques of antisubmarine warfare?" wondered Herbert A. Werner, then an ensign on the *U-557*, who was to survive the War as a U-boat commander. "We had no explanation."

In fact, Winston Churchill had already given fair warning of a change in the nature of the U-boat war. "We have got to lift this business to the highest plane over everything else," he had told his Navy chief, Admiral Sir Dudley Pound. "I am going to proclaim the Battle of the Atlantic." And on March 6, 1941, even as Prien, Schepke and Kretschmer were moving toward their final destinations, Churchill issued a major directive: "We must assume that the Battle of the Atlantic has begun," he said. "The U-boat at sea must be hunted, the U-boat in the building yard or in dock must be bombed."

Churchill's words were more than mere rhetoric. The British had begun to institute a number of measures that were eventually to produce results. The convoy escorts had been reinforced with 50 elderly but invaluable destroyers lent by America, with British destroyers released from other duties, as well as with corvettes, frigates and escort carriers. Ships and crews had been organized into unified escort groups and put through special training in antisubmarine tactics. Two naval bases had been established in Iceland, enabling escort ships to refuel there, thus extending their range. RAF Coastal Command planes had been put under the operational control of the Admiralty, making it possible to coordinate a two-pronged antisubmarine offensive by sea and air. And priority was given to the development of radar.

The effects of these measures were to be slow in coming, for—predictably—every technical and tactical advance by one side prompted a swift response by the other. When, for example, the Germans began using a new acoustic torpedo, designed to home in on the sound made by the propellers of enemy ships, the British replied with a noisemaking decoy; the devices—"damned rattling buoys," one U-boat man called them—could be towed at the end of long steel cables, luring acoustic torpedoes by generating a clapping sound. Similarly, when the British developed radar that could detect surfaced submarines even in heavy seas, the Germans answered with Metox, an instrument that detected radar waves and beeped a warning of approaching planes to its operator.

Thus, with the end of the Happy Time, the U-boat war settled into a deadly seesaw, both sides inflicting and suffering heavy losses, the blood and oil of hunter and hunted mingling on the seas, the grim daily drama of the men aboard the U-boats and the surface ships dictated by a silent struggle of technological thrust and counterthrust. This phase of the War would last almost two years, until the spring of 1943. The Happy Time was over, but the U-boats continued to be a deadly threat.

Admiral Dönitz, for his part—despite a profound personal grief at the loss of his aces—faced the new phase unflinchingly. His strategy was devastating in its simplicity: Probe the enemy's soft spots, strike where he was weakest and least wary, force him to stretch his defenses beyond the breaking point. The North Atlantic shipping routes obviously were the areas of highest opportunity because of the heavy traffic along them and their relative proximity to the U-boat bases in France. Yet, in keeping with the new strategy, Dönitz extended the War to other seas. U-boats now carried their scourge into the Mediterranean and the Black Sea, the Arctic Ocean and the Caribbean, the South Atlantic, the Indian Ocean and Far Eastern waters. Big new supply U-boats—the 1,700-ton Type XIV, nicknamed milch cows by their crews—refueled, rearmed and revictualed operational U-boats at sea (pages 124-129), thus doubling their range and endurance. Some U-boats made amazing voyages—the UB-107, commanded by Dönitz' son-in-law, Lieutenant Commander Günther Hessler, covered 22,000 miles in 135 days and set a World War II record by sinking 14 ships on a single patrol. ⚓

The motherly milch cows
that fueled the killers

For the first three years of World War II, U-boats could carry only enough fuel and provisions for a 7,000-mile voyage; if they crossed the Atlantic, they hardly reached the far side before they had to return. But in the spring of 1942, U-boat Command put into operation the first of 10 ingenious new submarine tankers designed to resupply U-boats out at sea, thus extending their field of action dramatically.

Designated Type XIV on the drawing board, the somewhat ungainly U-boat tankers—about six feet broader at the waist than their slender fighting sisters—were nicknamed milch cows by German submariners. A single milch cow could carry 700 tons of diesel oil and 45 tons of other supplies in her beamy hull, enough to keep a 10-boat wolf pack at sea for as long as four months. As one milch cow dried up, she sailed home to restock while another took her place.

A number of wolf packs, the first to be nursed by milch cows, conducted a successful blitz on Allied shipping deep in the Caribbean and the Gulf of Mexico in the spring and summer of 1942. U-boat Commander Karl Dönitz was exultant. "Thanks to the submarine tankers," he later recalled, "we were able to exploit a fruitful theater of operations, which was 3,000 to 4,000 miles from the Biscay bases."

Harassed right on its own doorstep, the United States Navy declared destruction of the tankers to be top priority. A bomber managed to locate and destroy one milch cow with a depth charge in August 1942; however, almost a year passed before any more were sunk. Eventually, Allied aircraft and ships would hunt down all 10 tankers built for U-boat Command, but until then the milch cows kept their wolf packs fueled, fed, armed and dangerously effective.

A milch cow's coveralled crewman (left) carries tinned provisions and a net bag of bread as he heads for his vessel. The tanker is being loaded in a concrete cavern of a bunker (right), taking on diesel fuel through a rubber hose while a truck-mounted crane hoists a torpedo aboard at the stern.

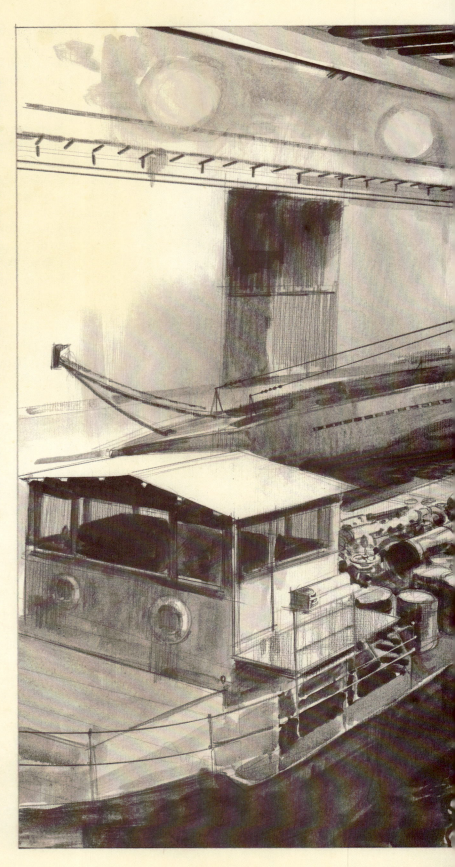

In foul Atlantic weather, a milch cow and two needy U-boats make their rendezvous. To find each other in the vast reaches of the ocean was a great test of seamanship and navigation. "At last we sighted the supply boat," recalled one crewman. "A piece of our country, a partner in our fate—what a moment it was."

Taking advantage of good weather, tanker crewmen refuel a parched hunter by means of a hose linkup and bring crated supplies on deck for transfer to the U-boat. An injured seaman is placed in a dinghy (background, right) to be moved to the tanker for transportation home.

Milch cow crewmen maneuver a 2,500-pound torpedo—swaddled in life jackets for added buoyancy—with a deck-mounted crane that will lower it into the sea. It will be transferred to the recipient submarine by a towline.

Interrupting a refueling operation, a United States Navy Wildcat fighter—which, as was sometimes the case, bears no markings other than the national insignia—swoops down to drop depth charges while a U-boat disappears in a crash dive. The milch cow, her hose prodigally spilling fuel into the sea, is left to face destruction. Milch cows were especially vulnerable to attacks from the air because of their capacious hulls, which were not designed for swift submerging.

Almost as soon as the United States came into the War in December 1941, Dönitz sent five U-boats into American waters in an operation he code-named the Drum Roll. Spearheaded by Lieutenant Commander Reinhardt Hardegen of the *U-123*, they contrived an unbelievable slaughter. The U-boat men were helped by the peacetime lack of blackout along the American East Coast: Towns were blazing with light; lighthouses and navigation buoys were still shining; even ships carried normal lights and used their radios freely, frequently signaling their position, so that the U-boats had no difficulty homing in on them. No convoy system existed, and antisubmarine defenses remained primitive and ineffective. U-boats penetrated the shallow waters, lying on the bottom during daytime, then coming up at night and calmly cruising the inshore shipping lanes, laying torpedoes as they went. At a conservative estimate, nearly 200 ships, totaling 1,150,675 tons, were destroyed by the end of April 1942—and just one U-boat was lost in the process. Only when the convoy system was instituted in American waters on April 1, 1942, did the U-boats meet any resistance. Then the number of sinkings fell dramatically, from

After falling victim to a U-boat off Cape Hatteras on April 5, 1942, the American tanker Byron D. Benson lies totally hidden beneath a boiling cloud of greasy black smoke. The pickings in the western Atlantic were so rich at first that German captains borrowed an American folk term and called operations there the "American turkey shoot."

Displaying a booty of rubber tires—a particularly valuable item for a nation cut off from such supplies—the U-156 returns to Lorient on July 7, 1942, after a successful mission against American shipping in the Caribbean. By the very nature of U-boat tactics, there was seldom any booty to take; in the first six months of 1942 alone, U-boats sent more than a million tons of Allied shipping to the bottom of the Atlantic.

128 ships in the first quarter of 1942 to a mere 21 in the second.

Retreating from American waters, Dönitz sent his U-boats south to devastate the Caribbean tanker lanes carrying petroleum to the war front. When convoys were formed there too, he switched his U-boats yet again, now detailing some to the South Atlantic. And there, about midway between South Africa and Brazil, a dramatic sequence of events in September 1942 brought a tragedy, compounded of human compassion and wartime ruthlessness, that changed the basic nature of the U-boat war.

Contrary to Allied wartime propaganda that portrayed U-boat captains and crews as war criminals who gloatingly machine-gunned helpless merchant sailors, atrocities had in fact been extremely rare in World War II. In the early years, U-boat crews often actually helped their victims. One commander, Herbert Schultze of the *U-48*, consciously or unconsciously emulating one of his World War I predecessors, went so far as to send radio messages to the Admiralty in London asking that a ship be sent to pick up survivors of a freighter he had just sunk.

No one made a more heroic effort to give mercy than Lieutenant Commander Werner Hartenstein, the 32-year-old captain of the *U-156*. On the night of September 12, Hartenstein torpedoed the British troopship *Laconia*, which was evacuating British servicemen and their families, together with some prisoners of war, from British Africa. On board were 463 British crewmen, 286 British servicemen, 80 civilians (some of them women and children), 1,800 Italian prisoners of war and 103 Polish guards. Hartenstein no sooner heard shouts for help than he began to pick the victims out of the water. SO FAR 90 RESCUED, he radioed to U-boat headquarters. REQUEST INSTRUCTIONS. Dönitz knew that torpedoing Italian soldiers could have a serious effect on Germany's relations with her Axis partner. He diverted two U-boats from off Freetown, Sierra Leone, to the scene; the Italians sent one of their own submarines, and the Vichy French in Dakar dispatched three warships to help pick up survivors.

For the moment, however, the *U-156* was alone. All through the night the boat cruised about, fishing people from the sea without regard for their nationality. Submarines were woefully unequipped for coping with such situations: There was hardly enough room below to handle the crew, much less extra passengers; moreover, survivors placed on the deck would be drowned if the submarine was suddenly forced to dive. At 4 a.m. the next day, Hartenstein sent out a radio message in English on the 25-meter international shipping distress band and the 600-meter commercial wavelength: IF ANY SHIP WILL ASSIST THE SHIPWRECKED LACONIA CREW, I WILL NOT ATTACK HER PROVIDED I AM NOT BEING ATTACKED BY SHIP OR AIR FORCES. I HAVE PICKED UP 193 MEN, 4° 52' S., 11° 26' W. GERMAN SUBMARINE. No ship came. But now the enemy knew the *U-156*'s position.

For two days Hartenstein struggled to keep the boats and survivors together. As far as he was concerned, the rescue operation was not a matter of military expediency but of humanitarian service. By now, 310 people were jammed on the *U-156*—Germans, Italians, British and Poles. An Italian doctor treated the sick and wounded, using the Germans' bandages, medicines and opium. Some of the Italians had suffered bayonet wounds in fighting with their Polish guards to escape the prison holds of the *Laconia*. Other people had severe injuries from shark bites.

At last the Freetown boats, the *U-506* and the *U-507*, arrived. They took some of the survivors from the *U-156* and removed others from lifeboats. Hartenstein now had 55 Italians and 55 British on board, including five women, and had saved the lives of some 400 people. The crews of the other boats behaved with equal concern, dispensing soup and coffee, giving up their berths to the women and the wounded. The U-boats began to gather lifeboats for the rendezvous with the Vichy French warships. While the *U-156* was thus engaged on the fourth day after the *Laconia* was torpedoed, disaster struck out of a clear blue sky.

At 11:25 a.m., while the *U-156*'s decks were crowded with survivors and many more were in tow in four lifeboats, a lookout reported hearing aircraft. A four-engined B-24 Liberator bomber with American markings was sighted approaching from the northeast. Hartenstein, anxious to show his peaceful intentions to the pilot, ordered a large improvised Red Cross flag to be spread over the 105-mm. gun and told the German crew at the antiaircraft gun behind the bridge to lie flat. At the same time, he ordered a signalman to send a Morse message to the plane in English: HERE GERMAN SUBMARINE WITH BRITISH SHIPWRECKED ON BOARD. IS THERE RESCUE SHIP

After torpedoing the British freighter Tweed off Sierra Leone in April 1941, the crew of the U-124 brings aboard survivors found clinging to an overturned lifeboat. The submariners righted and repaired the lifeboat, and then supplied the Tweed's men with such luxuries as chocolates, brandy and tobacco before pointing them on a course for shore.

IN SIGHT? When the pilot did not answer, a British officer asked Hartenstein if he could send a message with the signal lamp, since it might be understood better. The request was granted and the signal was duly flashed to the American pilot: RAF OFFICER SPEAKING FROM GERMAN SUBMARINE. LACONIA SURVIVORS ON BOARD, SOLDIERS, CIVILIANS, WOMEN, CHILDREN.

One British sailor recalled the scene with horror. "The most short-sighted of pilots could not have failed to appreciate the facts," he said. "Here was a submarine with four boats full of survivors in tow, the first about 20 yards from her." But again the pilot did not reply, then flew away—as was learned later, to pick up depth charges in Freetown.

At 12:32 the Liberator returned and made a low approach. As it swooped down, Hartenstein was dumfounded to see the bomb bay open. Two bombs dropped into the sea close by. Germans, British, Italians and Poles, momentarily united by a common if unexpected enemy, shouted execrations at the American plane. On the Liberator's second approach, a German sailor severed the lifeboats' towrope with one blow of an ax. It was too late. A bomb blew up one of the boats, killing a number of passengers. By now German crewmen were making for the antiaircraft gun, but Hartenstein shouted: "Not a man goes near the gun!"

The plane was coming at them again. One depth charge exploded directly under the control room. Women and children were screaming, and the control room and bow compartment were said to be taking water. Hartenstein had no choice: He must save his boat. "All British to leave the submarine at once!" he shouted. Then it was reported that the batteries were giving off chlorine gas; to clear the vessel of all but crew who could handle the emergency, he had to order the Italians off as well.

By now the plane had spent all its bombs, and left the scene. The *U-156* was so badly damaged that Hartenstein decided he had to break off the rescue and head back to base. Not until September 17, five days after the sinking, when two of the Vichy French warships finally arrived at the rendezvous, were the last survivors picked up from all the lifeboats.

Thus ended one of the most remarkable episodes in the U-boat campaign of World War II. The final tally of survivors was 450 out of 1,800 Italians, 588 out of 829 British, 73 out of 103 Poles. Of the U-boats that took part in the rescue, all were sunk by aircraft on later missions. Hartenstein was killed on the *U-156* east of Barbados in March 1943. Years later it was learned that the American pilot had correctly interpreted the rescue scene around the *U-156* but that the USAAF antisubmarine base on Ascension Island had ordered him to carry out the attack anyhow, on grounds that the U-boat remained a danger to ships in the area.

All too clearly, humaneness was no longer possible in the U-boat war. As a result of the Liberator attack on the *U-156*, Dönitz came to a far-reaching decision. "Never again," he vowed, "must submarines be exposed to the dangers of a rescue operation." To all U-boats he radioed an order that was to become notorious:

ALL ATTEMPTS TO RESCUE THE CREWS OF SUNKEN SHIPS WILL CEASE FORTHWITH. THIS PROHIBITION APPLIES EQUALLY TO THE PICKING UP OF MEN IN THE WATER AND PUTTING THEM ABOARD A LIFEBOAT, TO THE RIGHTING OF CAPSIZED LIFEBOATS AND TO THE SUPPLY OF FOOD AND WATER. SUCH ACTIVITIES ARE A CONTRADICTION OF THE PRIMARY OBJECT OF WAR, NAMELY, THE DESTRUCTION OF ENEMY SHIPS AND THEIR CREWS.

Britons, Italians and Poles pack the deck of the U-507 after being hauled from the South Atlantic on September 15, 1942. The U-156 had torpedoed the British transport Laconia on September 12. Discovering that Italian prisoners of war —Germany's allies—were on board, the U-156 called for assistance. The U-507 responded, and participated in one of the most bizarre rescues of the War.

Merciless now, with no quarter asked or given, the U-boat war moved into a winter that no one would forget. In the last three months of 1942, North Atlantic gales, seven of them at storm force 10, blew for 63 days out of 92. During that year, U-boats sank six million tons of Allied shipping—more than in 1939, 1940 and 1941 combined—and less than half of it was replaced by current production. In the savage battle of attrition, U-boat losses soared from 35 in 1941 to 87 in 1942. But Dönitz was now getting new boats at a rate of 17 a month, and by December 1942 he had 212 available for operations—more than at any previous time in the War. He used them to intensify his wolf-pack attacks, taking full advantage of the long, dark, stormy North Atlantic nights.

By March 5, 1943, B-Dienst, the German Naval Intelligence office, had learned from deciphered Royal Navy messages that three huge convoys were leaving New York for Britain. Designated by the Allies as SC-122, HX-229 and HX-229A, the three convoys totaled 141 ships from 10 countries and carried 920,000 tons of petroleum, frozen meat and other food, tobacco, grain, timber, minerals, steel, gunpowder, detonators, bombs, shells, trucks, locomotives, invasion barges, aircraft and tanks, together with some 9,000 seamen and 1,000 passengers. To intercept them, Dönitz deployed the largest concentration of U-boats in history—38 submarines deployed over an area covering 80,000 square miles.

With Kiel harbor faintly visible through its massive ribbing, a U-boat begins to take shape at Krupp's Germania Shipyard. U-boat chief Dönitz envisioned an all-out effort to build almost 30 new subs each month, but monthly output never exceeded 20.

A flood of freighters from American shipyards

President Franklin D. Roosevelt ruefully referred to them as "ugly ducklings," but these inelegant, 7,200-ton freighters—otherwise known as Liberty ships—proved to be the answer to Germany's U-boats. Mass-produced in American shipyards faster than the submarines could sink them, they carried more than 100 million tons of war matériel to the Allies.

The first United States-built Liberty ship, modeled on a beamy 1939 British prototype and christened the *Patrick Henry*, slid down the ways at Baltimore in September 1941. Another seven were completed during the next four months. But it was left to a California construction wizard named Henry J. Kaiser to realize the full potential of the simple, rugged design by applying the techniques of the automobile assembly line to the old-fashioned shipbuilding industry.

Kaiser knew so little about ships at first that he referred to the bow and the stern as the front and the back. But he did understand the techniques of designing machines with completely interchangeable parts, of prefabricating and stockpiling those parts, and of knocking them together without wasted effort. And he lost no time in securing for himself a government contract to produce Liberty ships.

Soon United States shipyards were turning out Liberty ships like so many Detroit flivvers. The average assembly time for the vessels, each with 30,000 parts, was reduced from 244 days in 1941 to an incredible 42 days in 1944. At one point four ships a day were being launched around the country.

All told, 2,710 Liberty ships were built, each one, in Roosevelt's words, "a blow for the liberty of the free peoples of the world," and in Henry Kaiser's, "a miracle of God and the genius of free American workmen."

Draped with a banner boasting her assembly time, the Liberty ship Robert E. Peary is launched in 1942.

Floodlights illuminate stacked deck sections at Baltimore's Bethlehem-Fairfield Shipyard, building site of 385 Liberty ships.

The wolf-pack tactics now brought to their zenith were a far cry from the lone exploits of the aces during the Happy Time. Dönitz organized his North Atlantic fleet in three groups, each given a name: Gruppe Raubgraf (Robber Baron), Gruppe Stürmer (Daredevil) and Gruppe Dränger (Harrier). Gruppe Raubgraf was to patrol off the Newfoundland coast. The other two were to locate themselves in the mid-Atlantic gap—the swath of ocean 200 to 300 miles wide that had so far proved beyond the range of Allied planes—spreading themselves out over about 600 miles from north to south. The boats were to act as the prongs of a giant rake, moving parallel to one another at distances of 20 to 50 miles apart. In the event that a U-boat sighted a convoy, it was forbidden to attack; instead it was to shadow the enemy, meanwhile sending regular signals from which U-boat headquarters could deduce all the vital facts—position, course, speed, number of ships, escort system and weather conditions—needed to convene the wolf pack for the kill. Only when the pack had gathered was the onslaught to begin.

As it happened, Convoy HX-229A swung around Gruppe Raubgraf and, except for losing one ship to an iceberg, made England safely. Convoys SC-122 (50 merchant ships, one rescue ship, nine escorts) and HX-229 (38 merchant ships, five escorts) were less fortunate.

Convoy HX-229 fell first into the vise between Gruppe Raubgraf, which caught the convoy from the west, and Gruppe Stürmer and Gruppe Dränger, sweeping from the east. In the early hours of March 16, Quartermaster Heinz Theen, who was in charge of the bridge watch on the U-653, made the first sighting. "The wind was very strong and it was very dark," Theen recalled later. "I saw a light directly ahead, only for about two seconds; I think it was a sailor on the deck of a steamer lighting a cigarette. I sent a message to the commander and by the time he had come up on the bridge we could see ships all around us. There must have been about 20; the nearest was on the port side between 500 meters and half a sea mile away. We did an alarm dive. As the ships of the convoy went over the top of us we could hear quite clearly the noises of the different engines—the diesels with fast revs, the steamers with slow revs and the turbines of the escorts with a singing noise. After about two hours we surfaced behind the convoy and sent off a sighting report."

Within minutes of receiving that report, Dönitz' headquarters flashed a momentous signal: ALL U-BOATS PROCEED WITH MAXIMUM SPEED TOWARD CONVOY GRID SQUARE BD 14. OVER 60 SHIPS COURSE NORTHEAST NINE KNOTS.

Their own radios chittering like jackals, 37 other U-boats turned toward the prey. Among them was the U-230, under Lieutenant Paul Siegmann. Throughout the day of March 16, the U-230 raced to catch up with Convoy HX-229. The submarine's first sighting came a few hours after sunset, when a lookout named Borchert, known for his keen eyes, reported: "Destroyer heading north, distance 4,000." The destroyer soon disappeared, and for the next two hours the U-230 sliced silently through the night. Then, at 10:40, Borchert reported: "Shadows on port, distance 6,500." Unable to restrain himself, he added: "It's the whole herd!"

Siegmann maneuvered for position, approaching the convoy from the southwest, to a point some 3,600 yards south and astern of the starboard column. There the boat steered a course parallel with the convoy's,

Admiral Karl Dönitz, head of the German U-boat arm, examines a map of enemy convoy positions with Chief of Operations Eberhard Godt (right) and Staff Operations Officer Adalbert Schnee. Dönitz esteemed Godt for his "unshakable imperturbability" and Schnee, who had sunk nearly 100,000 tons of shipping, for his experience in convoy battles.

while Siegmann peered through the darkness, assessing the enemy ships for their value as priority targets. At 11:30 a destroyer detached herself from the convoy and raced full speed across the U-230's wake, followed by a second escort. The U-230 turned, and then swung again into attack position.

"Destroyers astern, closing in fast," a watch officer reported.

But Siegmann was intent on his task. "Select your targets!" he shouted to his executive officer through the shrieking wind.

"Tubes 1 to 5, stand by!" ordered the officer.

"What are the fellows astern doing?" asked Siegmann. The destroyers were bearing down hard.

"Time is up," Siegmann yelled. "Shoot!" The executive officer pulled the firing lever five times, and Siegmann instantly began taking evasive action, first turning toward the tail of the convoy, then dodging into the cover of a snow squall. As he did so, explosions tore the night apart and three flaming ships fell out of line. Two of them broke up almost at once and the third drifted helplessly away into the North Atlantic darkness.

For the U-230, that was the end of the engagement; she had used up some of her torpedoes earlier in her patrol, and now the supply was exhausted. But as she turned for home, she left behind a battle that continued to rage in fullest fury, while the U-boats were cheered on by Dönitz, who signaled: BRAVO. KEEP AT IT. DO THE SAME AGAIN.

The night of March 16 was also a hard one for Convoy SC-122. Shortly after midnight the U-338 engaged Convoy SC-122, drawing so close—less than 200 yards—that the watch on the submarine bridge could see a man walking the deck of a ship carrying a flashlight. Four ships were torpedoed in this daring incursion. As 40 members of their British and Dutch crews were drowning or dying of exposure in the bleak watery wastes, the submarine crew celebrated with a breakfast of knackwurst.

The rest of that day, March 17, saw more sinking, more burning, more drowning, as the stricken convoy struggled eastward, given only partial respite by the inspired flying of a few new long-range Liberators from an RAF Coastal Command squadron base 900 miles away in Northern Ireland. These aircraft came out one at a time to cover the convoys, stretching their fuel reserves to the limits—one of the planes was airborne for an unprecedented 20½ hours—as they circled overhead and counterattacked the U-boats with depth charges and machine-gun fire, sometimes flying so low that their wing tips almost touched the waves. As the convoys drew slowly nearer to the shores of Britain, the air cover grew thicker and the U-boat attack began to let up. One by one, the U-boats peeled off and set a course for home. For them the attack had been a resounding success. On March 20, when the last U-boat withdrew from the surviving vessels of the shattered convoys, the combined wolf packs had sunk 22 Allied merchant ships of 146,596 tons; a quarter of the convoys' seamen and passengers had died. Only one U-boat had been sunk. To the returning U-boat men, Dönitz issued a triumphant message: "This is the greatest success ever achieved in a single convoy battle."

Dönitz would not long remain so jubilant—for almost overnight, in the immediate wake of the slaughter of Convoys HX-229 and SC-122, the tide of the U-boat war turned forever against the Germans.

Joyous homecomings for the undersea heroes

Recalling the cheering crowd of German Naval personnel that lined the quay when the *U-557* came home after its first war patrol in 1941, a crewman said, "And now we knew that we had jumped off the devil's shovel, and that life was sweet and rewarding." At U-boat bases all along the coast of occupied France—Lorient, Saint-Nazaire, Brest, La Pallice and Bordeaux—tumultuous scenes then awaited every submarine returning in triumph from a perilous mission against Allied shipping in the Atlantic. During the halcyon days of U-boat successes—from 1940 to 1942—Admiral Karl Dönitz himself was often on hand to greet his men and bestow Iron Crosses and combat badges. "I always visited the crews at once," remembered Dönitz. "When I saw them emaciated, strained, their pale faces crowned with beards and their leather jackets smeared with oil, there was a tangible bond between us."

The dockside celebrations, with their music and pretty servicewomen and congratulations from grinning senior officers, were only a foretaste of the pleasures the submariners could expect during their holiday from hell. Next, the men were escorted back to their quarters at home base for a steaming bath and a change of clothes, followed by a ceremonial dinner that lasted far into the night. But the real bonanza was a vacation lasting several weeks. The submariners might be sent to what they jokingly called the "U-boat pastures"—elegant French châteaux, and Alpine and seaside resorts, where their every whim was someone's command—or, if they wished, they might be granted home leave to visit their families in Germany.

Yet even as they sank into an idyll of rest and recuperation, the War stayed with them. "During the silent hours of solitude in my room," recalled one crew member on leave, "the memory of the fury and destruction we caused flashed vividly in my mind. The bellowing explosions of torpedoes, depth charges and bombs rang in my ears."

By mid-1943, as the tide of war changed and more and more U-boat nightmares became reality, the joyous welcomes grew less frequent. Returning to Brest in the spring of 1944, an officer of the *U-415* observed, "The pier was sparsely lighted. Only a few of the flotilla's brass found time to greet us." And by the middle of 1944 the dwindling numbers of returning crews often tied up at a quay that was as silent as the sea's own dim depths.

Bedecked with flowering branches and victory pennants, the U-552 docks at Saint-Nazaire after a successful mission in 1942. The white-capped commander is Erich Topp, third highest scoring German ace, who sank 193,684 tons of shipping. He was one of the relatively few U-boat men to survive the War.

Still wearing their coveralls, U-boat crewmen share a bottle of wine as they approach the port of Saint-Nazaire in 1942. "We were convinced," recalled one submariner, "that victory was only months away and that we had to hurry to sink our share of enemy vessels."

Wearing corsages given by their adoring public, crewmen of the U-558 feast on strawberries proffered by a German nurse at Brest. Fresh fruit was a delicacy submariners seldom enjoyed at sea; while on a combat mission they often had to make do on moldy bread and meat.

A group of just-returned submariners, the edelweiss insignia on their caps identifying them as the crew of the U-124, read German newspapers to catch up on the latest exploits of their comrades. Nazi propaganda persuaded the public and submariners alike that U-boat successes would bring the British to their knees.

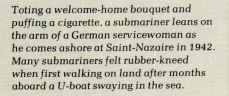

Toting a welcome-home bouquet and puffing a cigarette, a submariner leans on the arm of a German servicewoman as he comes ashore at Saint-Nazaire in 1942. Many submariners felt rubber-kneed when first walking on land after months aboard a U-boat swaying in the sea.

142

U-boat officers sunbathe at Le Treshier, a rest camp for submariners near Brest. "Life ran at full tide for me," one U-boat commander wrote of a sojourn in the South of France. "I lounged in the sun and swam with tanned French girls."

On leave in Lorient, U-boat crewmen inspect some delicate French lace at an outdoor stall. Submariners received bonus pay for their hazardous duty and could buy all manner of luxuries for wives and sweethearts, mothers and sisters.

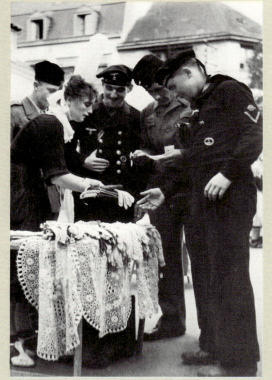

Carousing U-boat men drink and dance at a submariners' lounge in the summer of 1942. Admiral Karl Dönitz, chief of the U-boat arm, personally ordered the establishment of such luxury retreats.

Pausing between runs down an Alpine
slope, vacationing U-boat crewmen and a
pretty companion put their skis to
secondary use for a cat nap in the fresh air.

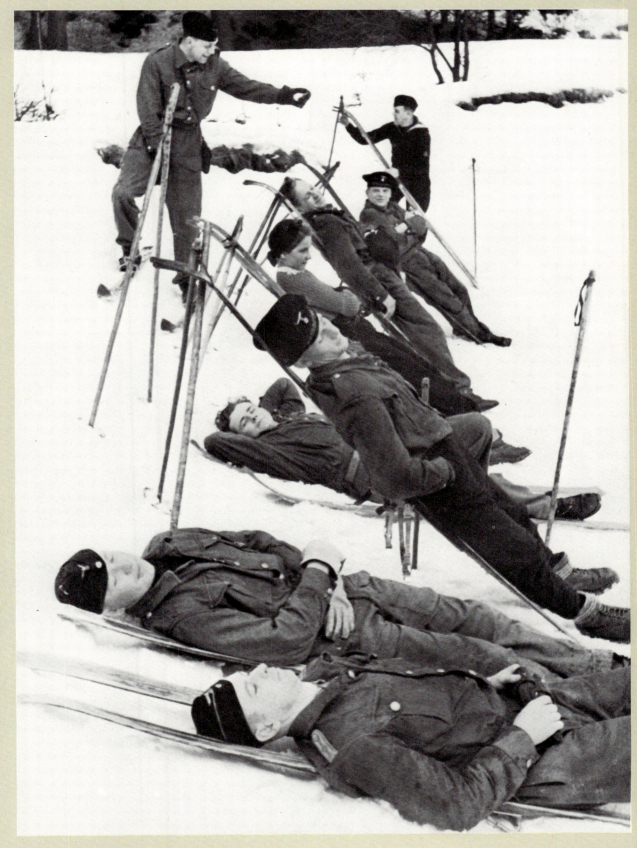

Chapter 6

Descent into nightmare

The Germans had scarcely six weeks to bask in the satisfaction of their great victories over the two Convoys SC-122 and HX-229 in mid-March, 1943. By the first week in May, Karl Dönitz—now promoted to the rank of Grand Admiral and installed in headquarters in Berlin—began to receive a succession of pitiful cries from the depths of the sea. Day after day, one U-boat after another radioed such distress signals as:

DESTROYER. ATTACKED. SINKING.

ATTACKED BY DESTROYERS. DEPTH CHARGES. LEAVING BOAT.

ATTACKED BY CORVETTE. SINKING.

AIRCRAFT. BOMBS. RAMMED BY DESTROYER. SINKING.

AIR ATTACK. SINKING 47 N. 5 W.

In their solitary worlds at sea, other U-boat men intercepted the signals and pondered their fateful meaning. Herbert A. Werner, first officer on the U-230, wondered: "What caused this sudden stream of messages that told us of nothing but dying?"

The answer—had Werner and his comrades only known it—would have devastated them. First, the British had managed to break the cipher in which Dönitz and his U-boat men communicated by radio; before much longer, their free transmission of radio messages, so crucial to the coordination of their wolf-pack attacks, was to be their undoing. Second, the full power of American might was beginning to tell. Third, British and American know-how had combined to produce a number of new wonder devices that would make it possible to hunt down and destroy the Germans in the farthest reaches of the sea. Together, the increase in manpower and matériel, the advanced technology and above all the heroic teamwork of the Allied antisubmarine forces were about to turn the tide of the War.

Perhaps the biggest coup of all in the new Allied counteroffensive, without which all the men, guns, planes, ships and devices could not have been nearly so effective, was the breaking of the cipher; it was an intelligence triumph of the first magnitude. That triumph hung on a wooden box no bigger than a suitcase—a mysterious box with a complicated and varied history.

As far back as 1926, German engineers had invented an electrical machine for enciphering messages. The device, simple to operate but complex in performance, was in effect a typewriter fitted with a set of three internal wheels that rotated when activated by electric impulses transmitted by the typewriter keys. Each wheel had 26 different contact points—one for every letter of the alphabet, but arranged in scrambled sequence. Depending on how the wheels were set, the punch of a lettered key would cause the first wheel to be engaged at some other specified letter; that wheel, in turn, would activate the two companion

Fatally stricken by a new Allied "Fido" acoustic torpedo dropped from a plane, the U-185, decks awash, rolls helplessly in the North Atlantic in August 1943. By that year the Germans were hard-pressed to keep pace with Allied technology; of all the branches of the German war machine, none was more severely affected by the struggle than the U-boat arm.

wheels, which in the end would light up still another letter on a board in front of the operator's eyes. As the operator typed out his message on the keyboard, he recorded the letters appearing on the board; these constituted the cipher, which could then be sent by Morse code to a receiver at some distant point. There someone with an equivalent machine and a code book of wheel settings would go through the process in reverse to decipher the message. For good and sufficient reason, the Germans called this contraption the Enigma.

The Enigma's three sequential wheels, each of which had its own scrambled pattern of letters, were interchangeable. There were six possible sequence combinations of the three wheels. Each new arrangement yielded a different permutation of the alphabet. Together, the various combinations made theoretically possible a mind-boggling three times 10^{18} settings for the machine. As the Enigma evolved during the 1930s, spare wheels were made available for use in the machine; with five spares, the number of possible wheel arrangements leaped from six to 336, and the number of settings rose accordingly to 209 billion. Another refinement came sometime later (it is not known exactly when) with the introduction of jacks and plugs similar to those on a telephone operator's switchboard; by increasing the number of electrical circuits, these devices increased the number of possible settings still further. In its final form, which it reached during the War, the Enigma machine had a total of three wheels, five spares and 10 different plugs, and an astronomical number of permutations—somewhere around 150 million million million.

By the beginning of World War II, the Germans had manufactured enough Enigma machines to start equipping the armed forces with them. Eventually the whole of Nazi-dominated Europe from the English Channel to the Volga River was in communication through Enigma-encoded radio signals; but because the Navy was in the vanguard, every ship and every U-boat carried an Enigma machine from the outset of the War. British listening posts could hear their ceaseless chatter by radio in Morse code that seemed to have no discernible pattern—for the Naval authorities changed settings every 24 hours (and the German high command assigned different settings to different branches of the armed forces). Nonetheless, the British were determined to unravel the mysteries packed into the Enigma box.

The daunting challenge fell to the Government Code and Cipher School—more informally known, after its initials, as the Golf, Cheese and Chess Society—located in a warren of offices in an ornate red-brick Victorian mansion at Bletchley Park in Buckinghamshire, some 60 miles from the nearest possible invasion beach. There, and in a cluster of corrugated-iron Nissen huts surrounding the main edifice, a brilliant collection of Oxford and Cambridge dons, mathematicians, linguists, chess experts and crossword-puzzle wizards labored over the German coding system for months on end.

The trail led back to Poland and the 1920s, a time when Europe was at peace and the Enigma machine was a commercial novelty—useful in confidential business dealings, for example—that could be purchased like any other hardware. One was bought by the Polish secret service. In the decade that followed, Polish inventors, working with the Enigma, developed another machine they called the Bombe, a protocomputer that enabled them to work out the calculations necessary for determining wheel settings on the Enigma. With the help of the Bombe, the Poles were able to make sense, at least occasionally, out of the various German communications that went over the airwaves as the Nazis rose to power during the 1930s.

By July 1939, Poland stood in danger of its life before the looming Nazi menace. Just in the nick of time—only a few weeks before Germany marched into Poland and opened World War II—a detail of Polish intelligence officials, acting on government orders, traveled to France with a set of technical drawings of the Bombe and how it worked, together with a Polish-built version of the German Enigma machine. In Paris they turned over their priceless burden to the head of French intelligence, who proceeded to Victoria Station in London. There he was met by his British counterpart, who in turn relayed the articles to the eager arms of Bletchley Park.

By now the contemporary German model, the Enigma M, was so versatile that it could handle a whole phalanx of cipher circuits for the different units that used it. The Navy alone had 13 cipher circuits (later the Navy would have 40); as the British would in time discern, each was known by a code name. Aegir was the cipher for surface warships in foreign seas. Tetis was for U-boats training in the Baltic. Hydra was for operational U-boats. The Bombe could by no means read them clearly; it was merely a tool for beginning to pry open the Enigma's secrets. "We seemed to be pygmies around a monster," one Bletchley Park section chief recalled. "We felt the tremor of a nerve, the flexing of a muscle, and then the great head moving toward a new prey."

It soon became evident to members of British Naval Intelligence that the only way of cracking Hydra was to acquire an up-to-date Enigma machine, complete with the current setting and all the secret Hydra cipher books and other relevant documents. The captains of Royal Navy warships were therefore given orders to take every opportunity of capturing German Naval vessels with their radio-signal equipment intact. Little by little, small heists, pulled off before the crews of the captured ships had time to destroy all of their secret communications gear, helped the pieces of the Hydra puzzle fall into place. In February 1940 an English vessel captured the *U-33* and bagged three Enigma wheels. In March 1941 another English vessel captured an armed German trawler that yielded another Enigma wheel. On May 7 still a third English vessel captured a German weather ship and with it a cipher book that gave some of the Enigma settings for the next three months. And just two days afterward, on May 9, came a grand coup and a prize whose value was beyond reckoning.

The victim was none other than Lieutenant Fritz-Julius Lemp, the man who had fired the first torpedo of the War and sunk the liner *Athenia* in September 1939. Now, more than a year and a half later, Lemp was pursuing a well-escorted eastbound convoy off the south coast of Greenland in the *U-110*, a brand new Type IX U-boat on her first patrol. At one minute before noon, Lemp launched a submerged attack on the convoy,

hitting two merchant ships with a fan of three torpedoes. The glow of the Happy Time had not worn off, and Lemp was overconfident. Instead of running away, he remained at periscope depth to watch the effect of the torpedoes on his victims. Within a minute or two, the periscope was spotted by the escort corvette *Aubretia*, which pounced at once and threw down a full pattern of 10 depth charges. Lemp escaped the blast by diving deep and altering course 90 degrees hard to starboard. But he was firmly held in the *Aubretia's* asdic beam, and about 20 minutes after the first counterattack came a second, which sent the *U-110* sinking by the stern to more than 300 feet before Lemp gave the order to blow the main ballast tanks.

By now two other escorts had joined the *Aubretia*, and they watched as the submarine rose from the depths and broke surface. Then they opened up with every gun they could bring to bear. Lemp and many of the U-boat men jumped into the sea. Others were hit as they poured out of the *U-110's* conning tower. Commander A. J. Baker-Cresswell was rushing the destroyer *Bulldog* in to ram when he suddenly realized that he might have a chance to capture the U-boat. Giving the order for full speed astern, he brought the *Bulldog* to a stop 100 yards from the wallowing submarine and at once commanded, "Away armed boat's crew!" A boarding party consisting of Sublieutenant David Balme and eight

A whaleboat is lowered from the British destroyer Bulldog to deliver a boarding party to the crippled U-110 on May 9, 1941, off the coast of Greenland. The U-boat's commander, Fritz-Julius Lemp (below), failed to destroy his Enigma ciphering machine and code books. Seized by the British, they contributed to one of the most significant intelligence breakthroughs of World War II.

men armed with rifles, revolvers and hand grenades rowed off toward the U-boat in a small whaler.

During the short interval since abandoning the *U-110*, Lemp had been encouraging his crew as they floated helplessly in the water. It was standard procedure to set scuttling charges inside a disabled U-boat, but for some reason the charges failed to detonate now. When Lemp realized that all his code books, cipher documents, marked charts and special equipment, including the vessel's Enigma machine, were about to fall into the hands of the enemy, he apparently took desperate steps.

Exactly what happened to him in the next few moments has never been made public. According to a deliberately vague British version put out after the War, when the exact significance of the capture was still a closely guarded secret, Lemp threw up his arms and committed suicide by drowning. But according to a later, more likely account he swam back toward the U-boat—perhaps with the forlorn idea of resetting the scuttling charges—and as he was attempting to clamber back on board he was shot dead by a member of the British prize party. At any event, it is certain that he was never rescued from the water. Thus perished one of the Third Reich's most aggressive U-boat commanders—who had now inadvertently made a monumental contribution to his country's final defeat.

The British captors found an eerie scene inside the abandoned submarine. Blue emergency lighting burned in the dank dark. "Coats were flung around and bunks half-made," wrote Sublieutenant Balme. In the surrounding sea other escorts were depth-charging other U-boats. "There was complete silence in the U-boat," Balme continued, "except for the continual thud-thud of our own ships' depth charges." Sound is five times louder in water than in air, and the shock waves were hitting the submarine's hull like a huge hammer. "This was a most unpleasant sound," Balme continued, "especially when the detonations came closer." There was a nasty possibility that those depth charges might detonate the explosive charges inside the *U-110*.

The boarding party wasted not a moment. Balme made straight for the code books and charts, while a signaler went into the radio office and took on the task of dismantling the heavy cipher machine. The British seamen then formed a chain and carefully passed the precious equipment and documents hand to hand up the conning-tower ladder and along the slippery deck to the whaleboat. After four tense hours of work the job was finished. Then the *U-110* was taken in tow, but she sank a day or so later.

On May 12 the *Bulldog*, with the U-boat's survivors on board and two large packing cases of Enigma material in the captain's cabin, entered Scapa Flow, now back in service as the Home Fleet base after Prien's raid nearly 19 months before. The ship was at once boarded by Special Naval Intelligence officers, who examined every item and carefully photographed every page of the documents. "This," one of them pronounced, with perfectly characteristic British understatement, "is what we have been looking for."

Four hundred men had witnessed the capture of the *U-110* and its Enigma machine, which was to make it possible for British intelligence at Bletchley Park at long last to comprehend German messages. While probably only a few realized what was being taken out of the sub, even the fact of the U-boat's capture had to be kept secret if the Germans were not to know that their cipher security had been penetrated. All the men were instructed not to talk about the matter. Not a single one of the 400 breathed a word of it for the remainder of the War. That in itself was a heroic feat, for in large measure the Allied successes that ensued were possible only because Dönitz and his staff never had an inkling that the British had an ear to the keyhole. Indeed, the whole affair remained secret for some 30 years, until the Allied governments began to release previously classified documents.

Meanwhile the British government expressed its gratitude in decorous fashion. Commander Baker-Cresswell was immediately promoted to captain, and he and all of his men were awarded medals of honor by King George VI—even while being sworn not to reveal to anyone why they received them.

The Enigma material, rushed from Scapa Flow to Bletchley Park, was a godsend. The machine was complete with almost all its daily settings for a three-month U-boat cruise, and these did not expire until the end of June. With immense speed the cryptanalysts penetrated the U-boat Hydra code. Within a week they could read operational U-boat radio traffic, deciphering some of it almost as swiftly as the German wireless operators to whom it was transmitted. It was like being suddenly blessed with the gift of hearing after a life of deafness. The U-boat war entered a new phase. The life cycle of a U-boat became an open book. Everything—a U-boat's whereabouts, targets, often even the amount of fuel that it had in its tanks and the number of torpedoes it had available for firing—was revealed.

The British made use of their new weapon by a system that was deceptively simple. The network of stations that monitored foreign wireless transmissions all over the world, called Y Service, passed on the U-boats' enciphered radio signals. Bletchley Park deciphered and translated them and passed them along by teleprinter to the Submarine Tracking Room, whose function was to collect, coordinate, analyze and disseminate any information that could throw light on German naval operations. This vital adjunct of the Operational Intelligence Center was buried deep underground beneath the Admiralty's concrete "Citadel" in the heart of London.

There the information became the province of one of the War's most unsung heroes—an obscure young ex-barrister by the name of Rodger Winn, a reserve officer in British Naval Intelligence with a twisted back and a limp. Together with a small band of associates in Britain—and later, America—Winn kept a vigil on the German U-boats, overseeing an undertaking that was referred to variously as "Special Intelligence," "Z" and "Fred." Churchill called the information produced by Winn's group the "golden eggs." This most precious intelligence of World War II finally ended up with the label "Ultra" (from "Ultra Secret," more secret even than "Hush Most Secret"). As passed on to Operational Command for direct action, Ultra turned out to be nothing less than a war-winning weapon.

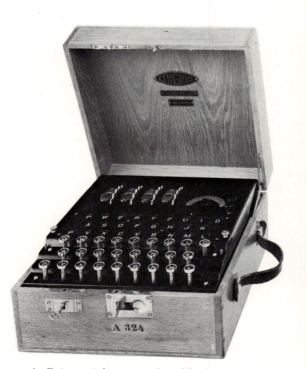

An Enigma ciphering machine like this one—a set of typewriter keys wired electrically to a number of rotors— enabled German cryptographers, by simply altering rotors and settings, to change the cipher for messages passed between ship and shore. The machine could express any communication in a near infinitude of letter combinations.

At Western Approaches Command
Center in Liverpool—nerve center of the
U-boat counteroffensive—top brass
and their staff keep watch on the war at sea.
Supplementing Allied reconnaissance
reports with intercepted German messages,
such teams plotted on a wall map 80
by 30 feet the position of every vital
vessel at sea, both friend and foe.

Naturally, it was not all clear sailing. The British had had the machine only nine months when it suddenly seemed not to be working any more; the signals were as much gibberish as before. The reason, it turned out, was that on February 1, 1942, the German Navy acquired a new model of the Enigma machine, and while he was at it Dönitz replaced the Hydra cipher with a new one called Triton. Bletchley Park worked for nearly a year before it was able to crack the Triton cipher—exactly how it was done has never been disclosed—and in that fatal interval Allied shipping losses soared catastrophically. During the first quarter of 1942, before the ciphering change-over was complete, Allied losses had amounted to 800,000 tons. In the quarter that followed, their losses almost doubled, reaching 1.4 million tons. And they kept on going up for the remainder of the year.

By the end of 1942, when Winn and his team were again able to follow the U-boat conversations, the Allies had the massed strength—more men and more and better matériel—to bring to bear on the German U-boats. At about this time the British Coastal Command was beginning to receive American-made Liberators that had been modified to fly at ranges of up to 800 miles—thereby enabling them to penetrate to the mid-Atlantic gap where U-boats had previously prospered with impunity from the air—and that were equipped with new, light 10-centimeter radar sets with a beam that could detect small objects on the ocean's surface. Moreover, the United States Navy by now had its own Ultra-fed Submarine Tracking Room, which was working in the closest possible cooperation with Winn's group.

But there were still occasional troubles to contend with back at Bletchley Park. In March 1943, just when Convoys SC-122 and HX-229 were preparing to sail out of New York waters for their ill-starred crossing to Great Britain, the U-boats changed over to still another new model, M4 Enigma, with four rotors instead of three. For a few crucial days while the convoys stumbled into the wolf-pack trap, Winn's vision was blurred by the decrypting complications that resulted from the change. But by a remarkable feat of cryptanalysis, Bletchley Park broke the new M4 ciphers in less than a fortnight. The results were almost immediate. The U-boats accomplished virtually nothing in April; May, with Bletchley Park back on the scent, would become known to the Germans as "the month of the lost U-boats."

The first strikes came in the opening days of that bloody month. Some 500 miles east of Cape Farewell, Greenland, a 20-boat wolf pack deployed at intervals of only eight miles lay in wait in heavy seas amid drifting icebergs, directly athwart the path of an eastbound convoy designated ONS-5, composed of 37 merchantmen escorted by two destroyers, one frigate, four corvettes and two rescue trawlers. As backup, 11 more U-boats took positions farther along the convoy's course. But the Allies, unknown to the U-boat commanders, were given advance warning of the ambush by Ultra's network and had already dispatched reinforcements in the form of five destroyers from St. John's, Newfoundland. Subsequently the sloop Pelican, three frigates and a cutter were also rushed to the scene.

During May 4, winds that had been blowing at gale force quieted sufficiently to permit Royal Canadian Air Force flying boats to cover the convoy; one of them promptly bombed and sank the *U-630*. By nightfall a deadly battle was joined as the U-boats retorted by sinking five merchant ships. Toward the end of the night, the firing briefly died away—only to resume at daylight on May 5, when the corvette *Pink*, which had been busily engaged in rounding up stragglers, sighted and sank the *U-192*. During the course of that day four additional merchant ships were torpedoed, and on the night of May 5 the U-boats, in the words of the convoy's senior commander, were attacking "from every direction except ahead."

The results were tragic—for the aggressors. The corvette *Loosestrife* pursued the *U-638* and sank it, and the destroyer *Vidette* made use of a new weapon, called the Hedgehog, to sink the *U-125*. The Hedgehog was a 24-barrel mortar that fired a pattern of small bombs ahead of the attack ships while the targeted U-boat was still held in the asdic beam. Unlike depth charges, these mortar bombs were designed to explode upon making contact with the U-boat's hull rather than on reaching a preset depth. Only a little later the destroyer *Oribi* spotted a U-boat as it slid silently out of the fog nearby; the *Oribi* rammed and sank the *U-531*. Finally, at 4 a.m., the battle came to an end when the sloop *Pelican* depth-charged and destroyed the *U-438*.

As the U-boats turned away from the battle, they left behind them 12 sinking merchant ships. But the wolf pack had lost six U-boats—plus a seventh sunk while heading for the rendezvous before the battle, when it was bombed by a Flying Fortress. In raw numbers the U-boats had won again. But American shipyards were by now launching 140 merchantmen per month, and the attritional exchange was one the U-boats could not for long endure.

A week or two later, in an attack against the 38-ship Convoy SC-130 out of Halifax, a 17-boat wolf pack lost six of its members without sinking a single merchant ship. Among those who went down was Dönitz' own son Peter, a member of the crew on board the *U-954*. The convoys, having been alerted by Ultra, zigzagged right around the wolf packs. For the rest of the month, the plight of the U-boats went from bad to worse. By the end of that terrible May, a total of 41 U-boats had gone down, most of them sunk by aircraft armed with new equipment—detecting devices that could pick up a submerged U-boat's magnetic field from aloft, and acoustic torpedoes that could be dropped from the air and could then find their way to submerging submarines by homing in on the sound of the U-boats' propellers.

Assailed both from the sky and on the surface, harried by depth charges and torpedoes that followed them to their lairs deep in the sea, the U-boat men now were suffering hardships of a sort they had not encountered before this time. Years later, Lieutenant Herbert Werner, who served aboard the *U-230*, was to publish a submariner's-eye view of a battle that took place on May 12. His U-boat was part of a wolf pack that was attempting to attack an eastbound convoy of more than 100 ships almost in the center of the Atlantic.

"0955: A startled cry at my back, 'Aircraft!' I saw a twin-engined plane dropping out of the sun. The moment of surprise was total.

A feisty guardian of convoys

Mike in hand, Walker coaches his sub killers.

"The best defence," Royal Navy Captain F. J. (Johnny) Walker wrote in 1942 of his convoy-escorting duties, "is to go out for kills." By then, Johnny Walker's right to strong opinions about his job was unimpeachable and he ultimately became the War's leading antisubmarine ace, with a record 21 kills. But for a time, his views about U-boat fighting—shaped while he was a lieutenant aboard a destroyer in World War I—had met little enthusiasm. Labeled a maverick by superiors, he was denied advancement to captain in 1938.

He finally was given an escort squadron in 1941 and immediately put his ideas to work. Not content to view escorts as defensive buffers, he introduced the risky but successful daytime practice of leaving the convoy partly exposed and sending escorts to chase U-boats sighted nearby. When a wolf pack attacked at night, his escorts moved into a prearranged formation, each ship blanketing an assigned zone with depth charges and firing flares over escape routes.

Walker's tactics paid off. On an early mission in the Atlantic in 1941, he directed the destruction of four U-boats in five days. His techniques were swiftly adopted throughout the Royal Navy, and his feisty confidence won him admirers in all Allied fleets. After he died—from a stroke when he was safe ashore in 1944—sub-chasing sailors still remembered his trademark exhortation: "Beat the pants off her."

" 'Alarrrmmm!' We plunged head over heels into the conning tower. The boat reacted at once and shot below surface. Four short ferocious explosions shattered the water above and around us. The boat trembled and fell at a 60-degree angle. I saw astonishment in the round eyes of the men. Where had the small plane come from?

"1035: The *U-230* rose to periscope depth. A careful check with our skyscope revealed no aircraft. We surfaced quickly. The hunt went on.

"1110: I detected a glint of metal between the clouds. It was a small aircraft, and it was diving into the attack.

" 'Alarrrmmm!' In 50 seconds four explosions rocked boat and crew.

"1125: The *U-230* surfaced. We drove forward and clung to the fringes of the convoy with grim determination. We raced in defiance of fear and sudden destruction—always forward, toward the head of the convoy.

"1142: 'Aircraft—alarrrmmm!' "

The *U-230* crash-dived yet again. Four explosions shook her hull. As the afternoon progressed, airplanes attacked the submarine four times more, twice surprising the U-boat so effectively that she did not have time to dive.

"The small aircraft grew enormous fast," Werner said of one of these attacks. "It dived upon us, machine-gunning the open rear of the bridge as the boat turned to starboard. Neither the mate nor I was able to fire a single bullet; our guns were jammed. The aircraft dropped four bombs, which I saw falling toward me, then roared over the bridge so close that I could feel its engine's hot exhaust brush my face. Four bombs in a row erupted alongside our starboard saddle tanks. Four high fountains collapsed over the two of us at the guns." That plane, having used up all of the bombs in its payload, flew away, but another one arrived on the scene about an hour later.

"Again it was too late to dive. The single-engined plane came in low in a straight line exactly over our wake. I fingered the trigger of my gun. Again the gun was jammed. I kicked its magazine, clearing the jam. Then I emptied the gun at the menace. Our boat veered to starboard, spoiling the plane's bomb run. The pilot revved up his engine, circled, then roared toward us from dead ahead. As the plane dived very low, its engine spluttered, then stopped. Wing first, the plane crashed into the surging ocean, smashing its other wing on our superstructure as we raced by. The pilot, thrown out of his cockpit, lifted his arm and waved for help, but then I saw him disintegrate in the explosion of the four bombs that were meant to destroy us."

During that afternoon of violence, Werner remembered, his submarine received radio distress signals from three other members of the wolf pack, the *U-89, U-186* and *U-456.* They had been hit and were sinking. "With a shudder," Werner wrote later, "I pictured what would happen to us once our own hull was cracked." At 4:38 p.m. the *U-230* at last reached a position from which she would be able to attack the convoy. "Tubes 1 to 5 stand ready," commanded Lieutenant Paul Siegmann, his eyes to the periscope. Then suddenly he shouted, "Down with the boat, chief, take her down for God's sake, destroyer in ramming position! Down to 200 meters!"

The U-boat dived and the depth charging began. The charges were

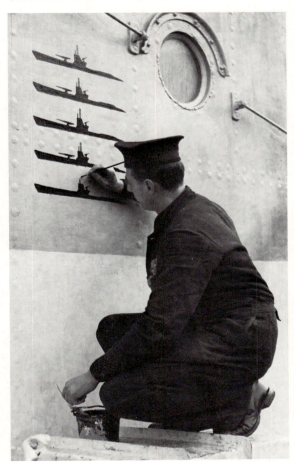

Meticulously painting a U-boat silhouette on the side of the wheelhouse, a seaman aboard the British destroyer Hesperus brings his ship's record up to date: five U-boat kills in May 1943. Allied forces, using increasingly sophisticated and coordinated air and sea attacks, sank an unprecedented 41 German submarines that month.

dropped in spreads of 24, a new spread surrounding the submarine with hull-jolting explosions every 20 minutes. The underwater bombardment went on and on.

"2000: We sat helpless 265 meters below. Our bodies were stiff from cold, stress and fear. The bilges were flooded with water, oil and urine. Our washrooms were under lock and key; to use them could have resulted in instant death, for the tremendous outside pressure would have acted in reverse. Cans were circulated for the men to use to relieve themselves. Added to the stench of waste, sweat and oil was the stink of the battery gases. The increasing humidity condensed on the cold steel, dropped into the bilges, dripped from pipes and soaked our clothes. By midnight the captain realized that the British were not going to let up in their bombardment, and he ordered the distribution of potash cartridges to supplement breathing." The purpose of the potash was to take carbon dioxide out of the air that the U-boat's crew breathed. "Before much longer, every man was equipped with a large metal box attached to his chest, a rubber hose leading to his mouth, and a clamp fastened on his nose. And still we waited."

The depth charging continued the next day, May 13, which was Werner's birthday. "I wondered whether it would be my last," he wrote. All that night the explosions kept coming. "By midnight we had approached the limit for boat and crew. We had reached a depth of 280 meters and the boat was still sinking. I dragged myself through the aisle, pushing and tossing men around, forcing them to stay awake. Whoever fell asleep might never be awakened."

Not until nearly dawn on May 14, some 35 hours after the attack had begun, did the escorts give up and make off. At 4:30 a.m. on May 14 the *U-230* surfaced. "Still numb from the murderous assault and stiff from the cold depths," Werner recalled, "we added up our account. Three U-boats in our group had been sunk. Well over 100 Allied ships had plowed past us, and we had not been able to sink a single one. We might now expect that some 700,000 tons of war matériel had safely reached the British Isles. It was not a pretty picture."

Grand Admiral Karl Dönitz, knowing what his men were enduring, and suffering with them, still felt bound to urge them onward. BE HARD AND RUTHLESS IN ACTION, Dönitz exhorted. ATTACK AND SINK. GIVE NO THOUGHT TO FUEL. After plugging the northern convoy route with four wolf packs in a staggered interception line, Dönitz radioed: WITH 31 U-BOATS SOMETHING CAN AND MUST BE ACCOMPLISHED. But nothing was. As yet another convoy threatened to slip through the U-boat net without suffering a single loss, Dönitz radioed: THE CONVOY ABSOLUTELY MUST BE FOUND AGAIN. DO YOUR BEST. SUCCESS MUST COME TONIGHT. But success did not come, and a frustrated Dönitz radioed his complaint: WE CAN SEE NO EXPLANATION FOR THE FAILURE.

But the Grand Admiral did, in fact, have an explanation of sorts, and he advanced it in a series of messages to all U-boats: OUR HEAVY U-BOAT LOSSES OF THE LAST MONTH ARE ATTRIBUTABLE PRIMARILY TO THE PRESENT SUPERIORITY OF THE ENEMY'S LOCATION DEVICES AND THE SURPRISE FROM THE AIR THAT THESE DEVICES HAVE MADE POSSIBLE. MORE THAN HALF OF OUR TOTAL LOSSES HAVE COME ABOUT AS A RESULT OF THIS SURPRISE.

Caught by a searchlight's beam, crewmen of the U-606 fall in a hail of fire from the U.S. Coast Guard cutter George W. Campbell during a wolf-pack attack on an Atlantic convoy in February 1943. The Campbell sank the U-boat, killing 36 of its crew. Combat artist Anton Otto Fischer was aboard the Campbell and later painted this scene.

Groping blindly from known effects to unknown causes, Dönitz and his experts speculated fruitlessly as to what exactly the Allied location devices might consist of. Was the enemy picking up some kind of ray emitted by the U-boat—infrared, heat rays, electronic rays of various kinds? Even the most outlandish suggestions were considered. For example, Lieutenant Hans-Helmuth Bugs, aboard the U-629, surmised that the Allies were cunningly using some sort of strange new aircraft; he reported that his vessel had been approached abeam by a flying disk that winked white, yellow and red.

In the end, U-boat headquarters attributed their losses to radar—and were so convinced they had arrived at the right answer that they dismissed all other possibilities. When the suspicion that the Allies might be reading U-boat radio traffic was so much as mentioned—as, inevitably, it was—Dönitz' experts scoffed at the notion. "An insight into our own cipher does not come into consideration," asserted one report from the U-boat staff. "Our ciphers were checked and rechecked," wrote Dönitz, "and on each occasion the head of the Naval Intelligence Service at Naval high command adhered to his opinion that it would be impossible to decipher them."

The U-boat Triton code thus remained unchanged, the British and

Americans continued to read German transmissions, and more U-boats were sunk. Finally, on May 24, 1943, after losing eight boats out of 33 sent against two convoys, without a single torpedo being fired, Dönitz transmitted a momentous signal to all U-boats: They were to retreat from the North Atlantic convoy routes to safer positions toward the south. This sudden move purported to be a tactical withdrawal to allow time for new weapons and better defenses to be found. In fact, it meant that after 45 months of being ahead in the U-boat war, Germany was losing her potency at sea.

For the most part, Germany's military leaders—including Adolf Hitler himself—failed to see just how grievously the U-boat weapon had been blunted. At a conference with Dönitz only a week later, Hitler, who had refused to give his Navy enough U-boats at a time when they could have made a decisive difference, agreed to step up production. "There can be no talk of a letup in U-boat warfare," the Führer insisted. "The Atlantic is my first line of defense in the west, and even if I have to fight a defensive war there, that is preferable to waiting to defend myself on the coast of Europe. The enemy forces tied up by our U-boat warfare are tremendous, even though the actual losses being inflicted by us are no longer great. I cannot afford to release these forces by discontinuing the U-boat warfare."

Dönitz' fleet of U-boats would continue the struggle for another two years, but they did so now without the slightest prospect of victory. Dönitz seemed to have some private misgivings, but he necessarily kept them to himself until after the War was over. "The question was," he wrote in retrospect, "would the U-boat arm itself appreciate the bitter necessity of continuing a campaign in which there was no longer any chance of major success, and would it be prepared to do so in a spirit of selfless devotion to duty?"

It would indeed—to the very end. During the dreadful months of dying that remained to the U-boats, their operations were sustained by the devotion of their captains and the superb spirit of their crews. They were also sustained by the fact that by this time many of the U-boat men had very little left to live for. Their hometowns were reduced to bombed-out rubble overrun by foreign armies. Their families and sweethearts were among the numberless civilian dead. Anonymous placards among the ruins echoed their own sentiments: OUR CITIES CRUMBLE, OUR WALLS COLLAPSE, BUT OUR HEARTS NEVER BREAK. U-boat men who discovered while they were on leave that their homes had ceased to exist curtailed their vacations and hurried back to their boats and fellow crewmen—the only world to which they now belonged. To them death seemed as inevitable as night. And by April they were going to their death at the rate of two or three boats a day.

Many of the captains—among them Lieutenant Commander Wolfgang Lüth, the second most successful U-boat commander of the War, with 43 ships and 225,712 tons to his credit—were keen students of human psychology. In a lecture given to a convention of naval officers in Weimar in 1943, Lüth told of some of the measures that he used to help maintain morale. He let his men have a look through the periscope or come up onto the bridge in turns to watch a steamer sinking or a whale

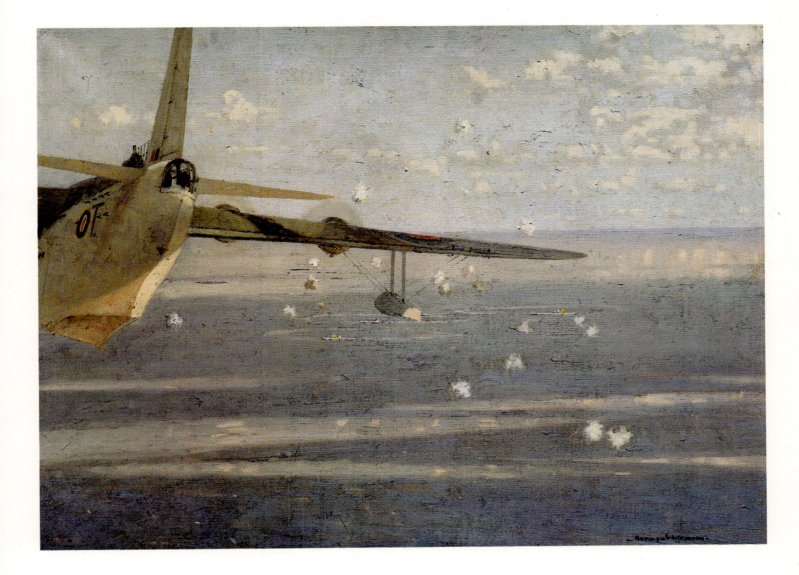

Disregarding flak, a British Sunderland swoops down to attack a submarine pack in this oil painting by Norman Wilkinson. With a 3,000-mile range and a formidable armament of depth charges, bombs and machine guns, the Sunderland played a vital role in the aerial campaign the Allies launched against the U-boats in 1943.

blowing or the aurora borealis high in the sky. He ran a ship's paper. He staged a chess competition, a tall-story championship, a funny-verse contest and a singing competition; first prize was to be allowed off a watch duty, second prize for a seaman was to start the diesel engine, and for a machinist a spell on the bridge running the ship in place of the captain. Lüth encouraged self-improvement on board and arranged lectures on such subjects as the Atlantic and its climate and fauna, the Gulf Stream, flying fishes and trade winds. At Christmas the crew would light candles on ersatz fir wreaths fashioned out of twisted towels and green toilet paper, and in the bow torpedo compartment a Santa Claus wrapped in a bed sheet would give each man a present of some candy and a personally inscribed book.

Miscreants were few, and Lüth rarely found it necessary to resort to disciplinary measures—fortunately, for there certainly was no way he could imprison a man on a U-boat, and there were few ways to restrict his liberty. For some offenses Lüth would occasionally deprive a subordi-

nate of his bunk and condemn him to sleep on the bow compartment's metal deck plates without a mattress or blankets for three days as a punishment. And on occasion he went so far as to threaten to send a man to a penal battalion on the Eastern Front at the end of a patrol. Yet he never lost confidence in his crew. "It is the duty of every captain to have faith in his men," he said, "even if they have disappointed him at one time or another."

Such faith went a long way toward keeping up morale. But it could not beat back the combined forces that beset the U-boats after their withdrawal from the North Atlantic convoy routes. The Allies had divided their theaters of responsibility, and during the summer of 1943 the brunt of the campaign against the U-boats in the whole of the South Atlantic fell to the Americans. Expanded, improved and reorganized since their humiliating defeats the previous year in their own waters, the antisubmarine forces of the newly formed United States Tenth Fleet took a savage toll of the U-boats that were now trying to rally west of the Azores. Dönitz had not had the foresight to anticipate the potential of aircraft carriers as convoy escorts.

Carriers acting as escorts now filled the mid-Atlantic air-cover gap that land-based planes had been unable to reach. Carrier-borne Wildcats and Avengers, put on the scent of U-boat movements by Ultra intelligence via the American Submarine Tracking Room, attacked U-boats with bombs, depth charges, torpedoes and cannon fire. Of 489 U-boats

Home from the hunt, a U-boat noses into a bunker in German-occupied Saint-Nazaire. Such U-boat pens, sited in ports around the Bay of Biscay, were roofed with reinforced concrete 16 feet thick, sufficient to withstand the most powerful bombs in the Allied arsenal.

sunk at sea from January 1943 onward, 93 were the victims of United States forces with the direct or indirect aid of Ultra. The American onslaught was so fierce that Dönitz found it prohibitive to form groups of U-boats and instead was forced to assign them individually. The day of the wolf pack was done.

Even so, there remained two focal points where Allied forces could find U-boats en masse. One was in the vicinity of the U-boat tankers, the milch cows around which the U-boats had to huddle for life-giving fuel during their long patrols in the South Atlantic (*pages 124-129*). By October 1943 the United States Navy had virtually smashed the entire fleet of U-tankers, thereby dramatically shrinking the operational area of the U-boats.

The other critical area was the Bay of Biscay, which all U-boats had to cross in order to gain access to their French bases. No sooner had the U-boats retreated from the North Atlantic than large British antisubmarine forces rushed in to concentrate their efforts on the U-boats' routes across the bay. U-boat kills there reached a peak of 18 in July 1943. They totaled 41 by early August.

By then U-boat Command was at its wit's end. "Diving is death," Dönitz admonished his commanders, reasoning that the speed of an attacking plane ensured that it would be able to drop a bomb or two on a diving U-boat before the vessel could get deep enough to escape. It was best to remain on the surface and fight. U-boats began crossing the bay in groups, with the hope that the combined firepower of their antiaircraft guns would be sufficient to drive the aircraft off. When that tactic failed, they were told to sneak home submerged through the inshore waters of the Spanish coast. But even for the U-boats that managed to elude Allied hunters near their bases there was no respite. As far away as the mouth of the Amazon, Lieutenant Commander Gerhard Thäter radioed from the *U-466* what was coming to be an all too familiar lament: AIR PATROL, AS IN BAY OF BISCAY. RADAR DAY AND NIGHT. Altogether, 237 U-boats were sunk during 1943.

In spite of the disasters that befell his fleet during that year, Dönitz had hopes for a revival of U-boat power. It had become clear that the only way a U-boat might be able to escape air attack was to operate submerged for prolonged periods. And by January 1944, the Germans finally had a means of achieving that purpose: they had put into operation what was perhaps the most significant of their many U-boat modifications—the snorkel (*page 161*).

The snorkel was a long tube, like a large periscope, which sucked in air from the surface and thus enabled the U-boat to run on its diesel motors at periscope depth, about 45 feet down, and to recharge its batteries while remaining submerged. To be sure, the snorkel had limitations. The U-boat could not use its diesels during an attack because their noise was easily picked up by the enemy. Nor was it possible for the submarine to cruise at more than six knots under diesel power because above that speed the wake created by the snorkel's head on the surface became too noticeable. But the simple and economical snorkel did vastly reduce the chance of detection from the air, thus giving the U-boats a new lease on

Pounded by bombs dropped from American aircraft, Saint-Nazaire erupts during one of the daily strikes flown against Bay of Biscay ports in the spring of 1943. "Not a dog, not a cat is left in these towns," observed Admiral Dönitz at the end of the ordeal. "Nothing remains but the U-boat pens."

life. As the American Submarine Tracking Room reported: "It was a half-way revolution in submarine warfare, a difference in degree but not in kind, a stage in the transformation of the U-boat into something like a true underwater cruiser."

The production of snorkels and their installation on existing U-boats became the U-boat Navy's top priority. But the process was agonizingly slow, and of the 61 U-boats collected in the Biscay bases at the beginning of June 1944 fewer than half were snorkel boats. By that time the Allies were ready to mount an enormous invasion of the Normandy coast. And on June 6, D-Day, when the invasion came, not a single U-boat got close enough to launch a torpedo against the Allied invasion fleet.

It was widely known that the Allies had something massive brewing. But the German Navy, like the rest of the German high command, had been utterly confused as to where the invasion would take place and, even as 5,000 Allied ships steamed across the English Channel, Grand Admiral Dönitz, fearing the move was a diversion, held his boats in the Biscay ports to await developments. Not until the evening of D-Day did 15 U-boats—eight of them without snorkels—sail out from Brest, under orders from their Grand Admiral that said: "Every boat that inflicts losses on the enemy while he is landing has fulfilled its primary function even though it perishes in so doing!"

The odds were overwhelmingly against them. Constant and intensive sea and air sweeps blocked both ends of the Channel leading to the invasion area. Of the U-boats that had originally sallied from Brest without snorkels, only three eventually returned to base—one of them so badly mauled that its chief engineer ordered nearly 500 major repairs. Snorkel U-boats fared a little better but did not achieve much. The intensity of air attack was so great, and the difficulties of snorkeling and navigating in the shallow waters and strong currents of the Channel were so tricky, that the average rate of progress over the ground was one and a half knots. Not until several days after the invasion did a solitary U-boat penetrate to the invasion area. Before being driven off, it managed to sink a tank-landing ship—but that was the total achievement of the U-boat Navy's hopeless and heroic effort to form Hitler's first line of defense in the west.

By the end of June, 12 U-boats had been sunk, the nonsnorkels had been driven forever from the waters around Britain, and it was clear that eventually the U-boat bases themselves would fall before the advancing Allied armies. Dönitz ordered his boats to abandon the French ports and fall back on bases in Norway, but since every one of the boats had to be fitted with a snorkel before there could be any hope of surviving such a journey, the transfer took time. The final scenes that were played out at the U-boat bases were a foretaste of Germany's ultimate disintegration: German civilians tried to bribe U-boat crews to take them along; rear-echelon Army officers arrogantly demanded accommodation for their French mistresses and private cargoes of champagne and wine; weeping French collaborators had to be prevented at gunpoint from rushing the U-boats in order to escape their impending fate. But on August 23 the last submarine sailed out of Bordeaux, and the U-boats were forever gone from France.

By the winter of 1944-1945, most of the 349 U-boats were established in the Norwegian bases at Bergen and Trondheim. Incredibly, Dönitz planned to launch from these mist-filled northern fjords an all-out, last-ditch campaign, which he called "total underwater warfare," against the same British coastal waters from which the German forces had already been so rudely driven.

U-boat commanders summoned to meet the Grand Admiral for this new undertaking found him changed. In his closely guarded headquarters complex in the pine woods to the east of Berlin, he looked old, seemed spent and diminished in stature, and spoke flatly—all in sharp

The snorkel: an adopted device that shifted the odds

The snorkel device that enabled submarines to take in fresh air while they were underwater was neither a German invention nor even a new idea. As early as 1897 a crude American sub ran its internal-combustion engine underwater by taking in air through a hose; the sub's mobility was severely limited, however, since the open end of the hose was held above the surface of the water by a float.

In the 1930s the Dutch Navy experimented with air pipes that could be closed when the submariners wanted to shut down their diesel engines and dive deeper. When the Germans overran Holland, they found the Dutch snorkels, and in 1943—spurred on by their worsening situation at sea—they began producing similar devices. In waters patrolled by Allied sub hunters, a snorkel-equipped U-boat had a chance—if only that—for survival.

Typically, a U-boat might cruise at a depth of about 180 feet during the day to avoid detection. When night fell, the sub would rise to just below the surface and extend its snorkel—a folding model on the standard Type VII U-boats and a telescoping model on the new Type XXI—so that the head valve protruded above the waves. A float in the valve dropped, admitting fresh air, which was pulled into the sub by a fan. The diesel motors were started, and the sub proceeded to recharge its batteries in preparation for the next period of deep running.

Snorkeling was a gingerly process. If the U-boat dipped too far below the surface, the head valve would shut and the diesels would gulp the air from the hull, creating a partial vacuum that could damage the crews' eardrums; if it ran too high, the snorkel might be detected and bring on a storm of depth

charges. Since the U-boat's delicate trim could be disturbed by even minor shifts of weight, crewmen could not move about without permission.

In theory, a U-boat equipped with a snorkel never had to surface at sea; one U-boat stayed submerged on patrol for 69 days. While few German submariners kept their vessels underwater for anywhere near that length of time, all who had snorkels made the most of them. "We owed our lives to the snorkel," said one U-boat commander, "as surely as hundreds of U-boats owed their deaths to the lack of it."

On the Type XXI U-boat, the snorkel was kept lower than the periscopes to leave the view unobstructed. The separate intake and exhaust pipes were joined at the snorkel head for strength, and a coating of synthetic rubber on the head absorbed radar signals and made detection by an enemy less likely.

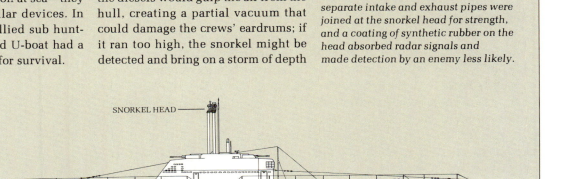

SNORKEL HEAD

contrast to his crisp style of earlier years. But they also found him to be as resolute as ever. At one point he recalled the example of a Polish-Prussian fortress commander named G. R. Courbière von Graudenz, who had refused to surrender to the French in 1806. When told that further resistance was useless since the Kingdom of Prussia no longer existed, the man had stoically replied: "Then I am King von Graudenz, for I know no other duty than to defend this fortress." Somehow even amid the wreckage of his hopes, Dönitz managed to instill his spirit in the U-boat men. "We believed," recalled one of the U-boat captains, "we trusted and we continued to sail."

Dönitz' plans for total underwater warfare were based on the coming into service of two new types of wonder boat—Types XXI and XXIII electroboats. Both had large storage batteries that gave them the power to operate submerged at higher speeds for longer periods than the earlier boats. But heavy Allied air raids devastated Germany's communications and production networks, severing the canals along which prefabricated sections of the new boats were shipped and delaying their delivery to the Navy. By Christmas 1944, German shipyards had managed to turn out 90 of the big, sleek Type XXI boats and 31 of the tiny Type XXIII, which carried only two torpedoes. Then the Navy faced another setback: It was difficult to retrain the crews for these very specialized high-speed boats in the heavily mined waters of the Baltic. The first Type XXIII boat did not go out on combat operations until January 29, 1945. She soon succeeded in sinking a merchant ship off Sunderland, England, and during February and March five more Type XXIII boats accounted for the loss of six other enemy vessels, bringing the Germans their first ray of hope in many a month.

It was only in late April that a Type XXI put to sea. She went under Commander Adalbert Schnee, a talented and successful U-boat commander who had won his oak leaves back in 1942 and had been serving since that time as an officer on Dönitz' personal staff. Now Schnee was given command of the *U-2511*, a sophisticated piece of weapons technology that was fully up to the requirements of modern submarine warfare and that represented a phenomenal improvement in the combat potential of the U-boat arm.

The *U-2511* was nearly twice as big as the old Type VIIC; it had a streamlined hull, spacious living quarters and a deep freezer in which to store food. All of its six bow torpedo tubes could be automatically reloaded in just 12 minutes at the press of a button (reloading the tubes on older vessels took 10 to 20 minutes for each tube), and as many as 18 torpedoes could be fired in 20 minutes from a depth of 150 feet. Its hydrophones were capable of picking up a ship at a distance of 50 miles. It could dive as deep as about 650 feet, some 60 feet farther than the old submarines, and it could reach an underwater speed of 16.5 knots, more than twice the speed of its predecessors. The Type XXI was the total submarine—utterly lethal and almost invulnerable. At long last Dönitz had a weapon that was a match for any enemy.

But it was already too late. Schnee's vessel was the only Type XXI U-boat that ever put to sea. On April 30, 1945, Adolf Hitler committed suicide—having named as his successor none other than the commander of the U-boat arm and Commander in Chief of the Navy, Grand Admiral Karl Dönitz. Now, for the first time in his professional life, Dönitz was burdened with responsibilities that by far outweighed those of the U-boat war in the Atlantic. At 3:14 p.m. on May 4, when Dönitz had ruled his nation for only four days, it was clear to him that any further resistance was utterly futile. He sent a radio signal to his beloved fleet: ALL U-BOATS. ATTENTION ALL U-BOATS. CEASE FIRE IMMEDIATELY. STOP ALL HOSTILE ACTION AGAINST ALLIED SHIPPING. DÖNITZ. And the next day the U-boats received a final valedictory from their commander:

"My U-boat men, six years of war lie behind you. You have fought like lions. An overwhelming material superiority has driven us into a tight corner from which it is no longer possible to continue the War. Unbeaten and unblemished, you lay down your arms after a heroic fight without parallel. We proudly remember our fallen comrades who gave their lives for Führer and fatherland. Comrades, preserve that spirit in which you have fought so long and so gallantly for the sake of the future of the fatherland. Long live Germany. Your Grand Admiral."

The U-boat campaign, the longest of all the World War II campaigns, had come to an end.

On May 7, the day of Germany's unconditional surrender, Dönitz sent out a new order instructing the U-boats to surface, report their positions and then proceed to certain ports that had been designated by the Allies. That same night, Lieutenant Commander Emil Klausmeier, on his first patrol as captain of the *U-2336*, having failed to receive Dönitz' radio message, fired the final torpedo of the U-boat war, sinking a Canadian freighter off the east coast of Scotland. The freighter was the last casualty of the war at sea.

Slowly and grudgingly, one by one over the next few weeks, most of the U-boats obeyed Dönitz' order to surrender *(pages 166-171)*. Dönitz himself came face to face with retribution on May 23, more than a fortnight after the German capitulation, when a squad of fully armed British soldiers burst into the morning conference at his government headquarters at Flensburg shouting, "Hands up!" In a preplanned ritual of official degradation, every one of the Germans present, including Dönitz, was forced to strip and undergo a minute body search, presumably for cyanide capsules. As soon as they had dressed, they were marched into a courtyard with their hands above their heads. There the prisoners were photographed and filmed by more than 60 Allied reporters while their rooms were searched and looted. Then they were bundled into waiting trucks and, with an escort of between 30 and 40 armored vehicles, driven off at high speed toward captivity—and, for Karl Dönitz, trial as a war criminal.

In the massive Palace of Justice at Nuremberg, Dönitz and 20 other leading Nazis were to sit in the dock for nearly a year, from November 1945 to October 1946, before eight British, American, French and Russian judges of the International Military Tribunal. Throughout that time there was a strong possibility that Dönitz would finish his life at the end of a rope. When at last the trial ended on October 1, 1946, the first 10 defendants stood, one by one, to hear the verdicts and their sentences. Each was pronounced guilty and sentenced to death by hanging. Then

A terror-stricken young U-boat crewman is rescued from death in the Atlantic after his submarine was pursued and sunk by the aggressive Canadian frigate Swansea late in 1944. Seizing the initiative in the Battle of the Atlantic, Allied U-boat killers found their prey crewed by ever-younger, less-experienced German sailors, unprepared for the horrors of submarine warfare.

Karl Dönitz arose. He was found not guilty of conspiracy to wage war. But he was pronounced guilty of waging war—as indeed he had—and of two highly tangential war crimes: failure to rescind Hitler's Commando Order, by which all suspected saboteurs found inside the German lines were to be killed immediately, without any questions asked, and failure to prevent the employment of slave labor in the U-boat shipyards. Upon hearing that he was being sentenced to 10 years in prison, Karl Dönitz silently pursed his lips.

Dönitz' captors kept him in the forbidding gray prison in the Spandau section of Berlin until 10 years had ticked away. Throughout that time there remained within him a spark of the man who had sailed with the U-boats in one world war and had sent them to sea in another. As in World War I, Dönitz' U-boat Navy had met the end of World War II less in abject submission than in defiant surrender; they were in fact the only arm of the German forces not to be defeated. In both wars the U-boats had come perilously close to forcing the British to terms, and although they had sunk a smaller number of ships in World War II (2,828 as against 4,837 in World War I) they had destroyed more tonnage (14.5 million tons against 11 million).

During the course of that second great struggle, the steadfast courage of Dönitz' U-boat men had won the admiration of even their bitterest enemies. No compulsion had been needed to force them to sail out in their iron coffins. They remained to the very end loyal to their commander in chief, their fatherland—even to their capricious Führer. Some quiet inward stratum compounded of resignation and adamantine dutifulness was the bedrock of the U-boat arm.

Much of that spirit came from Dönitz himself—a fact that was widely known. During the dark days of his confinement, more than 100 American captains and admirals wrote to tell him that he had served Germany as they had served the United States—by fighting honorably and well. In the end, Karl Dönitz could still find it within himself to say, "I have nothing to apologize for and would do everything all over again just as I did then."

When Dönitz uttered those words, the U-boats that he had fathered and reared had gone off to their own destinies. By the end of June 1945, the Allies overseeing the surrender operation had accounted for 377 U-boats; only two were still at large. One of them was the *U-977* under Lieutenant Commander Heinz Schaeffer; along with many of his men, he had decided to sail away from the ruins of war in the hope of starting a new life on the other side of the world. After putting ashore the married men and any others among the crew who still felt ties to the conquered fatherland, the *U-977* cast off from her moorings in a Norwegian fjord and slipped out to sea in early May. Thus began a curious odyssey that was to last 104 days.

Staying submerged, she snorkeled her way around the northern reaches of the British Isles, down the European coast as far south as Spain, and past Gibraltar. Approaching the Cape Verde Islands, she surfaced for the first time in 66 days. Next she headed westward, and only then, because she was well out to sea, did the crew relax their guard. They slung hammocks from the guns, sunbathed on the conning tower,

Admiral Karl Dönitz, having succeeded Adolf Hitler as Germany's head of state after the Führer's suicide, is taken prisoner and led away by a British soldier on May 23, 1945. Later, in his memoirs, the stoic Dönitz recalled: "Feeling that our fate was inevitable, my companions and I remained perfectly calm."

water-skied from the bowlines and sang chanteys beneath the Southern Cross in the tropic night sky. Finally, on August 17, 1945—three months after the War had ended—they made landfall off the South American coast. Expecting asylum in Argentina, they approached the harbor mouth at Rio del Plata and flashed a signal in English: GERMAN SUBMARINE.

They did not get the welcome they expected, however. First they found that they had come in right on the heels of the only other missing U-boat, the *U-530*. Stories were wildly circulating that Hitler was still alive and had been smuggled out of Germany—and what better way to do the evil job than with a U-boat? By one account he was supposed to have been dropped off in Antarctica, where he was already setting up new headquarters.

For Schaeffer and his shipmates, the dream of life in the sun was soon dashed. They were promptly transported to Washington, where they were severely interrogated before they succeeded in convincing their captors that the stories about Hitler were pure fantasy. Eventually they were returned to Germany and repatriated without incident. Nevertheless, their sorry odyssey had proved a point. The last of Dönitz' U-boats had behaved entirely in character—spreading fear of malefaction to her very last port of call.

An armada of new Type XXI U-boats clog the slipways of the Blohm & Voss shipyard in bomb-battered Hamburg in May 1945—too late to send their lethal might against the Allies. A month earlier, about 120 of these vessels were all but ready for action—but only one of them ever went into combat.

Bloodied but unbeaten, the sea knights dismount

Equipped with advanced snorkel-type submarines, improved armaments and a variety of new defensive devices, the undaunted gray wolves of Germany's U-boat service were bracing to launch a fresh offensive against the encroaching Allies in the spring of 1945—just as the rest of the Third Reich collapsed around them. Undefeated, but obedient as ever, the U-boat men followed orders and surrendered their deadly iron vessels to the enemy. For most of them it was a bitter moment; for some it was a time for a last act of defiance, however fruitless.

Forty-five U-boats were at sea when Admiral Karl Dönitz issued his cease-fire order. On May 7, the day Germany surrendered, he ordered them to surface and set course for ports stipulated by the Allies.

Grudgingly, one by one over the next few weeks, most U-boats complied with the order; 23 sailed into British ports, three to the United States, four to Canada, two to Argentina, the rest to Norway or Kiel. Two were scuttled by their crews off Lisbon; one ran aground off Holland. On the *U-2511*, Commander Adalbert Schnee infiltrated a British cordon north of the Faroe Islands, lined up a heavy cruiser in his sights, simulated a last torpedo attack undetected, then bitterly returned to base and internment.

The U-boats lying in northern European bases at war's end—377 submarines in all—were given their surrender orders by the British Admiralty. They were commanded to proceed on the surface to designated British anchorages. The order was obeyed by the crews of 156 U-boats. The men were interned, and thereafter most of their vessels were towed 30 miles north of Malin Head, Northern Ireland, and sunk. But the crews of 221 other U-boats decided independently to defy the enemy's ritual of defeat, and scuttled their boats themselves.

The cost of their struggle had been terrible. Of the 1,162 U-boats built between 1939 and 1945, 784 had been lost—632 of them sunk at sea. Of the 40,000 crewmen who served on U-boats, 28,000 had been killed and 5,000 captured. But they had come astonishingly close to defeating Britain and altering the outcome of the War. Their audacity and dedication had sometimes been shaken but had never failed. And in the end they created a legend of potent force scarcely rivaled in the history of war at sea.

Heads bowed in sullen grief, crewmen of the U-291 under Captain Hermann Neumeister avert their faces from a British photographer as their submarine ties up alongside a jetty in Wilhelmshaven and other U-boats enter the harbor behind them.

Under the watchful eye of a Navy blimp, United States officials board the U-858 in American waters, about 15 miles off Cape May, New Jersey. The U-858 was one of 10 U-boats kept by the United States as war prizes under the terms of an agreement among the Allies.

An incongruous sight under Big Ben
and the Gothic spires of the Houses of
Parliament, the U-776 cruises up
the Thames after her surrender. She lay
alongside London's Embankment as
a public curiosity for a while and then was
taken off to Northern Ireland and
scuttled with more than 100 other U-boats.

Bibliography

Auten, Harold, *Q-Boat Adventures*. London: Herbert Jenkins, 1919.

Bailey, Thomas A., and Paul B. Ryan, *The Lusitania Disaster*. Free Press, 1975.

Buchheim, Lothar-Günther, *The Boat*. Alfred A. Knopf, 1975.

Campbell, Gordon, *My Mystery Ships*. London: Hodder and Stoughton, 1928.

Chatterton, E. Keble, *Q-Ships and Their Story*. London: Conway Maritime Press, 1972.

Clark, William Bell, *When the U-boats Came to America*. Little, Brown, 1929.

Craig, Gordon A., *Germany, 1866-1945*. Oxford University Press, 1978.

Dönitz, Karl, *Memoirs: Ten Years and Twenty Days*. Greenwood, 1976.

Frank, Wolfgang, *The Sea Wolves: The Story of German U-boats at War*. Rinehart, 1955.

Fritzsche, Hans, *The Sword in the Scales*. London: Allan Wingate, 1953.

Gibson, R. H., and Maurice Prendergast, *The German Submarine War, 1914-1918*. Richard R. Smith, 1931.

Grant, Robert M., *U-Boat Intelligence, 1914-1918*. Archon Books, 1969.

Gray, Edwyn, *The Killing Time*. Charles Scribner's Sons, 1972.

Gretton, Peter, *Crisis Convoy: The Story of HX231*. London: Peter Davies, 1974.

Hashagen, Ernst, *The Log of a U-boat Commander*. London: Putnam, 1931.

Hoehling, A. A., and Mary Hoehling, *The Last Voyage of the Lusitania*. Henry Holt, 1956.

Horton, Edward, *The Illustrated History of the Submarine*. Doubleday, 1974.

Hoyt, Edwin P., *From the Turtle to the Nautilus*. Little, Brown, 1963.

Hughes, Terry, and John Costello, *The Battle of the Atlantic*. Dial Press (James Wade), 1977.

Lewin, Ronald, *Ultra Goes to War*. McGraw-Hill, 1978.

Macintyre, Donald:
The Naval War against Hitler. Charles Scribner's Sons, 1971.
U-boat Killer. United States Naval Institute, 1976.

McKee, Alexander, *Black Saturday*. Holt, Rinehart and Winston, 1959.

Middlebrook, Martin, *Convoy*. London: Allen Lane, 1976.

Neave, Airey, *On Trial at Nuremberg*. Little, Brown, 1978.

Neureuther, Karl, and Claus Bergen, eds., *U-boat Stories*. Richard R. Smith, 1931.

Preston, Antony, *U-boats*. London: Arms and Armour, 1978.

Reynolds, Clark G., *Command of the Sea*. London: Robert Hale, 1974.

Robertson, Terence, *Night Raider of the Atlantic*. E. P. Dutton, 1956.

Rohwer, J., and G. Hümmelchen, *Chronology of the War at Sea*. Vol. 1, *1939-1942*. Arco, 1972.

Roskill, S. W., *The War at Sea 1939-1945*. Vols. 1, 2. London: Her Majesty's Stationery Office, 1976.

Showell, Jak P. Mallmann, *U-boats under the Swastika*. Arco, 1973.

Simpson, Colin, *The Lusitania*. Little, Brown, 1972.

Snyder, Gerald, *The Royal Oak Disaster*. London: William Kimber, 1976.

Spiess, Johannes, *Six Years of Submarine Cruising* (transl. by Hyman Rickover). Office of Naval Intelligence, 1926.

Thomas, Lowell, *Raiders of the Deep*. Doran (Doubleday), 1929.

Watts, A. J., *The U-boat Hunters*. London: Macdonald and Jane's, 1976.

Werner, Herbert A., *Iron Coffins*. Holt, Rinehart and Winston, 1969.

Winton, John, ed., *The War at Sea 1939-1945*. London: Hutchinson, 1967.

Picture Credits

Acknowledgments

The index for this book was prepared by Gale Partoyan. The editors wish to thank the following: Roy H. Andersen, artist, and Karl-Wilhelm Grützemacher, consultant (pages 124-129); John Batchelor, artist, and Antony Preston, consultant (pages 22-23, 33-35, 46-47, 70); Thomas O. Paine, consultant (page 161); Bill Hezlep, artist, and Karl-Wilhelm Grützemacher, consultant (page 97); and Peter McGinn, artist (page 120 and endpaper maps).

The editors also wish to thank: In the Netherlands: Den Helder—Commander Philip Bosscher, Lecturer, The Royal Netherlands Naval Academy. In Switzerland: Zug—Kirk Kirchhofer. In Germany: Bonn—Captain Kurt Diggins (Ret.); Wilhelm Baumann, Karl August Hüpper, Klaus Schubert, Marine-Offizier-Vereinigung; Aumühle—Grand Admiral Karl Dönitz (Ret.); Berlin—Dr. Roland Klemig, Heidi Klein, Bildarchiv Preussischer Kulturbesitz; Axel Schulz, Ullstein Bilderdienst; Bremerhaven—Arnold Kludas, Librarian, Deutsches Schiffahrtsmuseum; Coblenz—Dr. Matthias Haupt, Bundesarchiv; Cologne—Dr. Hanswilly Bernartz, Inge Sturm-Prien; Düsseldorf—Jochen Brennecke; Essen—Martin Weber, Press Department, Fried. Krupp; Feldafing—Lothar-Günther Buchheim; Freiburg—Dr. Gerd Sandhofer, Bundesarchiv; Hamburg—Dr. Jürgen Meyer, Altonaer Museum; Jochen Ahme, Deutscher U-Bootfahrer Verband; Kiel—Admiral Eberhard Godt (Ret.); Munich—Ulrich Frodien, Süddeutscher Verlag, Bilderdienst; Georg Högel; Mürwick—Franz Hahn, Librarian, Marineschule; Oberwinter—Rear Admiral Erich Topp (Ret.); Oldenburg—Hans Wessels; Rastatt—Henning Volle, Ulrich Schiers, Curators, Wehrgeschichtliches Museum; Remscheid—Gerd Rose; Stuttgart—Dr. Jürgen Rohwer, Director, Bibliothek für Zeitgeschichte. In Belgium: Brussels—Jean Lorette, Chief Curator, Army Museum; Commander Philippe van der Stichelen, Belgian Air Force. In the United Kingdom: London—Terry Hughes; J. Lucas, E. Hine, M. Willis, J. Pavey, Department of Photographs, D. Nash, Department of Printed Books, J. Simmonds, Art Department, Imperial War Museum; P. Russell, Lloyd's Register of Shipping; Joan Moore, Photographic Sales Department, National Maritime Museum; David Brown, M. W. Thirkettle, Alan Francis, Naval Historical Branch; M. Willis, Radio Times Hulton Picture Library; Karl Heinz Wahnig; Guildford—N. T. Davies; Maidenhead—J. Adams Newton, Commonwealth War Graves Commission; Portsmouth—Richard Kerr; Chief Petty Officer Knibbs, RN, Submarine Museum, H.M.S. Gosport; Lieutenant Commander R.S.C. Robinson, RN, H.M.S. Vernon; Sherborne—Rear Admiral B.C.J. Godfrey Place, V.C., D.S.C., RN (Ret.); Telford—Jak P. Mallmann Showell; Winchester—Martin Brice; Stenness, Orkney, Scotland—Peter Leith. In Canada: Vancouver—Ed Ogle, Chris S. V. Rose. In France: Paris—Jacques Alaluquetas; Hervé Cras, Director for Historical Studies, Denise Chaussegroux, Researcher, Marjolaine Mathikine, Musée de la Marine. In Italy: Rome—Lieutenant Commander Flavio Serafini, Ministero della Marina; Countess Maria-Fede Caproni, Museo Caproni; Bologna—Arrigo Barilli.

The editors also wish to thank: In the United States: Washington, D.C.—Jerry L. Kearns, Head, Reference Section, Prints and Photographs, Elena Millie, Curator of Posters, Library of Congress; Donald S. Lopez, Assistant Director for Aeronautics, Robert C. Mikesh, Curator of Aircraft, National Air and Space Museum; James Trimble, Bureau of Ships, Harry Rilley, Modern Military Branch, William Leary, Paul White, Still Pictures, National Archives; Charles R. Haberlein Jr., Agnes Hoover, Photographic Section, John C. Reilly Jr., Ships History, U.S. Naval Historical Center; Brielle, New Jersey—Herbert A. Werner; Carrollton, Texas—Robert C. Stern, Squadron/Signal Publications; Cicero, Illinois—Greg Schröder; Groton, Connecticut—Carl H. Hochstetler, Director, Terry Cass, Librarian, Submarine Force Library and Museum, Naval Submarine Base; Los Angeles, California—Commander Donald D. Foulds, USN (Ret.), Northrop Corporation; New York, New York—John E. Costello; Nashville, Tennessee—Gerald W. George, Director, American Association for State and Local History; Salem, Massachusetts—The Peabody Museum of Salem; Upper Montclair, New Jersey—Hellmuth Walter.

Particularly valuable sources of quotations were When the U-boats Came to America by William Bell Clark, Little, Brown and Company, 1929; The Killing Time by Edwyn Gray, Charles Scribner's Sons, 1972; The Lusitania by Colin Simpson, Little, Brown and Company, 1972; The Royal Oak Disaster by Gerald Snyder, William Kimber, 1976; and Iron Coffins by Herbert A. Werner, Holt, Rinehart and Winston, 1969.

Index

GREENLAND

Cape Farewell

CANADA

NORTH AMERICA

NEWFOUNDLAND

St. John's

Halifax

Boston

New York

Philadelphia

Atlantic City

Baltimore

Cape May

Washington

DELAWARE BAY

CHESAPEAKE BAY

Cape Henry

Cape Hatteras

UNITED STATES OF AMERICA

BERMUDA ISLANDS

New Orleans

GULF OF MEXICO

ATLANTIC OCEAN

WEST INDIES

Puerto Rico

Barbados

CARIBBEAN SEA

Trinidad

PACIFIC OCEAN

SOUTH AMERICA